C000007101

AFRICAN APPROPRIATIONS

AFRICAN APPROPRIATIONS

CULTURAL DIFFERENCE, MIMESIS,

MEDIA

MATTHIAS KRINGS

INDIANA UNIVERSITY PRESS

Bloomington and Indianapolis

This book is a publication of

Indiana University Press
Office of Scholarly Publishing
Herman B Wells Library 350
1320 East 10th Street
Bloomington, Indiana 47405 USA

iupress.indiana.edu

♾ The paper used in this publication
meets the minimum requirements of the
American National Standard for
Information Sciences—Permanence of
Paper for Printed Library Materials,
ANSI Z39.48-1992.

Manufactured in the United States of
America

Cataloging information is available from
the Library of Congress.

ISBN 978-0-253-01625-6 (cloth)
ISBN 978-0-253-01629-4 (paperback)
ISBN 978-0-253-01640-9 (ebook)

1 2 3 4 5 20 19 18 17 16 15

CONTENTS

ACKNOWLEDGMENTS AND PREFACE

THIS BOOK presents material I gathered during the past twenty years spent doing research in and out of Africa. The first chapter goes back to what in retrospect looks like the initial spark of my academic career—a year spent in northern Nigeria from 1992 to 1993. At the time, I was a graduate student of anthropology and African languages and had intended to study abroad for two semesters at Bayero University Kano. When the university went on strike only two months after my arrival, I began to develop a research project of my own and ended up studying *bori,* the Hausa cult of spirit possession. I became particularly interested in the Babule spirits, who when embodied by their human mediums in ritual performances, represented mimetical interpretations of European alterity. During the first nine months of 1993 and another three months in 1994, Usman Mohammed Dakata, Husseini Gandu, Saminu 'dan Jan Dutse, and the late Lawan na Kawari introduced me to the world of bori spirit possession. Husseini and Lawan also kept me up to date on bori matters in subsequent years (1998–2001), when I stopped over in Kano en route to my new fieldwork site in Borno state, where I conducted research for my Ph.D. project (not presented in this book). In Kano, I enjoyed the hospitality of Aminu Shariff Baffa and his family, who was my host in the Sabuwar K'ofa neighborhood, where I found numerous friends among the bachelors of the quarter who kept me company, helped me improve my Hausa, and assisted me in so many other ways. I cannot name all here, but I mention Usman Aliyu Abdulmalik, Ibrahim Shariff Baffa, Abdulhamid Yusuf Jigawa,

Abdulkadir Maje, and Kabiru Maje. In this neighborhood, I was in no way the only *Bature,* as "Europeans" are called in northern Nigeria. In fact, I shared this "field full of researchers"—as Katja Werthmann, among them, once called it in retrospect—with numerous others, including Douglas Anthony, Conerly Casey, Rudi Gaudio, Jan-Patrick Heiß, Alaine Hutson, Tae-Sang Jang, Brian Larkin, Esther Morgenthal, and Jonathan Reynolds. I thank all of them for the many lively discussions we had which enriched my more general knowledge of Nigeria and Hausaland in particular.

In 2003, I returned to Kano for a research project on Hausa video film, which I carried out under the auspices of the Forschungskolleg Medien und Kulturelle Kommunikation at the University of Cologne. During my fieldwork on Kanywood, Ahmed S. Alkanawy assisted me in many ways, most notably by connecting me to his numerous friends and acquaintances in the Hausa movie "industry." Among them, I am especially indebted to Abdulkareem Mohammed, chairman of the Moving Pictures Practitioners Association of Nigeria (MOPPAN), and to the filmmakers 'Dan Azumi Baba, Ishaq Sidi Ishaq, Hamisu Lamido Iyan-Tama, and Ibrahim Mandawari. Shu'aibu Idris Lilisco and Aminu Bizi taught me what it's like to act in front of a camera by casting me in minor roles in their movies *Salam Salam* and *Jinjirai 99,* respectively. Abdalla Uba Adamu inspired me through his own research and prolific writing on Hausa films, and his generous sharing of information helped me to keep track of the latest developments in Kanywood in subsequent years. The same holds true for Ibrahim Sheme and Carmen McCain, without whose blogs I would never have been able to follow up on the censorship crisis after 2007.

I am also indebted to Brian Larkin, whose work on media in northern Nigeria has inspired my own and who was kind enough to share his knowledge and experiences with me on several occasions. In Cologne, colleagues at the Forschungskolleg facilitated my initiation into the world of film and media studies—among them Friedrich Balke, Ilka Becker, Gereon Blaseio, Michael Cuntz, Cornelia Epping-Jäger, Gisela Fehrmann, Erika Linz, Frank Thomas Meyer, Jens Ruchatz, Gabriele Schabacher, Leander Scholz, Erhard Schüttpelz, and Brigitte Weingart.

My research on the appropriation of foreign media in Tanzania began in 2006, when I visited Dar es Salaam for the first time during a short reconnaissance trip. I returned for longer stays in 2007 and 2009, and eventually headed a project researching the negotiation of culture through video movies and Bongo flava music in Tanzania from 2009 to 2011. I thank the team of researchers—Claudia Böhme, Gabriel Hacke, and Uta Reuster-Jahn—who made this project a success and from whose work, insights, and friendship I profited enormously. In Tanzania, we were affiliated with the Department of Fine and Performing Arts at the University of Dar es Salaam. I am very grateful for the kind assistance of its staff on numerous occasions and thank its consecutive directors, Amandina Lihamba, Herbert Makoye, Frowin Nyoni, and Imani Sanga. Vicensia Shule was always ready to share her knowledge of Tanzanian theater and media culture with me and also facilitated my research in multiple other ways. Deoglace Komba introduced me to various aspects of life and work in Dar es Salaam and assisted me as an interpreter. I also owe a great many thanks to Rose Nyerere, who put me up in her house in 2007 and one day took me along to visit her late father's residence on the shores of the Indian Ocean, which I always will remember as an almost mystical experience.

Mtitu Game was always ready to talk about Swahili movie production and his latest projects; Captain Derek Gaspar Mukandala, aka Lufufu, introduced me to the "translation" of foreign films during a number of practical dubbing lessons and subsequent conversations. I thank both of them. Special thanks are due to Amandus Mtani, who allowed me to appropriate the cover of his *Titanic* graphic novel for the cover of this book. My research into the history of *African Film*, the 1960s photo-novel magazine featuring the adventures of Lance Spearman, also began in Tanzania, where I was able to buy used copies of the magazine and interview several of its former readers, including Simon Chupa, Athumani Hamisi, Mike Mande, Chahya Mtiro, Joseph Mwamunyange, Hashim Nakanoga, Richard Ndunguru, and Abdul Sawe. Accessing more issues of *African Film* magazine was made possible with the help of Randall W. Scott of Michigan State University Library, East Lansing, and Toyin Alade from Lagos, both of whom swapped copies with me; James Orao was kind enough to retrieve several issues from the Kenyan National Archives for me.

The last two chapters of this book, which focus on internet-related phenomena, afforded a certain amount of technical finesse and a new methodological tool kit. I acknowledge the help of Jan Beek, who joined me during the initial steps of my exploration of cybercrime in 2008 and whose clever reading of scam letters inspired my own. I am also grateful to Jan Budniok, who gave me a crash course in Facebook, making it much easier for me to navigate the Facebook pages of the three musicians whose work I discuss in chapter 8. Special thanks are due to Espen Sørensen, aka Mzungu Kichaa, and Eric Sell, aka EES, who were generous enough to meet me for interviews in 2013 in Hamburg and Cologne, respectively.

I also express my gratitude to the conveners of several conferences, panels, and seminars where I presented part of my work at various stages of completion and from the discussion of which I gained a lot: In 2005 and 2006, Birgit Meyer invited me to participate in two wonderful conferences as part of the Pioneer Project in Mass Media and the Imagination of Religious Communities that she ran at the University of Amsterdam; Carmen Birkle and Nicole Waller encouraged me to develop a first version of the "Black *Titanic*" paper for their seminar series on transatlantic encounters at Johannes Gutenberg University Mainz in 2006; and Mahir Şaul and Ralph Austen convened the African Film conference, which took place at the University of Illinois in 2007 and where I was able to discuss first findings on the remediation of Nollywood in Tanzania. I also thank Onookome Okome for organizing with me the Nollywood and Beyond conference at Johannes Gutenberg University Mainz in 2009, where I could discuss part of my work on the remediation of Nollywood films by Tanzanian video narrators with an audience of international experts on Nigerian video film. Heike Becker and Dorothea Schulz invited me to take part in the panel (Un)making Difference through Performance and Mediation in Contemporary Africa, which they convened at the Fifth European Conference on African Studies in Lisbon in 2013. The panel encouraged me to write a first draft of the last chapter of this book.

I also acknowledge the effort and moral support of those who read and commented on the manuscript or parts of it in various stages of preparation—as friends and colleagues, or as external reviewers, or both—Abdalla Uba Adamu, Gerd Becker, Hauke Dorsch, Cassis Kilian, Carola Lentz, Birgit Meyer, Peter Probst, and Bob White. I am most grateful to all of them. I also want to mention Jonathan Haynes, whose work I admire. I gleaned a lot more about Nigerian video film from our conversations—whether in Kano, Cologne, Mainz, or wherever else we met. John McCall was so kind to send me a copy of the *Osama Bin La* video; Bärbel Freyer allowed me to photograph her collection of bin Laden posters; Johannes Harnischfeger always shared firsthand information about Nigerian current affairs with me; Jigal Beez brought the *Titanic* graphic novel and the *Omereme* photo novel to my attention; Léon Tsambu Bulu helped me clarify the history of events surrounding the *Titanic* video clip by Wenge BCBG. I am indebted to all of them. Claudia Böhme, Uta Reuster-Jahn, Vicensia Shule, and Solomon Waliaula helped me with translations from the Swahili, which I greatly appreciate.

In addition, I acknowledge Sabine Lang and particularly Pauline Bugler for their wonderful copyediting of the manuscript, as well as Dee Mortensen and Sarah Jacobi of Indiana University Press for their generous support during all preparatory stages of the book. Three of the chapters are revised versions of essays which have been published previously: chapter 2 appeared as "A Prequel to Nollywood: South African Photo Novels and Their Pan-African Consumption in the Late 1960s," in the *Journal of African Cultural Studies* 22, 1 (2010), and is reprinted by permission of Taylor & Francis Group (www.tandfonline.com) on behalf of the *Journal of African Cultural Studies;* chapter 5 was published as "Nollywood Goes East: The Localization of Nigerian Video Films in Tanzania," in *Viewing African Cinema in the Twenty-First Century,* edited by Mahir Şaul and Ralph A. Austen (2010), and is used by permission of Ohio University Press (www.ohioswallow.com); and chapter 6 was published in German as "Marke Osama: Über Kommunikation und Kommerz mit Bin-Laden-Bildern in Nigeria" in *Peripherie* 113 (2009), and is reprinted by permission of Verlag Westfälisches Dampfboot (www.dampfboot-verlag.de).

Financial support for my research and writing came from a variety of sources. The German Research Foundation sponsored the bulk of the research that went into the book, including fieldwork in Kano in 2003 and the Tanzania-related project from 2009 to 2011; Johannes Gutenberg University Mainz sponsored my initial two journeys to Dar es Salaam in 2006 and 2007, and also granted me a sabbatical during the winter semester of 2013–2014, which enabled me to make final revisions to the manuscript. The German Academic Exchange Service sponsored a Hausa language course I took at Bayero University Kano in 1994. My parents, Christa and Werner Krings, and my late-grandfather Wilhelm Krings sponsored my first two trips to Kano, in 1991 and from 1992 to 1993. Their support, moral and otherwise, and the tolerance they showed despite my outlandish field of study still command my respect. My deepest gratitude goes to my wife, Evelyn, for her compassion, love, and support throughout these years, and to our children, Marie and Luis, who tolerated the occasional absences of their father necessitated by the researching and writing of this book.

AFRICAN APPROPRIATIONS

Introduction

ONE FRIDAY MORNING in August 2009, beautiful choral voices filled the air of the Kamunyonge Seventh-day Adventist Church in Musoma, Tanzania. Touched by the powerful force of this spontaneous live performance and deeply impressed by the professionalism of the choir, I sat at the table of honor provided for me and listened to the song. The female members of the choir set in singing, in Tanzania's national language, Swahili: "Unfortunately, it was false and stupid, nothing can have a beginning without an ending." The men replied: "Men built a huge ship called *Titanic*. They trusted and believed that it would never sink." Together we sailed along on this journey, moving ever closer to the disastrous demise of the ship, and they ended their hymn by reminding me and the other listeners that "Now the world is just like the *Titanic*—about to sink. And even if it is difficult to believe that the world is coming to its end—that is the truth. The world will sink and men will perish." This was not my first encounter with this song. Three years earlier, I had bought a tape recording of it in a music store in Dar es Salaam, also in Tanzania. Attracted by the cassette's cover, with an image of the ship taken from James Cameron's *Titanic* (1997), I was excited to add another piece of this Hollywood film to my growing collection of African appropriations. By that time I had already come across a Nigerian video remake, a Tanzanian comic book, and a Congolese music video clip. Later on I was to discover still more references to it, from names of video stores and barbershops to those of buses and boats. What is so fascinating about this particular material is that it highlights some of the myriad ways a *single* cultural product may be appropriated—that is, interpreted, reworked, and adapted to suit new social contexts, interests, and media environments once it has entered transnational media circuits.

Simply speaking, this book is about African ways of dealing with cultural difference. These approaches to cultural difference may take place through what we conventionally consider to be media—audiocassettes, videotapes, and comic books. They may also occur through more traditional forms of mediation—live performances, such as ritual, dance, song, and theater. Both may be considered the means through which cultural producers might translate and transmit practices and symbolic elements rooted in life-worlds different from their own. They thus constitute "contact zones" (Pratt 1991) situated between two life-worlds which are experienced as being different from each other. Therefore, if this is to be a book about African ways of dealing with cultural difference, it also needs to be about the accompanying media. In fact, most mediations of cultural difference I discuss in the following chapters are at the same time remediations (Bolter and Grusin 2000). African cultural producers mediate between two contrasting life-worlds, and this frequently occurs on the basis of a difference in the media employed. Colonial military parades are thus turned into rituals; foreign films become photo novels, comic books, and songs; and the news coverage of international media houses is made into stickers, posters, and even scam letters.

Seen from a slightly different angle, I am interested in one of several possible effects of what in older anthropological writing has been dubbed "culture contact." This needs some explanation. Unlike older anthropology, I am avoiding any essentialist or substantialist reification of "culture" as a homogeneous and neatly circumscribed entity. Instead, I conceptualize "culture" first and foremost as an ideological construct that comes into play whenever groups with different social norms, values, and beliefs (embodied in corporeal practices and material objects) come into contact with one another. Fredric Jameson (1993: 33) writes, "Culture is not a 'substance' or a phenomenon in its own right, it is an objective mirage that arises out of the relationship between at least two groups. This is to say that no group 'has' culture all by itself: culture is the nimbus perceived by one group when it comes into contact with and observes another one." Despite numerous attempts to save the concept, I doubt that "culture" can any longer serve anthropology well as an analytical tool (Abu-Lughod 1991; Kuper 1999; Trouillot 2003). The idea that something like "culture" really exists, however, is a reality that is out there, a reality which anthropologists have had a hand in shaping and which we encounter more than once in this book. Seen in this light, an inquiry into the effects of "culture contact" is a misnomer. We might more aptly speak of the *experiences of cultural difference* that crop up when people come into contact with other "possible lives" (Appadurai 1996: 53), and the effects of such experiences. When using "contact," I am referring both to situations experienced in real life, such as a visit paid by a colonial officer to a village head or a public parade of colonial soldiers observed by a local audience, and to mediated forms of contact brought about by audiovisual media, that is, by fragments—or "copies"—of other life-worlds, such as American and Indian films sold as pirated video copies almost everywhere in Africa, or world news broadcast by international media houses via satellite and watched by global audiences, including many people in Africa. Such contact with difference may stimulate local copies of what has been encountered, from the young Bills of Kinshasa, who took their inspiration from cowboy movies and the emblematic figure of Buffalo Bill, roaming the streets of the Belgian Congo's capital in the 1950s (Gondola 2009), a black James Bond featured in South African photo novels of almost Pan-African circulation during the 1960s (chapter 2), to a Nigerian Shah Rukh Khan, acting in northern Nigerian melodramas in the early 2000s (chapter 4). Such copies, again, allow access to, participation in, and the experience of—essentially, contact with—other "possible lives." The imagined possibilities offered by foreign media are therefore brought even closer to a local audience. Such mediations between the foreign and the familiar contribute to the construction of local modernities which do not deny their difference from the life-worlds they copy from; by copying from and contacting these very life-worlds, however, they also express a difference from their own past. The underlying operational logic of contact and copy and copy and contact, which has been set forth by Michael Taussig (1993) and which I cover in more detail later on, not only organizes ways to deal with other life-worlds in Africa. Its very attractiveness is owed to the fact that it can be understood as the governing principle underlying the mimetic faculty of mankind per se.

The cassette which I bought in 2006 in Dar es Salaam and which in-spired me to travel, in search of the composer and the singers of the *Titanic* song, all the way to Musoma, a small town situated on the shores of Lake Victoria, turned out to be a veritable catalyst of contact in its own right. Not only did it bring me directly to those who had produced the song, it also connected the American film industry to the Tanzanian music busi-ness, a founding myth of Western modernity to apocalyptic Adventist belief, and in the process, linked a tragedy far removed in space and time to a very recent disaster close by. On my way to Musoma, I passed the cemetery where a number of those lie buried who drowned in May 1996 when the ferry M.V. *Bukoba* sank on Lake Victoria near Mwanza, claiming about 700 lives. This disaster not only provided the local context of recep-tion for Cameron's film (which came out only a year later) but also for the production and reception of local appropriations of that film, such as the song by the Kamunyonge choir. While talking to members of the church board, I learned that two German missionaries, who in 1909 founded a mission station at nearby Majita, had brought Adventism to this part of Tanzania. Actually, the centenary of this founding was to be celebrated the very weekend after my visit. Here I stood, or rather sat, for as guest of honor I had been placed at a table next to the head of the church elders, and I felt somehow uncomfortable: a German anthropologist in a "contact zone" of sorts, attempting to unravel the multiple layers of contact and copy and copy and contact embodied in a simple audiocassette, its jacket, and its musical content. Part of my answer to the task of unraveling this particular web of contacts is to discuss it in connection with cases that are somehow similar but different enough to broaden the picture. The *Titanic* adaptations, which I cover in more detail in chapter 3, are part of the much broader sphere of the mediation of cultural difference that takes shape in and through various genres of African popular media. I explore such mediations of difference in this book.

MEDIA AND MEDIATION

Media came rather late to anthropology as a new field of inquiry. Dur-ing the greater part of the twentieth century, anthropologists were almost blind to the presence and use of modern media among the people they studied. Media were associated with the societies most anthropologists came from, and thus with the self rather than the other. Media meant contagion with modernity (Probst, Deutsch, and Schmidt 2002), and despite a recurring interest in understanding the processes of "acculturation" and "culture contact," many anthropologists tended toward the "traditional." Some notable earlier exceptions notwithstanding (Carpenter 1972; Powdermaker 1962), it was only at the beginning of the 1990s that the anthropology of media, along with the anthropology of globalization, firmly took root. Meanwhile, roughly two decades later, this has grown into a veritable subdiscipline, built on a number of canonical texts, textbooks, introductions, and readers (Askew and Wilk 2002; Ginsburg, Abu-Lughod, and Larkin 2002; Peterson 2005).

Media anthropology is composed of a number of different research strands that sometimes feed into one another but are often kept separate. Three of these strands are particularly relevant for this book and worth mentioning here. The first draws on theories of active audiences, which were among the leading paradigms of media and cultural studies during the 1970s and 1980s. This new paradigm reversed the then-prevalent conception about the distribution of agency between media texts and audiences, insofar as audiences, who since the days of the Frankfurt School had been viewed as mere passive recipients of media texts, were now attributed agency in their consumption of films, TV serials, and music (Ang 1996; Hall 1992). Anthropologists took up this new conception and applied it to the study of how audiences made meaning out of media content produced in societies different and often far away from their own. What today reads almost as a truism—that audiences interpret media content against the backdrop of their everyday lives and the social and historical context of the particular society they live in—was established by anthropologists who studied how Papua New Guinean villagers made meaning out of Rambo movies (Kulick and Willson 1994), Trinidadians dealt with American soap operas (Miller 1992), Nigerians approached Indian movies (Larkin 1997), and Senegalese audiences viewed Latin American telenovelas (Werner 2006).

The second line of research relevant for this book is media anthropology's discovery that like media texts, the different forms of media on their own are not necessarily stable entities or neutral technologies, which are used identically throughout the world. This approach rests on an older line of thinking in media studies which declared content irrelevant to the social effects of media; instead, it turned to the physical and sensory properties of media to explain media's effects on social life. Marshall McLuhan's dictum "the medium is the message" has become shorthand for this line of thought. Anthropologists, however, while picking up McLuhan's message about the capacity of media to impose new social relations through their formal properties, had considerable difficulty coming to terms with the inherent technological determinism of this approach. Instead, inspired by the new material culture studies of the 1980s and the debate about "the social life of things" (Appadurai 1986), anthropology discovered the "social life of technology" (Ginsburg, Abu-Lughod, and Larkin 2002: 19) and explored the "cultural concretization" of media, as Tobias Wendl (2004a) has termed the process undergone by media following their arrival in new social contexts and previously established media environments. "Technologies are unstable things," says Brian Larkin (2008: 3), summing up the findings of this line of research. "The meanings attached to technologies, their technical functions, and the social uses to which they are put are not an inevitable consequence but something worked out over time in the context of considerable cultural debate" (3). The spectacular rise of the small-medium video from a recording technology used in private first-world households and co-opted in a big way by African film industries is an apt example of this, and one I discuss in several of the subsequent chapters.

One way to look at African popular media is to explore them as products of "cottage culture industries" (Peterson 2005: 214–218)—the third strand of anthropological media studies relevant to this book. These industries, artisanal as they may be, have been built up around small media, with video being the most prolific. In contrast to big media, such as film, television, and radio, which depend on large budgets, small media are relatively affordable and therefore accessible to many. Moreover, such technologies are difficult to control, a feature that encourages their proliferation as a primary vehicle of discourse, countering that of state-owned mass media. African cottage media industries are commercially oriented. Since they depend on the market, they keep an ear out for popular discourse, reworking it in their products, which are in turn fed back onto the streets.

The Nigerian video industry is the most prolific and best-known example of such an industry in Africa (Haynes 2000; Krings and Okome 2013a).

These different strands of media anthropology inform my own studies to varying degrees. In my attempt to explore how people in Africa appropriate and make meaning out of foreign life-worlds—at this point, read: "foreign media content"—I do not confine myself to audience ethnography but, taking appropriation more literally, turn instead to local adaptations, or "copies," of such content. Moreover, I understand such appropriations as the material result of local interpretations—namely, by those producing these copies and who in so doing articulate their "readings" of the foreign "originals." The paradigm of the active audience thus gets a specific spin in this book, where it is translated into the agency of those who make meaning out of the foreign material by remediating it in the context of a local universe of meanings and by using locally specific methods. In other words, such remediations are the result of both their producers' interpretation of the foreign templates and the technological means of (re)production. Media do not represent neutral technology, but as media studies teach us, they shape the content produced and transmitted through them. They are not stable entities either. As the anthropology of media demonstrates, they are socially shaped means of production. My discussion therefore addresses the "copies" as texts and as forms shaped by specific media in local use.

In an attempt to better understand the current use of media as discernible in Africa (and elsewhere), anthropologists have recently invoked the concept of mediation, which is what media do. Calling the work of media "mediation" implies that media are not conceptualized as mere vehicles or means of transporting messages. Rather, "underlining the centrality of the *medium* (that which occupies the middle)" serves, according to Régis Debray (2000: 111), "to highlight the efficient dynamism of the *mediate* (that through which one thing relates to another)." Its two connotations, "means" and "middle," turn the *medium* into something that is located in between *a* and *b,* enabling *a* to contact *b* or vice versa. Viewed in this light, mediation is no longer confined to technological media but pertains to objects, the human body, and social practice as well. This is why William Mazarella (2004: 353) states: "Rarely is it acknowledged that mediation . . . necessarily precedes the arrival of what we commonly recognize as 'media': that, in fact, local worlds are necessarily already the outcome of more or less stable, more or less local, social technologies of mediation." Looking at media technologies in terms of their relationship to social technologies of mediation allows us to explore "the intersections of two or more systems of mediation" (353). Birgit Meyer's (2005) work surrounding Ghanaian video films illustrates this point. She argues that Pentecostal videos may be understood as "religious remediations" (160). They remediate older forms of mediating the divine and the demonic previously associated with other media, such as the Bible, sermons, and church services. Remediation, of course, implies a relationship between the new and older systems of mediation, which is far more complex than the mere portrayal on video of priests delivering sermons and congregations holding services. The intermediality of Ghanaian video films is owed rather to the fact that they are made to work just like sermons, and that these films enable their audiences to have visions, just as church members do in Pentecostal services (Meyer 2003). Nowhere, however, do social technologies of mediation come as close to media technologies as does spirit mediumship (chapter 1). As a social technology of mediation, spirit mediumship is intimately linked with the human body, which is employed to serve as a conduit. Through their bodies, spirit mediums enable contact and communication between humans and spirits. They either transmit verbal messages thought to originate from a realm of spiritual beings, or embody and thus represent such beings in complex rituals. Spirit mediumship merges mediation and mimesis.

MIMESIS AND MIMICRY

Mimesis, which roughly translates as "imitation," is another key concept of my study. It embraces ritual, dance, music, theater, art, media, mediation and representation, and above all requires alterity, or otherness, as a *conditio sine qua non*—because a difference between imitator and imitated, the representation and the represented, must always be given in speaking of mimesis in a meaningful sense. At once product and process, mimesis bridges the gap between alter and ego, original and copy. Etymologically, the term *mimesis* goes back to the Greek word *mimos*, denoting a "mime." As early as the era of Plato and Aristotle, whose writings form the basis of mimesis theory, the term's primary meaning—the imitation of animals and humans in speech, song, or dance—had expanded to incorporate "the imitation of persons or things in an inanimate medium" (Gebauer and Wulf 1995: 28). For a study that sets out to explore human encounters with representations of alterity and the reworking of such encounters in ritual, media, and works of art, mimesis is a particularly promising concept. Throughout the chapters of this book, though, we encounter a fundamental ambiguity that comes along with the practice of mimesis that is rejected and considered dangerous as often as it is valued and embraced.

This ambiguity marks Plato's (2008) treatment of the topic. In *The Republic*, written around 380 BC, Plato dwells at length on the relationship between mimesis and its audiences. He observes that mimetic poetry as performed by storytellers can be employed for educational purposes as it engenders imitation by the audience. This, however, implies that it is censored lest it impacts the spectator's virtues negatively. Plato drafts an enormous catalog of topics, characters, and expressions poets must avoid (386a–392c). According to Plato, imitation affects both the spectator's character and that of the imitator. Therefore, similar precautions need to be taken with regard to plays performed by young people, who are the future guardians of the state. They need to be prevented from imitating such characters as women, slaves, evil men, or fools lest they take on their qualities. Young people should instead imitate courageous men and warriors only (395c–396b).[1] In book ten of *The Republic*, Plato talks about the relationship between works of art and reality. The danger of mimesis, for Plato, lies in the fact that it tricks spectators easily into believing that they are facing reality. Like a mirror that produces only reflections of existing things, a painter produces mere appearances, not true things. According to Plato, material objects originate in the realm of ideas created by God. The artist's representations are even twice removed from the truth of the ideas, as they are second-degree imitations. The carpenter who builds a bed, to quote one of Plato's famous examples, beholds the true rational idea as created by God, the "natural author"; the painter merely copies the object built by the carpenter without any understanding of the original idea (597b). The same holds true for poets, "beginning with Homer," they "are only imitators; they copy images of virtue and the like, but the truth they never reach" (600e). On the basis of its deceptive nature, Plato dismisses mimesis, as opposed to truth, and bans it from his utopian state.

Plato's disciple, Aristotle (1987), writes in defense of mimesis. In his *Poetics* (360–320 BC), he develops the idea that mimesis, which becomes synonymous with art, enables spectators not only feelings of pleasure but also understanding. This is achieved through an effect of distancing, brought about by the very mediality of art: "We take pleasure in contemplating the most precise images of things whose sight in itself causes us pain—such as the appearance of the basest animals, or of corpses" (34). The single topic elaborated most in the *Poetics* is tragedy. While Plato (2008) dismisses tragedy for "feeding and watering the passions instead of drying them up" (606d), Aristotle assigns the "arousal of pity and fear," tragedy's most distinctive element, a positive meaning because it effects "the *katharsis* of such emotions" (37). *Katharsis* should not be understood as "a notion of pure outlet or emotional release," contends Stephen Halliwell (1987), one of Aristotle's most prominent interpreters, but rather as "a powerful emotional experience which not only gives our natural feelings of pity and fear full play, but does so in a way which conduces to their rightful functioning as part of our understanding of, and response to, events in the human world" (90). For Aristotle, emotions do not exclude cognitive experiences of the world but rather operate as a part of reason. Tragedy invites pity from its audience because spectators sympathize with the dramatic characters, and it elicits fear because spectators recognize that what happens to the fictional characters could also happen to them. This fear, however, is pleasurable, as it is mediated by the staged play and thus kept at a safe distance, allowing for contemplation.

In ancient Roman and Renaissance thought, mimesis took on yet another meaning. As Matthew Potolsky (2006: 7) explains, the notion of "rhetorical imitation"—that is, "the imitation of exemplars and role models"—was instrumental in supplementing "the Greek focus on art as an imitation of nature with theories about the way artists should imitate one another." In the Latin, *imitatio*, mimesis was advocated as an artistic practice, a way to learn from a canon of classical works. There is a rich body of ancient treatises on the subject, which indicates that imitation was viewed as a creative practice aiming at transformation rather than mere reproduction (54–57). Through imitation, artists were thought to become inspired by their precursors and to participate in their talent. From the Renaissance to the eighteenth century, imitation continued to inform European art practices, before it was devalued by the romantic notion of the artist as a "genius" who sought inspiration from within rather than the work of others.

Much of this latter European uneasiness with imitation is also present in the writing of postcolonial theorists who were troubled by the figure of the colonial African who dons European clothes and copies cultural practices associated with the colonizer. In his treatise *Black Skin, White Masks,* Frantz Fanon (1967) interprets such imitative behavior in psychological terms, as an expression of an inferiority complex bestowed on black people living under colonial conditions. In their fight for the revalorization of African cultural practices, African nationalists were equally embarrassed by those they considered to have a "coconut problem" and whose very conduct they considered "to confirm the claim of the racist colonizer: that 'African' ways were inferior to 'European' ones" (Ferguson 2002: 553). Significantly, postcolonial theorists refer to such phenomena as *mimicry,* rather than mimesis. While both terms share the same Greek root and may be roughly translated as imitation, mimicry, via its conceptualization in biology (cf. Pasteur 1982), has come to denote a mode of representation that is associated with camouflage, duping, and subversion.[2] Homi Bhabha (1984), in his influential essay *Of Mimicry and Man: The Ambivalence of Colonial Discourse,* draws on Jacques Lacan and states: "Mimicry is like camouflage, not a harmonization or repression of difference, but a form of resemblance that differs/defends presence by displaying it in part, metonymically" (131). For him, mimicry is an effect of a "flawed colonial mimesis" (128). While the British Empire was driven by a "mimetic imperative," as Graham Huggan (1997/1998: 95) calls "the desire to reproduce its culture in the colonies as so many faithful copies of the originary model," it rather produced the mimicry of its colonial subjects. Bhabha (1984: 128) observes the emergence of a mode of representation "between mimesis and mimicry" that is subversive, in as much as it mocks the power of the colonizer's culture to act as a model. While Bhabha restricts his analysis to written representations, some of his exegetes have extended its meaning to apply to colonial everyday life as well. Huggan (1997/1998: 96) equates it with parody and finds its traces "in performative acts of simulated obedience, as colonial subjects bow in mock-deference to their metropolitan 'masters,' tacitly resisting subordination by appearing to embrace it."

Anthropologists who studied imitative appropriations of European conduct in African dance, ritual, and plastic art were equally keen to point out the subversive, deeper meanings of these phenomena and interpreted them as acts of resistance to colonial or neo-colonial power relations (Friedman 1990a; Lips 1937; Stoller 1984). In a recent revision of such interpretations, James Ferguson (2002: 555) argues that such analysis, despite being "ingenious," may still fall short of accounting for the desire for similarity expressed by most (post-)colonial mimetic phenomena. He suggests that these need to be understood in terms of claims to membership—historically, to colonial society, and more recently, to world society—rather than acts of subversion. While I am reluctant to discard the subversive potential of mimesis outright, as we see at least some such cases in subsequent chapters, I find compelling Ferguson's interpretation that mimesis is an attempt to participate in the imitated. This connects well to a strand of mimesis theory I further explore by taking recourse to the work of Walter Benjamin, Fritz Kramer, and Michael Taussig.

On the Mimetic Faculty is the title of a short essay written in 1933 by the German critical theorist Walter Benjamin (2005). Inspired by the anthropological writing of his time, Benjamin inquires into the cultural history of mimesis, at the base of which he assumes a human faculty for sensing and producing similarity.[3] The essay opens with the following lines: "Nature produces similarities; one need only think of mimicry. The highest capacity for producing similarities, however, is man's. His gift for seeing similarity is nothing but a rudiment of the once powerful compulsion to become similar and to behave mimetically. There is perhaps not a single one of his higher functions in which his mimetic faculty does not play a decisive role" (720). Benjamin is interested in the resurfacing and transformation of the mimetic faculty within modernity. While he seeks to trace the mimetic roots of "man's higher functions," language and writing, for example, in the context of the human capacity for producing "nonsensuous similarities" (such as those observable in astrology and divination), I am instead concerned with "sensuous" similarities (such as those observed in the mimetic relationships between originals and copies that I focus on in this book). Benjamin broaches the sensuous only briefly by referring to play and dance. What interests me about Benjamin's conception of mimesis is the "powerful compulsion to become similar and to behave mimetically" that he insists on. Unfortunately, however, he does not say anything about what triggers this compulsion, for even "the ancients" cannot have felt a compulsion to behave mimetically in the face of each and every phenomenon they encountered.

In his seminal study *The Red Fez: Art and Spirit Possession in Africa,* Fritz Kramer (1993) provides an answer to this question. His object is the representation of alien others in African plastic and performing arts. According to Kramer, the unity of such representations lies in their display of realism, which prior to the colonial encounter was absent from the idealist traditions of African art. Borrowing his concept from Erich Auerbach's study of mimesis in literature, Kramer defines realism as the "interpretation of the real by mimesis" (ix). The spirits of European alterity, which we encounter in chapter 1 of this book, where I discuss Hausa rituals of spirit possession in Nigeria, are part of this realist tradition. Drawing on Godfrey Lienhardt's cosmology of the Dinka, Kramer interprets such spirits as images of *passiones,* as ritual representations of external forces that moved and overwhelmed not only the Dinka but also other Africans (58–59). Kramer, who speaks of a compulsion to imitate in the face of alterity, takes recourse with Plato and calls mimesis "a basic form of human behavior which is not primarily purposive" (251). Though we still need to learn more about the specific contexts of such imitations, this conceptualization already helps us understand why copies of European conduct and technology in African arts and ritual should not be regarded as intentional buffoonery or parody, as suggested by Lips (1937) and Stoller (1984), respectively. A shorthand for Kramer's argument would be that contact with alterity likely triggers copying. This, however, is only half of what is at stake in such mediations, for the copy thus obtained might as well serve a number of purposes—to connect with what has been copied, for example.

CONTACT AND COPY

In his book *Mimesis and Alterity,* Michael Taussig (1993: xiii) defines the human mimetic faculty as "the nature that culture uses to create second nature, the faculty to copy, imitate, make models, explore difference, yield into and become other." He goes on to explain that the "wonder of mimesis lies in the copy drawing on the character and power of the original, to the point whereby the representation may even assume that character and that power" (xiii). Inspired by Benjamin, Taussig broadens the former's theme of the surfacing of the primitive within modernity to some extent by showing that the complex dialectics of mimesis and alterity have governed "primitive" encounters with alterity no less than "civilized" ones, with anthropology being the most prominent among the latter. Taussig traces the logic of contact and copy back and forth between Cuna healing figurines, Frazer's sympathetic magic, mimetically capacious machinery (such as the phonograph and the camera), situations of first contact, and both ethnographic writing and film. The all-too human idea that contact with something may be established by means of its copy may likely be traced back to physics and physiology, and is therefore grounded in nature. Contact and copy turn out to be steps in the process of sensing. Taussig (1993: 21) writes: "A ray of light, for example, moves from the rising sun into the human eye where it makes *contact* with the retinal rods and cones to form, via the circuits of the central nervous system, a (culturally attuned) *copy* of the rising sun. On this line of reasoning, contact and copy merge to become virtually identical, different moments of the one process of sensing; seeing something or hearing something is to be in contact with that something." Media, especially those producing image and sound, are "mimetically capacious machines" (243). They can make copies of physical realities appear, which are then sensed by human spectators or audiences. Their mimetic capacity combines with that of the human users. "A camera copies a physical reality through a form of contact with it (light reflected by an object makes an impression on film); this copy—the film image—contacts the retinal rods of the eye and forms a second copy that connects the spectator with the invisible original" (Yanoshak 2008: 1052). Insofar as media can create copies of absent originals, they connect such copies with their originals through the eyes of the beholder. Therefore, obtaining a copy of something means being in contact with that something, even if this contact is established only through sight or sound because looking at something means "touching" it with the eyes, and listening to something, "touching" it with the ears. In terms of film, Laura Marks (2000: xii) calls this the "tactile and contagious quality of cinema."

But what about the copies I explore in this book? Within the physical and physiological chain of contact and copy just sketched, they seem to multiply the processes involved, and turn out to be copies of copies of copies of copies. Take, for example, a Nigerian video remake of an Indian movie (chapter 4). The latter is a copy of physical reality, experienced through a second copy produced within the sensory apparatus of the spectator, who in our case is the producer or director of the remake. This spectator now transforms his copy into physical reality again—that is, into human action on a film set he directs (most likely mediated by a screenplay or some other written plot). This action in turn is copied by a camera onto a storage medium (most commonly digital tape), which if watched by a spectator, produces yet another copy. This situation is further complicated by the fact that the Indian original is most likely also a copy in yet another sense, as Indian films are often adaptations of Indian mythology. Apparently, the status of "original" has to be considered a relational thing: an original is only so in relation to its copy, and not in any absolute or ontological sense. Most originals thus turn out to be "original copies" (Fehrmann et al. 2004: 8), which in fact depend on copies to lay claim to their originality. "It is the copying that originates" (Geertz 1986: 380).

In terms of enabling encounters with "other possible lives," this video example harbors still another problem. The Indian "original copy" is based on mimesis—showing actors acting as if they were others. Hence, Nigerian directors and their actors base their own copies on at least twice-mediated representations of "other possible lives." A very tempting shortcut is to just ignore the complex process of mediation involved in either the mimesis of the first or second degree, as is sometimes done in Nigeria and elsewhere. In his book *Street Dreams and Hip Hop Barbershops*, Brad Weiss (2009: 169–196) discusses how young Tanzanian urbanites relate to American TV serials. According to Weiss, these audiences frame the American soap opera as some sort of "live" show—not in the sense of a live broadcast but in the sense of portraying the true lives of real people (in contrast to performances by actors embodying fictitious people), therefore ignoring the mimesis of the first degree. As if attesting to the Platonian critique of mimesis, Nigerian audiences of Indian films also tend to ignore the mediated nature of such films, despite being well aware that they are watching performances by actors. These films are in fact conceptualized as windows permitting views onto a foreign "culture." The play of Indian actors thus appears to be synonymous with "Indian culture," which Hausa directors and actors in Nigeria then copy in their own films.

All case studies in this book involve copies that are not really faithful, in a conventional sense, compared to their originals. Just like the copies Taussig (1993: 17) discusses in *Mimesis and Alterity*, my own examples, too, slide "between photographic fidelity and fantasy, between iconicity and arbitrariness, wholeness and fragmentation." While I do not use the word *copy* purely metaphorically, I do not take it at face value, either—that is, assigning its narrowest meaning. This would imply faithfulness to an original, matching it as closely as possible, in the way a medieval transcript matches its script or a photomechanical reproduction its original document (Schwartz 2000). The mediations of cultural difference I am interested in are most often based on selective copying. The fragments copied from another life-world are elements perceived as different, in comparison with the appropriator's own life-world. For example, a certain style of dress, way of talking, type of food is copied—and in the eyes of the copiers, these fragments are sensed as emblematic, if not essential, features of those other life-worlds. What unites the copies I discuss is the fact that they do not deny their origins but seek to establish or maintain contact with their respective originals.

AFRICAN APPROPRIATIONS

The African cultural producers whose works we encounter in subsequent chapters appropriate alien cultural forms, which are also often commodities, and repurpose them for their own ends. The term *appropriation*, which derives from the Latin verb *appropriare*, "to make one's own," has currency in debates about ownership on various scales (Strang and Busse 2011). It is frequently evoked in studies about authorship, copyright, and intellectual property (Boon 2010; Coombe 1998), and also features prominently in debates about the restitution and protection of "cultural property" (Coombe 2009; Noyes 2010). In their introduction to *Borrowed Power: Essays on Cultural Appropriation*, Bruce Ziff and Pratima Rao (1997: 3) point out that even though the meaning of the term *appropriation* is somewhat open-ended, it generally connotes "some form of taking" and therefore indicates a "relationship between persons or groups." Ziff and Rao further explain that appropriation is primarily regarded as an act of taking "from a subordinate into a dominant culture," and while they acknowledge that the "subordinate" may also appropriate, they view this as a "complementary opposite" and call it "cultural assimilation" (5). I take issue with this viewpoint for two reasons: First, it calls a single practice (taking something out of one context and putting it into another) by two different names; and second, one of these names, *cultural assimilation,* evokes the holistic conception of "culture" as a bounded and homogeneous entity to which "intruding" alien elements need to be assimilated—that is, stripped of their alterity so as not to endanger cultural homeostasis.[4] In Ziff and Rao's terminology, *cultural appropriation,* which is practiced only by hegemonic groups, values alterity, and the appropriated object retains part of its difference (even though much of it is imagined), whereas *cultural assimilation,* practiced by "subaltern" groups, supposedly aims at effacing the alterity of the object that is taken into the "culture." Second, this conceptualization grants those who "assimilate" considerably less agency than those who "appropriate." If *appropriation* is defined as "the act of claiming the right to use, make, or own something that someone else claims in the same way" (Boon 2010: 204), why should members of marginalized societies—that is, in terms of global politics and economy—appropriate things from elsewhere differently than members of hegemonic societies? And why should they not also thrive on the "borrowing of power" through their acts of appropriation?[5]

While I think it is important to discuss the politics of appropriation and the power relationships at stake, we should not lose sight of the manifold forms of re-signification involved in appropriation. Appropriation means taking a cultural form, a symbolic representation, for example, out of one context and putting it into another, whereby shifts of meaning most likely occur. And it is such shifts in meaning and their social and cultural consequences that I focus on particularly in this book. No doubt, legal issues are at stake when African cultural producers appropriate, for example, Cameron's *Titanic,* by turning the movie into a quarry for their own productions. The ease with which this is done is reminiscent of traditional forms of creation that have been recently labeled "open source" (Noyes 2010: 2) or "Read/Write," in contrast to "Read/Only," culture (Lessig 2008: 28)—terminology that highlights the fact that popular creativity in the digital age has its antecedents in historical forms of creation.[6] While the changing regimes of ownership rights in cultural property in Africa (Comaroff and Comaroff 2009; Diawara 2011) and the legal dimensions of cultural appropriation are fascinating topics in themselves, for the present study I privilege an inquiry into the semantic and medial dimensions of cultural appropriation.[7] I thus adopt a refined concept of appropriation, which defines the word not exclusively in legal terms but as hermeneutic practice. Arnd Schneider (2003) advanced this reconceptualization. He frames appropriation as a practice of understanding and interpretation, with reference to the French philosopher, Paul Ricoeur (1981), whom I quote through Schneider: "An interpretation is not authentic unless it culminates in some form of appropriation (Aneignung) if by that term we understand the process by which one makes one's own (eigen) what was initially other or alien (fremd)" (178, in Schneider 2006: 26; German terms in original). While Ricoeur focuses on the operations of understanding by the interpreting subject, who following Ricoeur, ideally reaches "a new self-understanding" through appropriation, Schneider claims that "anthropology, which owes by its very nature . . . to the producing, 'originating' cultures, cannot stop here." This is because Schneider, like Ziff and Rao, locates cultural appropriation exclusively within the domain of "the powerful" (26), whereas I seek to establish it as a term that applies equally to such practices, if carried out by people who are conventionally considered less powerful—that is, for the very phenomena which hitherto have been labeled "cultural assimilation." Perhaps it makes sense to bracket the seemingly commonsensical ethical (and therefore political) dimensions of appropriation talk for a moment. While Schneider (2006) continues his discussion, searching for a concept that reconciles "the element of 'understanding'" with the "element of agency" (i.e., the agency of the creator of the artifact that is being appropriated), I am concerned with the appropriator's agency. Though I also subscribe to the notion of appropriation as an intermediary practice linking the appropriator via the appropriated artifact to the latter's producer, I contend that the interpretation of alien artifacts, such as Cameron's *Titanic* by African cultural producers, takes place very much on the terms of the latter. And as we see, hermeneutic fidelity is not necessarily what individual appropriators are aiming for, rather considerable re-significations are the order of the day. Schneider (2006) arrives at a definition of appropriation "as a hermeneutic procedure that, consequently, implies not only that cultural elements are invested with new signification but also that those who appropriate are transformed, and ultimately construct and assume new identities" (29). While I am wary of identity talk (cf. Brubaker and Cooper 2000), the notion of "transformation," which derives from Ricoeur's hermeneutics, matches the uncanny power of mimesis. Like the interpreting subject, who is transformed through understanding, mimesis confers some of the original's qualities on the copy (and on its producer). In this sense, the African appropriations I look at in this book should be viewed as "mimetic interpretations"—a coinage that combines mimesis with the notion of appropriation as hermeneutic process.

Calling African *Titanic* remakes (and the like) appropriations allows me to stress the agency their producers display vis-à-vis the source material. All too often such appropriations have been dismissed under the rubric of "cultural assimilation." This terminology is problematic because it turns African appropriators of non-African cultural forms into mere victims of European or American "cultural imperialism," despite the considerable agency and creativity such practices of appropriation engender. Attributing agency to African appropriators, however, does not mean that their appropriations necessarily subvert the alien "originals"—comparable to the "writing back" of postcolonial literatures (Ashcroft, Griffiths, and Tiffin 1989). In an essay on the appropriation of the Western film genre in Africa, Lily Saint (2013) argues along similar lines. She contends that such appropriations "need neither be categorized as resistant nor as repressive." She continues: "Instead, they should be geographically and historically situated to be understood on their own terms, re-conceptualized outside of debates on authenticity and mimicry, and examined instead as critiques or comments on those very debates" (211). This contention mirrors very much my own conviction. In this book, I focus on the appropriation by African cultural producers of alien cultural objects, such as performances, music, texts, still images, and films. While most of the appropriated objects I look at originate outside of Africa, some have African sources. In particular, I am interested in appropriations that display a certain deliberate play with difference and strive for a symbolic "borrowing of power," from that which has been appropriated. To highlight this aspect of appropriation, I rely on the term *mimesis,* as this implies some sort of relationship to an "original" (understood here simply as that to which a "copy" relates) and the borrowing of some of its qualities. The embodiment of spirits clad in European uniforms in Hausa rituals in Nigeria (chapter 1), *Titanic* songs sung by Tanzanian choirs (chapter 3), and the mimicry of bureaucracy by Nigerian cyber scammers (chapter 7) are all aimed at invoking contact—in quite a number of ways—with their originals by means of the fabricated copies, as is apparent throughout this book.

THE STRUCTURE OF THE BOOK

Most of the appropriations I discuss herein are related to the two African countries where I spent most of my time as a researcher—that is, Nigeria and Tanzania. To a minor extent, reference is made to Congo, Ghana, Namibia, Niger, and South Africa as well. Each chapter addresses the case of a different copy, thus covering a wide range of examples in terms of media—from mimetic interpretations of the European other by African spirit mediums during the early decades of the twentieth century to the pastiches of blackness in music video clips produced by cosmopolitan "crazy white men" at the beginning of the twenty-first century. In each chapter I focus on the copy as text, the context that was conducive to its production, and the media involved, along with its social effects. The degree to which I discuss each of these parameters, however, varies from chapter to chapter.

Chapter 1 focuses on what I have called an "*ur*-scene" of the mediation of cultural difference in Africa. I recollect my own experiences in northern Nigeria during the first half of the 1990s with spirit mediums possessed by Komanda Mugu—the Wicked Major—and other spirits said to be of European descent. I trace the origins of these ritual copies of Europeanness to French colonial West Africa, in about 1925. Reconstructing the context of their early manifestations in rituals of spirit possession, a social technology of mediation well established in this region of Africa at the time, allows me to explore the relationship between original and copy specific to this corporeal form of mediation, and to speculate about the social functions allotted to the copies. The possessed embodied the essence of European difference and colonial power, represented through their spirits' military comportment, and sometimes also took the form of specific colonial personnel—such as Horace Crocchichia, a French *commandant de cercle* (district commander), immortalized as Komanda Mugu, the Wicked Major. The ritual copies, I argue, were used to connect with the invisible power hidden behind European force. The power acquired in this way, however, was not used against its source to mock or resist the French colonial regime as has been contended by several contemporary observers. Instead, it was used against local forms of amoral power and illegitimate authority—that is, to resist witchcraft and colonial African chiefs. In the early days, the spirits played an important role both as witch-hunting agencies and as spiritual guides of a revitalization movement whose purpose it was to rebuild local society by imitating certain aspects of colonial modernity. Over time and with changing social contexts, the functions of these spirits changed. When I encountered them in Kano, Nigeria, in the 1990s, they were integrated into the pantheon of the *bori* cult of spirit possession, where they appeared to be just one of several categories of foreign spirits. Unlike the others, however, they "embodied colonial memories" (Stoller 1995) and were sought after when it came to curing afflictions or solving problems somehow associated with modernity by their local clients: misuse of hemp, compulsivity in gambling, and failure in school.

Chapter 2 addresses the remediation of Western modernity through *African Film,* a magazine of photo novels that enjoyed almost Pan-African circulation during the second half of the 1960s. Produced by South Africa–based Drum Publications Ltd., each issue of this twice-monthly magazine was read and looked at by about half a million people in English-speaking Africa, between South Africa and Uganda, Kenya and Nigeria. Devoted to the adventures of Lance Spearman, an African crime fighter inspired in equal measure by James Bond and the hard-boiled private eyes of American films noir, *African Film* introduced an African visual modernity and provided a stylish streetwise character with whom a readership of young Africans could readily identify. The magazine's language and images allowed people to imagine how an urban modernity, with which many readers had come into contact through American or European films, might look if inhabited exclusively by Africans, and what it would mean to live in this kind of modernity. Drawing from interviews I conducted with former readers in Tanzania and from comments gathered on the internet, I look into reading practices and some of the magazine's social effects, as well as the sensation it stirred up in its fans. I assume that at a time when commercial African filmmaking was almost absent from the continent due to the costs involved, this magazine of photo novels served as a surrogate for film, as is suggested by its very title, *African Film*. The photo novels of the late 1960s, with their openness to borrowing from American and European popular culture, as well as their commercial orientation and transnational circulation, have much in common with current Nollywood video films, some of which we encounter in several subsequent chapters.

Chapter 3 focuses on four African remediations of a single American film—James Cameron's *Titanic* of 1997. The film, itself being the most recent, expensive, and successful version of a story that has been told through various genres and media of Western mass culture many times before, was immensely popular among African audiences, who saw it via legal screenings or pirated videos. I suggest that Cameron's "original copy"—that is, the film's mise-en-scène which sets the stage for high melodrama to play out openly the conflict between collective social norms and the individualistic and potentially antisocial force of love—accounts for at least half of the film's appeal to African audiences. Beginning with the Onitsha market literature of the 1950s (Obiechina 1973), popular genres all over Africa have reflected, along similar lines, on the social conflict inherent to African modernities. Moreover, the film's appeal is doubtlessly due to the fact that sinking ships lend themselves to plays of thought and therefore make excellent material to be used allegorically. The four copies I discuss—a Nigerian video remake, a Congolese music video clip, a Tanzanian comic book, and the song of the Kamunyonge choir—focus on one or both of these aspects. All four copies also aim to capitalize on their original's fame. Like most of the copies I discuss in this book, they are commodities which have been produced and distributed by African cottage culture industries. To boost sales, and sometimes also an ideology or belief promoted by their products (the Musoma Adventist choir's apocalypticism, for example), cultural producers may tie their own products to a foreign best seller. They hope that their products thus partake of the popularity and fame of the original, which may also translate into economic gain. Finally, by snitching film sequences from Cameron's "original copy" and intercutting these with their own material, the producers of the Nigerian remake and the Congolese clip also connect with Cameron's *Titanic* quite physically.

American film, however, is by no means the only foreign cinema African cultural producers appropriate. Films made in Kanywood, the Kano-based video industry of northern Nigeria, which I discuss in chapter 4, are frequently inspired by Bollywood movies. Such feature films, shot in the Hausa language, provide glimpses of a local Islamic modernity modeled after Indian films, in which lovers negotiate the opposing forces of their individual desire and traditional social norms, as in the case of fixed marriages. In the musical sequences of Hausa videos, women and men dance together, occupying the same visual space. This stylistic device, which is likewise inspired by Indian films, has sparked considerable controversy. Against the backdrop, over the past decade, of northern Nigeria's Islamic revitalization, which advocates an Islamic hygiene of local social practice, films that overtly mediate between a local and a foreign life-world are eyed suspiciously by conservative factions of society; after all, such movies establish contact between things that according to the new local cultural policy, should remain separate, including unmarried women and men, and Hausa and Indian "culture." Copies of other possible lives may have polluting effects on local youth, or so goes the Islamic rationale—this is the quintessence of local critique. My discussion of Kanywood under duress focuses on the consequences of this critique, such as censorship, the burning of videocassettes by clerics, and two total bans on video production for several months during the past decade. Within the overall theme of this book, chapter 4 shows that the contact implied by a copy is not always viewed in a positive light; it may also be considered dangerous and therefore highly contested.

In Tanzania, I observed a case of contact and copy which prompted a local critique akin to concerns in northern Nigeria over protecting local cultural identity. Interestingly enough, the influence of Nigerian Nollywood films on local Swahili video film production has come under fire by an intellectual elite in Tanzania. In chapter 5, I discuss such local copies of Nollywood movies in the context of the rapid spread of Nigerian video films across Africa within the past decade (cf. Krings and Okome 2013a). Tanzanian audiences are fascinated by Nigerian movies for the very reason that they depict an African life-world similar to their own—and yet different enough to evoke a sense of novelty. Similar to Hausa fans of Indian films, Nigerian video films provide their Tanzanian viewers with images of a "parallel modernity" (Larkin 1997). For Tanzanian audiences, however, Nollywood films shot in English pose one major problem: language. A number of cultural producers in Dar es Salaam capitalized on this and provided translations into Swahili by remediating Nollywood films. I discuss three distinct examples involving remediation: a photo novel based on screenshots of a Nigerian video film, with speech bubbles in Swahili; a Nollywood film with a cinema narrator whose Swahili voice-over simultaneously provides commentary, explanation, and translation; and, finally, *Dar 2 Lagos,* a video film produced by a Tanzanian and shot with a mixed cast of Tanzanian and Nigerian actors in Dar es Salaam and Lagos.

In chapter 6, I return to Nigeria and look at how local cottage culture industries have reworked the newscasts of global mass media related to 9/11 and America's subsequent "war on terror." In this case, it is not other possible lives that are remediated by African copies but rather the life of a single person—Osama bin Laden, who has become an icon of radical Islam. Soon after 9/11, a plethora of bin Laden merchandise flooded the northern Nigerian markets—posters, stickers, badges, key-ring pendants, T-shirts, baseball caps—all of which bore his image, as well as video films and tape-recorded songs that praised him. I argue that Nigerian cultural producers have not only capitalized on bin Laden's cult status among radical-minded Muslims but also provided the very material that established him as a brand of radical Islam. I distinguish two different meanings attached to this brand by local Muslims, corresponding with the communicative function of menacing gestures directed at two different addressees. Within the ethno-religious politics of the Nigerian nation-state, images of bin Laden connected the Muslim north with a radical Islamic force from outside. I see this as an attempt to tap the potential of a powerful other to increase Muslim agency and northern Nigerian bargaining clout at a time when the country was headed by a Christian president. Within the Muslim north, which underwent a massive Islamic revival at the time, images of bin Laden were meant to remind local elites of their duty to share their wealth with their less-affluent brothers in faith, just as bin Laden was alleged to have done. Given the millenarian hopes that were associated with the reintroduction of sharia law, the type of copy and contact at play here is, in a way, reminiscent of that employed by the spirit mediums I describe in chapter 1. Both seek to contact a power from outside through locally produced copies of that power, to gain agency in local projects of radical social reform.

Copies of newscasts and other genres of dominant global mass media are also key to the strategies of African cyber scammers, which I discuss in chapter 7. To lull their victims, the majority of whom are from America or Europe, Nigerian advance fee fraudsters mimic the common forms of Western representations of Africa. And sure enough, the stories made up by scammers in these unsolicited emails tie in very well with Western stereotypes of Africa, and are deliberately meant to do so. As the scam goes, some ex-dictator or corrupt government official offers to pay for the privilege of moving millions of dollars out of his country, in exchange for a bank account number. The copy has to be as faithful to its original as possible if the scammers are to succeed. Indeed, this is a special case of contact and copy, in which the copy is not only used to evoke its original but actually turns against those who are associated with the original's production—a perfect example of mimicry as a form of "mischievous imitation" (Huggan 1997/1998: 94). Along the lines of such scams, more forged copies are important as well, such as copies of bureaucratic paper-work and international business procedures. As I learned through online interviews, scammers justify their crimes as "retribution" for Africa's co-lonial and postcolonial exploitation by Europe and America. Scamming turns former "masters" into *mugus,* or "fools," as the victims are called in Nigerian scammer parlance. If the so-called savage ever hit back with a form of imitation, it is precisely through this orientalist mimicry and not through alleged parodist sculptures, as Julius Lips assumed in his study *The Savage Hits Back* (1937).

In chapter 8, I discuss the work of three white musicians who appropriate African popular culture to differing degrees: Mzungu Kichaa (Crazy White Man), a Dane who grew up in East Africa, performs Tanzanian pop music and sings in Swahili; White Nigerian, a Nigerian national with Levantine roots who has built his career as both a musician and comedian on his ability to speak Hausa and pidgin English; and EES, or Namboy, a German Namibian who performs Nam-Flava, a Namibian version of Kwaito music. What sets the performances of these musicians apart from mimicry is not only that they address their audiences in Tanzania, Nigeria, and Namibia, respectively, but also the pastiche-like nature of their artistic work. I view their performances as deliberate plays on difference and sameness. While their skin color makes them stand out from the masses of other musicians in Africa, their conduct and command of African languages signify just the opposite: sameness. Thus, they thrive on the (un)doing of difference, and I argue that it is exactly this feature that accounts for their popularity among African audiences. Paying special attention to technologies of mediation is important here, as I argue that their popularity is very much linked to visibility and therefore to the emergence of digital visual media and the recent rise of the video clip in African music. With this chapter, the book comes full circle: while it begins with a discussion of Africans imitating European conduct and technology in rituals of spirit possession during the colonial era, it ends with a chapter about postcolonial imitations of African performances by white men who are disseminating their mimetic appropriations via digital media and the internet.

I conclude this introduction with a cautionary note: the phenomena under discussion in this book touch on practices, discussed under the terms of *appropriation, mimesis,* and *media,* which I deem crucial for any kind of cultural production—not just African. The fact that I have limited myself to a discussion of exclusively African examples can only be accounted for by the contingencies of my biography and the place anthropology holds in the disciplinary rubrics of the academic system. The products of the anthropologist's profession, ethnographic texts and films—mimetic interpretations of other life-worlds—are perhaps appropriate examples for

FIGURE I.1

Author in costume of female bori spirit, Bagwariya, together with two friends, Kano 1993.

highlighting the fact that the human desire to mediate cultural difference through mimesis is certainly not limited to people in Africa or to forms of popular culture. And aren't there many of us anthropologists who, under certain circumstances, feel an urge or even the compulsion to dress, talk, or act like a typical member of the communities among whom we conduct our research? A photograph of my younger self, taken in Kano in 1993 and a bit embarrassing today, shows me clad in the ritual dress of a bori spirit—a female, pagan spirit, for that matter (see figure I.1). Photographs of Franz Boas dressed as an Inuit and of Frank Hamilton Cushing in Hopi regalia are better-known examples of our mimetic inclinations. The desire to experience other possible lives, at least temporarily, by dressing as they do, is no less an expression of the human mimetic faculty than that displayed by Nigerian spirit mediums who host the spirits of colonial Europeans, Hausa actors who mime Indians, South African James Bond impersonators, and Tanzanian video film stars who act "Nollywoodish."

The Wicked Major

EMBODYING CULTURAL DIFFERENCE

IT WAS GETTING close to midnight when the musicians finally intoned the hymn of Magajiyar Jangare. The amplified sound of the *garaya,* a two-stringed lute, distorted and cracking through the megaphones that served as loudspeakers, sent shivers down my spine. I had witnessed a number of public bori possession dances before and knew that this was the sign for the spirit mediums to begin their preparations. On that night in December 1992, Idi and his group had been performing in Unguwa Uku, one of the bustling quarters outside the old city of Kano, Nigeria, since the last prayer, at about eight that evening. For hours, Idi had sweetly praised women and men among the audience with words sung to the tunes of the spirit hymns. Those who were praised had reciprocated with cash, thus expressing their close relationship to particular spirits as well as their acknowledgement of Idi's praise. Now Idi sang the lines which prompted those willing to come forward to serve as the spirits' "horses," or mediums, on that very night: "Children of bori, come forward, your mother has arrived, the one with the large *zane*-wrapper." The six-gourd rattle players sitting in front of Idi gave their best and sped up the rhythm. Clad only in single cloths tied around their waists or above their chests, the nine "children of bori," six men and three women, came up and sat down in the middle of the makeshift dance floor, an open space surrounded by more than 300 people. Soon some of the mediums began to yawn. With trembling bodies and bulging eyes, groaning and frothing from their mouths, they produced the physical signs of possession trance. The scene grew wilder by the minute. As if violently thrown across the dance floor by invisible hands, some mediums traversed the open space half-crawling, half-jumping—raising clouds of dust. Finally, when the spirits had fully mounted their horses, the scene calmed down again. Each medium now moved and spoke according to the personality of the particular spirit he or she embodied.

Two of the mediums, whose spirits had treated their bodies with particular harshness, stood erect—their legs apart, hands on their hips—and announced who they were by shouting their *kirari,* a form of self-praise, in a wild mixture of French, English, and corrupted Hausa:

> What's up, Monsieur spirits!? Come forward, Monsieur spirits! Only we of the governor, the lads of the governor! We conquer the town; we pass the town; we go into hiding as if we weren't there! One wants us to come; one wants us to leave! We come to town; the town falls empty; we leave the town, and the town falls empty! We are pagans who go to sleep at half past ten and rise at ten! We are pagans who turn the next day into "tomorrow"! We are killing. People say it's Allah—Allah is killing. People say it's us! Ocho!

When they had finished, the two mediums were led outside the circle and got dressed. When they came back, one of them was wearing a red uniform, the other a green one with red applications; both men also wore sashes across their chests, as well as berets and heavy boots. While one of them used his whip and Thunderer whistle to push back the audience and rearrange the dance floor, the other greeted the dignitaries among the audience with military salutes and handshakes. As I learned from someone standing next to me, the one in red was Kafaran, the "Corporal," and the one in green Komanda Mugu, the "Wicked Major." Both belonged to the family of Babule spirits who are said to be of European descent.

The two Europeans, who temporarily occupied the bodies of their African mediums, were almost naturally drawn to the only other European present, the one "who occupied the body of an anthropologist"—to borrow a phrase from Paul Stoller (1994: 646). They came over to me. After we shook hands and someone translated the greetings the spirits had uttered in corrupt Hausa, Kafaran ordered a bench to be brought for his superior and himself, and they sat down next to me. Together we watched the dance of the other spirits, who belonged to different families, including hunters, aristocrats, Fulbe, Tuareg, and Maguzawa, or pagan Hausa. Not only were the three of us among the few who had been offered a bench to sit on, but as I soon discovered, we had a number of other things in common, such as smoking cigarettes, drinking bottled soft drinks, and taking notes.

My new friends were the last to be called on to perform in front of the musicians. "Black ones, lads of the governor, one can see your whiteness, one can see your blackness," sang Idi in their praise, exclaiming, "Let's drink fire, let's taste the whip! Come forward, the one of Halima, owner of a thousand bullets!" Marching more than dancing in their heavy boots, they transformed the dance floor into a military parading ground. Their performance climaxed in a powerful demonstration of their superhuman invulnerability to fire. By stroking their bare chests with burning torches, they "washed [themselves] with fire," and when they "drank fire" like fire breathers, they lit up the surroundings by sending large balls of fire up into the night sky. Soon after they had finished their performance, the music stopped and the audience began to disperse. The spirits, however, far from swiftly leaving the bodies of their mediums, stayed on for a while outside in the dark, where people consulted them about their personal problems. Suddenly, I was approached by one of the Babule's helpers, who told me that Kafaran wanted to see me. I followed him to a dimly lit spot where Kafaran, about to leave his medium, was waiting. "Did you get what you came looking for in Nigeria?" he asked me, and I said, "Yes, almost." "What about *maganin kwarjini*, a 'medicine' which will ensure you the respect of others?" I had to confess that I had not come across it yet, and he offered: "I will give it to you!" However, he made clear that he expected something in return: "What will you give me?" "Twenty naira," I replied. He took a deep, roaring breath and said, "Fifty naira!" We made a deal, and he asked me to give the money to his "horse," who would prepare the "medicine" for me and from whom I should collect it the next day. I handed the money to his helper, shook hands with the spirit, and watched him dismount his medium. The moment he left, the medium fell to the ground. Gradually regaining control over his body, the medium, a young man called Isa, inspected himself and the scene around him, and then he asked us in astonishment what had happened and how he had gotten to where he found himself now in the early hours of the morning.

In this chapter, I focus on spirit possession as a primary technology for the mediation of cultural difference in Africa, which is based on the conception that the human body can serve as a medium for spirits. Recollecting my own experiences from 1992 to 1994 with Babule spirits in northern Nigeria (Krings 1997), I trace the origin of these ritual copies of Europeanness to French colonial West Africa in 1925. The spirits that first manifested themselves during possession rituals in the Hausa-speaking regions of southwestern Niger embodied the essence of colonial power and European alterity. "We copy the world to comprehend it through our bodies," writes Stoller (1994: 643) in his discussion of Michael Taussig's take on spirit possession and Cuna healing figurines. With reference to Adeline Masquelier (2001), who further developed this argument with regard to the Babule, I argue that the early Babule mediums did not only copy to comprehend but also to acquire some of the qualities of those on whom their ritual copies were modeled. The power thus acquired, however, was not used against its source to mock or resist the French colonial regime, as has been contended both by contemporary observers and some more recent interpreters (Stoller 1984), but against forms of amoral power and illegitimate authority—that is, witchcraft and local chiefs installed by the colonizers. I argue that the Babule spirits, far from being ritual caricatures of colonial Europeans, rather, have to be conceptualized as embodied pastiches, as particular spiritualized copies of powerful others, who transferred some of the qualities of the colonial Europeans to those possessed by the Babule spirits.

What becomes obvious by following the traces of the Babule spirits to the present, as I set out to do, is that they change their meaning according to respective historic contexts and the social functions of the rituals of possession they are associated with. What began as a revitalization movement inspired by embodied pastiches that formed its spiritual backbone, in Niger in 1925, became a religious institution around which Nigerien immigrants to southern Ghana organized their communities and social life in the 1950s. In northern Nigeria, where the Babule had been integrated into the pantheon of bori spirits early on, they acted according to the logic of a typical cult of affliction: during the 1990s, they were the source as well as the remedy for serious afflictions and mundane problems alike, which were somehow associated with local modernity, and they enabled their adepts to make a living by performing as their vessels during public possession dances and administering "medicines" to clients during private consultations. What these different forms have in common is that they make use of alterity to articulate and legitimize certain functions of the self.

REWIND: NIGER 1925–1927

The early Babule spirits manifested themselves in southwestern Niger during a period marked by the intensification of French colonial rule. Since the turn of the century, Kurfey and Arewa, the two neighboring Hausaphone regions that were to produce particular strongholds of Babule followers, had each experienced dramatic political and economic changes. In search of traditional rulers who would help govern the peasant population, the French had installed "district chiefs," or *chefs de canton,* among people who hitherto had had no dealings whatsoever with centralized political institutions, such as the egalitarian Kurfeyawa, or expanded the power of traditional political authorities which had formerly been checked by a fragile system of power sharing, such as in Arewa (Fuglestad 1975; Latour 1992). In both regions, the new local authorities had proven to be particularly efficient helpers of the French. They had helped fight revolts, forcefully recruited men to serve in the French army during World War I and as laborers for construction work, exacted aliments, and levied taxes (Echard 1992: 96; Fuglestad 1975: 211). In 1925, such coercions became even more burdensome when the French decided to develop Niamey, which would become Niger's administrative capital. To realize their plans they needed manpower, foodstuffs, and animals for transportation, all of which they exacted particularly from the regions near Niamey. The Babule spirits first made their presence felt in Tudu Anza, a village of the Arewa region (Echard 1992) during the dry season of 1925.

In that village, a woman called Shibo became possessed by an unknown female spirit who turned out to be Batura (female European).

Nothing is known about the immediate context in which this happened. It is also unclear why Shibo, daughter of the *chef de village* of Shikal in the neighboring canton of Kurfey, went to that particular Arewa village. The spirit, however, must have struck a chord with the villagers who flocked to the séances Shibo began to organize. Soon, more villagers, especially young people, became possessed, and the number of spirits grew. Embodying spirits such as the Governor, Commandant de Cercle, and Capitaine, the possessed "became invulnerable, swallowing cinders, flogging each other with torches and so on" (Fuglestad 1983: 129). When Shibo and her followers began to agitate against the chef de canton, Tassao Gao, the French stepped in with a number of unsuccessful disciplinary measures. The spirits and their cult then spilled over into neighboring regions, and by May 1926, had already spread among the Hausa-speaking Mawri of the subdivision of Dogondoutchi. Meanwhile, Shibo, who had returned together with a number of followers and musicians to Shikal, her home village in Kurfey, continued to initiate new adepts into the cult of the strange spirits. By February 1927, the cult had spread across the whole of Kurfey. Like before in Arewa, they also began to agitate against the chef de canton of Kurfey, Gado Namailaya. A French official described the situation as follows: "A woman of Shikal, Shibo, and her father, Ganji, have invented a sect that copies our administration. Young boys and girls come together, found villages, name governors, commanders, doctors, exercise with wooden rifles, arrest the native guards. . . . Shibo enters into trance, preaches insubordination, urges people to stop paying taxes and to refuse to work" (Scheurer, in Olivier de Sardan 1984: 282; my translation). To reassert their presence among the peasants, the French decided to carry out a population census of the Kurfey canton. Led by a young and inexperienced official keen to break the passive resistance of the population, this census turned into a punitive expedition. However, the administration at Niamey disapproved of this development and decided to compensate the victims, among them also followers of the Babule spirits (Echard 1992; Fuglestad 1975). The Babule adepts and their followers claimed this success as their own and as proof of the power of their spirits. According to Fuglestad (1983), two further events must have contributed to a growing conviction among the peasants that the tables were beginning to turn: the death of the chef de canton, Gado Namailaya, who was *the* most proximate symbol of colonial rule and who died in March 1927, and the assault on the military post of Tessaoua in June of the same year, which went unatoned. When the cult started spreading among the Songhay-Zerma and Tuareg of the neighboring cantons later that year, the colonial administration arrested Shibo and several hundred of her followers.

On the orders of the French commandant de cercle, Horace Croccichia, Shibo, and about sixty of her followers were brought to Niamey and imprisoned. According to Jean Rouch (1960), who in the 1940s conducted research into the Hauka (as the Babule spirits were called by their Songhay-speaking adepts), Croccichia locked up the spirit mediums without food for three days and three nights. When he called them out of their cells, they danced and became possessed by their spirits, and Croccichia slapped them one after another until each admitted that there was no such thing as Hauka spirits. Rouch reports on a second version of this incident as well:

> "Dance, I want to speak with Hauka!" said Croccichia. So they performed a ceremony in front of him. They became possessed, and he asked the gods to weep and to take their tears and put them on the Hauka. The possession crisis stopped immediately, of course, and the commissioner said, "You see, there are no more Hauka, I am stronger than the Hauka." Then he put them all in jail. When they were in jail, one man became possessed and said, "I am a new Hauka, I'm Corsasi (The Wicked Major)" . . . , and the man said, "I'm stronger than all the other Hauka, we have to break out of jail." (Rouch 1978: 1008)

Some of Rouch's interlocutors believed that this jailbreak was actually successful and that the spirit mediums were able to flee to the Gold Coast. Adeline Masquelier (2001) recorded a similar version from Nigerien Babule adepts in the 1990s, who turned the historical defeat into a success. In this version, Croccichia "never had a chance to display his power by beating the troublemakers," for the mediums became possessed soon after their imprisonment and "in a matter of minutes" knocked down the prison walls with their bare fists and escaped "before anyone realized what was happening" (175). The historical facts, however, read much more prosaically. The majority of the Babule mediums were discharged after two months and allowed to return to their villages. But Shibo and some other prominent figures of the "sect" were deported to Upper Volta and

Ivory Coast, where Shibo was to return to Kurfey only after nine years (Echard 1992; Fuglestad 1975). Though the so-called Babule movement has since lost its political implications, the veneration of the foreign spirits never ceased to exist. Migrant workers from Niger took them to the colonial Gold Coast where the cult was further elaborated and its pantheon expanded. Back in Niger, the spirits were integrated into the pantheon of two older cults of spirit possession—the *holey* of the Songhay-Zerma and the bori of the Hausa (Echard 1992; Krings 1997; Rouch 1960).[1]

IMAGES OF *PASSIONES* AND EMBODIED PASTICHES

Faced with distorted images of themselves and a ritual display of military routines that looked like parodies, French colonial officers felt ridiculed by colonial subjects who "aped" their colonial masters (Fuglestad 1975: 205). The Annual Political Report for Niamey County of 1925 thus talks about "young people who under the influence of *bori* spirits . . . have formed groupings that parody our military institutions," and adds that "the imposition of some punishments . . . suffice[d] to restore the calm" (in Olivier de Sardan 1993: 172; my translation). Perhaps the French officers experienced the unsettling moment referred to by Michael Taussig (1993), when the boundaries between self and other collapse and "the self enters into the alter against which the self is defined and sustained" (273). On top of this psychologically disquieting experience, French officials soon began to sense a political motive behind the activities of Shibo and her followers. Thus, the "movement" was banned in 1927, demonstrating that the colonial administration took the potential threat to colonial order quite seriously. This interpretation, later adopted by Paul Stoller (1984) on the basis of his early encounters with the Babule/Hauka as a young Peace Corps volunteer in Niger during the late 1960s, is both right and wrong. I argue that Babule adepts likened themselves to the colonizers not to ridicule them but to become like them. Although Jean-Pierre Olivier de Sardan (1993) has cautioned us about taking the reports of colonial officials too literally and also warns against political "over-interpretation" of the Babule, I find it difficult not to call the Babule follower's actions political (173). What else, if not political, is the refusal to pay taxes, the

refusal to lend one's body to forced labor, and the audacity to "openly declare that the rifles [of the French] are only good enough to shoot water,
that there are no chiefs in the Kurfey any longer, and finally that the moment has come for Gandji and Shibo to take over their places" (Annual
Political Report for Niamey County, 1927, in Olivier de Sardan 1984: 283;
my translation)? While such actions were just one aspect of the Babule
adept's activities, they were the biggest worry for the French, and for that
reason colonial observers may have exaggerated their frequency and effect. Equally important were activities that might be viewed as religious,
such as the Babule follower's witch-hunting, which according to Nicole
Echard (1992), took place every night.

The Babule followers were in fact far more concerned with the effects
of colonial rule on their immediate social environment and personal lives
than with the European colonizers as such. The colonizers were at a distance. The effects of their power, however, were mediated by local African
authorities—the chefs de canton and the *gardes de cercle* (police), who
shared a certain amount of power with the French and used it not just to
enforce French orders but also for personal gain (Echard 1992). And these
locally accessible and highly visible agents of colonial hegemony were the
main targets of Babule actions. For example, the Babule were said to have
arrested the guards de cercle or kept them out of their villages (Fuglestad 1975). Likewise, witches, whose activities were felt to have increased
immensely since the advent of colonial rule, were experienced as agencies of dangerous and amoral power that needed to be contained for the
common good. In my view, this suggests that despite its political effects,
the so-called Babule movement is not to be regarded as a political revolt
but rather a "doctrine of resistance and hope" (Worsley 1957: 26), which
included utopian attempts at building a new society based on a radically
different social order in the face of social crisis. Intrinsically considered,
it has much in common with revitalization movements, defined by Anthony Wallace (1956: 265) as "deliberate, organized, conscious effort[s]
by members of a society to construct a more satisfying culture," which
are often centered on a sacred message proclaimed by a prophet. Cargo
cults are particularly apt examples of such movements. Like the Babule
adepts, the followers of several Melanesian prophets stopped working

in the fields and organized their communities according to the model of the colonizers, borrowing military ranks and military comportment from them.[2] The refusal to be counted and to supply labor were common forms of passive resistance among Niger's peasantry (Olivier de Sardan 1993); however, imitating the colonial military and using its system of ranks as a model for a new social order was anything but common. I turn to this aspect now and moreover to the fact that the spirits—who were the spiritual resources of the "movement" and as such are comparable to the transcendental forces that spoke through the prophets of revitalization movements elsewhere—took on French military ranks, sometimes even the personal names of colonial officers, and were generally believed to be Europeans.

Historian Finn Fuglestad (1975) argues that in the eyes of the Nigerien peasantry, the French colonizers were associated with an unusually powerful force that had enabled them to conquer the vast territory of the central Sudan, and that this force could only be explained as emanating from spiritual sources. Despite Olivier de Sardan's (1993: 177) nagging critique, who calls this explanation speculative and "intellectualistic," and thus implicitly likens it to the "if-I-were-a-horse" speculations of nineteenth-century evolutionists (Evans-Pritchard 1965: 24, 43), it may not be too far-fetched, especially if we take into account that the idea that warriors were protected by spirits who accompanied them in battle was a common belief among the Kurfeyawa and Arewa of precolonial times (Masquelier 1993). According to Fuglestad (1975: 213), the possession dances constituted "a means to 'capture' that new force" and made the adepts, if not invulnerable, "at least the equals of the French."

I find intriguing the idea that the Babule followers hoped to acquire some of the colonizers' qualities, and further elaboration on the topic is warranted. First, let us consider why the spirits resembled the French. Following Fuglestad's (1975) line of thinking, it would seem logical that the spirits, who lent the French their force, would resemble them in some way. Adeline Masquelier (2001) has proposed a somewhat more sophisticated answer. Unlike Fuglestad and his scholarly adversary Jean-Pierre Olivier de Sardan, who is equally inattentive to that matter, Masquelier (2001), in her take on the Babule, places special emphasis on the human body as an important tool of kinesthetic learning and understanding. She argues that among the Arewa and Kurfeyawa "understanding is often embedded in praxis" and thus more corporeal than textual:

> For the young men and women who became possessed by Baboule spirits, getting a grasp of the colonial situation involved imitating the bodily movements and attitudes of the men who had conquered the central Sudan through military force and who would subsequently administer the newly founded colony of Niger. In the pre-literate, pre-Islamic society where educating oneself and learning were mostly based on direct observation and imitation . . . , coming to an understanding of the colonials' power and learning to be strong like them was thus a matter of using one's body the way the French did. (185–186)

Copying the French with their own bodies and therefore internalizing, as Masquelier (2001) describes it, "what they took to be embodied forms of foreign selfhood and authority" meant not only "understanding and mastery over the alien universe of French colonial rules" (163) but actually acquiring certain qualities of the French—their force perhaps, as Fuglestad (1975) would have it, or whatever had turned the foreigners into such powerful human beings. What we observe here is a particular instance of copy and contact, in which the possessed imitated the powerful others to acquire some of their qualities.

Let me further complicate this by addressing the question of agency I have overlooked so far. According to the local conception, mediums do not produce spirits at will, and spirits are thought to be entities endowed with agency of their own. They are believed to have existed since time immemorial, and only at the time of their revelation, when they choose to reveal themselves to humans, are they known. Bori mediums are conceptualized as "horses" (*doki*, masculine; *godiya*, feminine) of the spirits. The spirits "mount" (*hau*) their mediums during rituals of possession. "Babule ya hau Shibo" would be one way of expressing that "a Babule spirit mounted Shibo," marking the spirit an agent and its medium a passive instrument, or "patient." How, then, can we grasp the relationship among the model, its copy, and the one who copies (the French and the Babule spirits and their human mediums) without ignoring this emic conception and the distribution of agency it implies? With the help of Fritz Kramer (1993: 58–59), we may draw on Godfrey Lienhardt's interpretation of the cosmology of the Dinka and therefore conceptualize the Babule as images of *passiones*, as ritual representations of external powers by which the peasants of southwestern Niger felt moved. Lienhardt (1961: 151) uses the Latin word *passiones* "to indicate an opposite of actions in relation to the human self," something that is lost in the modern English term *passion*. Following this terminology, the Babule are "the images of human *passiones* seen as the active sources of those *passiones* (151)." But how are these images related to the actual experience the Nigerien peasants had with the French? Fritz Kramer (1993: 251) draws on Plato's conception of mimesis—imitative representation—and defines it as "a basic form of human behavior which is not primarily purposive." According to Kramer, mimesis can be triggered by the experience of cultural difference in the confrontation with alien others, who in appearance and behavior are marked by a strong alterity vis-à-vis the self. The sheer difference and "unfamiliarity of the other can overwhelm and compel mimesis (251)." Kramer (1993) goes on to say:

> Possession is experienced not merely as non-independent action, but in fact as an express compulsion to "imitate," to resemble an other which is different to the subject and which wishes to be represented. Although this "other" is considered to be not the visible reality as such, but rather "spirit," here "spirit" is understood as an "image of a *passio*," as a piece of reality which has detached itself and become independent, often being that which makes the visible entity the member of its class. The spirit host seems to have ceased to be his self; he acts and speaks *as an other*; and precisely this is also the oldest and probably most original distinguishing feature of mimesis in the European tradition. (249)

Spirits may be understood as refractions of reality or, to be more precise: as externalized refractions of reality as experienced by those who become affected by it. Within the Hausaphone societies of Niger and Nigeria, new spirits have appeared quite frequently in the past (Echard 1992; Masquelier 2001), and have continued to do so until recently (Casey 1997). Of the hundreds of spirits that may appear, only a small number are recognized beyond the immediate context of their first apparition and therefore make it into the bori pantheon. These are the spirits that strike a chord among those who take part in the process of establishing their personality and meaning, the shaping of which occurs after a spirit's first spontaneous manifestation (Echard 1992). In the complex negotiations that play out during numerous séances, the new spirit, speaking through the mouth of its medium, and the nonpossessed bori adept, talking to the spirit, each has equal share in establishing the spirit's personality, paraphernalia, and ritual.

Possession by alien spirits, such as the Babule, is a practice which, like spontaneous mimesis, is not primarily purposive in itself, but "'irrational,' even though it appears in contexts which are otherwise determined by rational actions" (Kramer 1993: 247). But once the spirits have been properly established and are recognized as meaningful by others, they may be used for all sorts of purposes. They may empower those who lack power; they may give a voice to those who otherwise must remain silent; or they may be employed to heal or harm, to entertain, or to make a living. After all, it is a pious fiction that the agency lies solely with the spirits, and bori mediums know very well how to manipulate their spirits. Therefore, the relationship between humans and spirits in ritual may not only be expressed by a phrase such as "Babule ya hau Shibo" (a Babule spirit mounted Shibo), but likewise by saying, "Shibo ya hau Babule," which literally translates as "Shibo mounted a Babule spirit," providing Shibo with considerably more agency and making the spirit her "patient." Hence, even within the local conceptualization of possession, the relationship between humans and spirits is seen as being quite mutual.

To claim that the French provided the cause of and at the same time (a model for) the remedy for the crisis, which the local societies experienced since the French colonizers intruded into their life-worlds, is bewildering, to say the least. Since the French had proven to be the most powerful force within the life-world of the peasantry, it is perhaps only consequential that the Babule spirits, to be effective—that is, stronger than the traditional spirits and able to endow those who venerated them with qualities the older spirits could not provide—garnered their inspiration from the ever-powerful French. Given the nature of the relationship between original and copy under discussion here, in which the original is valued for certain qualities thought to be transferred onto the copy, I propose to conceptualize the Babule as embodied pastiches. Richard Dyer (2007: 1) has defined *pastiche,* as "a kind of imitation that you are meant to know is an imitation." I wish to extend this definition, which he reserves for a particular type of relationship—that between works of art, which applies equally to the relationship between staged performances, such as drama or spirit possession, and real-life models. Dyer's definition implies that the beholder of a pastiche "gets" the references to the absent model while looking at the pastiche. I suggest that the Babule spirits worked exactly this way. Speaking "French," holding military ranks, exercising, and handling weapons (or at least imitations of the latter) were actions that made their relationship to the French blatantly obvious. The fact that everybody "got" the reference accounts for their massive followership and impact among young people. Pastiche has also been defined as "a way of learning one's art" (Dyer 2007: 8), and as such, this form of imitating goes back to the ancient philosophers, who believed that through imitation "certain emanations are conveyed from the genius of the men of old into the souls of those who emulate them" (Longinus in Dyer 2007: 36). Possession by Babule spirits is based on the same logic, on empowering through emulation. As embodied pastiches, or corporeal emulations of the French, the Babule spirits were sought to convey "certain emanations" from those they were modeled after "into the souls" of those who became possessed by them.

But what about the Babule spirits' handling of fire and the fact that their mediums, even while embodying the spirits, remained quite obviously and visibly African in appearance? According to one of its earliest definitions, a *pastiche* is "neither original nor copy" but constitutes something in between, being neither something entirely new nor a simple imitation of something that already exists (Dyer 2007: 22). The Nigerien peasants possessed by the Babule spirits displayed "copies" of Europeans through the medium of their own bodies. The copies were thus shaped by the very "media" that produced them, and like the content of any medium, the European spirits inevitably carried features of their African "media." However, the Babule were not only shaped by the very corporality of their human horses but likewise by the ritual framework of bori "spirit possession," in which the mediums performed. The Babule spirits' characteristic "washing with fire" (*wankin wuta*) has a number of referents: by translating the awesome power of the French and the spirits associated with them into a symbolic language, it bespeaks the fact that the Babule are more than "simple" imitations of something that already exists; it signifies the power the spirits bestow on their mediums, who become invulnerable while possessed; it serves as proof that the mediums are indeed possessed and not just pretending (and as such it is comparable to similar proofs with regard to other categories of bori spirits); and finally, it attests to the "truth" of the spirits (which in the beginning were very much contested among traditional bori priests; Echard 1992: 97). Shibo and her followers were able to externalize their *passiones*, their painful experiences of French colonial rule, in the gestalt of the Babule spirits. This was not so much a conscious but rather an involuntary process, and as such nonpurposive. However, the epistemological framework and moreover the practices associated with spirit possession provided them the means with which to use the spirits for certain ends. In this way, the Babule became embodied pastiches that could be used by their adepts as sources of power in their resistance to colonial rule and their fight against its devastating effects on the local societies.

FORWARD: GHANA 1950s

According to Jean Rouch (1956: 78), the Gold Coast—that is, colonial Ghana—became the "Mecca" of the Babule. From 1929 onward, young male Zerma migrant laborers traveled to the Atlantic Coast, taking their spirits with them. There, the expanding pantheon of the Hauka (as the Babule spirits were called among the Zerma) accommodated the immigrants' experiences with British colonial modernity. Unlike rural Niger, where the cult had remained marginal in comparison to traditional religious practices and Islam, it transformed into a central religious institution among the immigrant communities of Ghana. The traditional spirits of the Zerma, being mostly associated with rural subsistence activities, were of little help in the urban environment of the Gold Coast, and since their typical mediums were female, despite the vast male majority of immigrants, they even lacked enough "horses" to make their presence felt. Rouch (1956: 175) writes: "Unlike the classical spirits of Niger, the Hauka have become inseparable from the Gold Coast: their mythology is a transposition of the grand adventure of the immigrants; their gods have come straight from a modern Africa; their rites are 'brutal and gallant' like the young immigrants themselves. This is a religion of the modern

world, the 'religion of the force,' which—born in a tiny village of Niger—
has found its true terrain in the Gold Coast" (my translation). Elsewhere,
he estimates that at least 30 percent of up to 100,000 Nigerien migrant
laborers, who went to Ghana each year, were Hauka mediums, "but all the
others were followers, 'the faithful,' who were there every Saturday and
Sunday seeing an entertainment which was better than cinema" (Rouch
1978: 1007). The quick and successful implantation of the cult into the life
of the immigrant communities was due to the charismatic personality of
Ousmane Fodé, a Zerma who had gone to the Gold Coast much earlier in
the century and had fought in the British army during World War I. Himself possessed by Dongo, the Zerma spirit of thunder and lightning, who
was considered to be the Hauka's host among the traditional spirits (Rouch
1960), Fodé became the chief priest (*zima*) of the Gold Coast Hauka mediums. According to Rouch (1956), his prestige among the immigrants was
so great that he even installed a huge number of local chiefs within the
Zerma community of Ghana. During Fodé's time, the cult of the Hauka
seemed to become far more institutionalized than ever before. Rituals were
refined and places of worship fixed, sacrifices took place each Friday, and
possession dances were held on Sundays. Even during the week, Hauka followers were expected to comply with certain rules, such as wearing proper
clothing, staying away from fights, and sharing their money (Rouch 1956).
To me, this reads as if some of the utopian elements of the early Hauka
movement had finally become reality in the Ghanaian diaspora.

Even though this golden age of the Hauka had already passed when
Jean Rouch shot *Les maîtres fous* (The mad masters), his film presents a
vivid picture of Hauka rituals.[3] Filmed in and around Accra in 1953, the
documentary follows a group of Hauka mediums from Accra as they perform an annual ritual that takes place outside of the city in the compound
of Mountyéba, a cocoa farmer who is their chief priest. The compound is
decorated with rags called Union Jack. There is a termite hill painted in
black and white called the Governor's Palace and in front of the hill is a
wooden sculpture representing the Governor, with mustache, saber, rifle,
and miniature horses. The ritual commences with public confessions by
those who have sinned against the Hauka. One medium confesses that he
has had sex with a friend's wife, another pleads guilty to "never washing
and never dressing elegantly," and a third to having flashes of apostasy:

"I don't care about the Hauka. Sometimes I say that the Hauka do not exist and that I am not part of them!" A sacrifice of a chicken and a ram, whose blood is poured over the Governor's Palace, is meant to appease the spirits. The culprits promise to better themselves: "We ask our Hauka to kill us should we relapse!" Guards armed with wooden rifles and whips ensure that the misdemeanants are taken away into the bush where they are made to remain until their spirits possess them.

The second part of the ritual begins when the mediums start to walk in a circle to the tune of a monochord violin until their spirits take possession of them. Some are thrown violently to the ground while mounted by their spirits, others seem to have less difficulty undergoing the transformation. Gasping for breath, saliva dripping from their mouths, the possessed speak a mélange of broken French and pidgin English in staccato style. Depending on their spirits, some mediums wear pit helmets and red sashes, others women's dresses. The Wicked Major is among the arriving spirits. The General orders him to use a big burning torch to prove his truth: "Burn yourself like the others! Show them that you truly are the Wicked Major!" The Governor and other military spirits, such as Capitaine, Caporal de Garde, and Private Tiémoko, take possession of their mediums, too. But there are also spirits who represent the immigrants' urban experience: Mai Mota, the Truck Driver; Hanga Beri, the Locomotive, who forces its medium to writhe back and forth continuously across the dance floor; and Madame Lokotoro, the Doctor's Wife. The sacrifice of a dog marks the culmination of the ritual. Rouch (1978: 1007) interprets this breaking of an Islamic food taboo as being symbolic of the colonial Europeans' alterity: "Europeans are not supposed to be afraid of anything. They don't care, they break taboos, they do what they want, and I think that the Hauka represent the same behavior." In the film, when the spirits start to quarrel over their share, some already sucking the blood from the dead dog's body, the Governor calls a "roundtable conference" to decide whether the dog is to be eaten raw or cooked. The Wicked Major and Capitaine argue that it needs to be cooked so that those who had to stay back in Accra may also get their share. As the meat boils in the pot, the possessed grab their share with their bare hands and start to chew away on the half-cooked pieces. Soon after, the spirits leave their mounts. Only the Locomotive refuses to go. He calls for Moukayla Kiri, the informal leader of Accra's Hauka mediums who did not enter the trance during the ritual, and tells him: "Moukayla, the feast was great this year. But next year we have to have two such feasts and that way we, the Hauka, will be very content!"

Most of the Zerma migrant laborers traveled back to Niger every year to cultivate their fields. The Hauka spirits of Ghanaian origin were thus brought back to Niger, where they enriched the pantheon of the earlier Hauka and Babule spirits. Among the Hausa of Niger, the spirits continued to spread east. They reappear under yet another name, Mushe (from the French *monsieur*), in the writings of Ralph Faulkingham (1975), who conducted fieldwork from 1968 to 1975 in a village near Madaoua in Niger. Faulkingham encountered two exclusive cults of spirit worship that existed alongside each other. Bori ceremonies were reserved to venerate indigenous, inheritable spirits, while the ceremonies of the 'yan Mushe, the followers of Monsieur spirits, were dedicated to the European spirits. According to Faulkingham's (1975: 40) interlocutors, the cult of the Mushe had been installed in their village "over half a century ago." At the time of his research, the 'yan Mushe were headed by a retired soldier, Abdu 'dan Umma, who had fought with the Free French in North Africa during World War II, paralleling the case of Ousmane Fodé, the chief priest of the Hauka on the Gold Coast. During the rituals, Abdu 'dan Umma embodied Kabran Sakitar (Corporal Secretary), and "brandishing his whip, he barked commands to his troops in French (Allez!, viens! Vite! Vite!; non ce n'est pas ca). With each utterance they filed in order, stopped, then turned about. When they reacted slowly, Abdu shouted, 'I am Kabran Sakitar; do as I say!'" (Faulkingham 1975: 43). Among the thirteen Mushe spirits listed by Faulkingham, we meet our old acquaintance Komanda Mugu, the Wicked Major, as well as Lisidan (from the French *adjudant*), Ba'kin Bature (Hausa for "black European"), and Halima, the "wife" of the Babule. It is interesting to note that the Mushe spirits had taken over some of the traditional spirits' responsibilities: they were sought after during bad times, such as a long dry spell in the rainy season, and they were believed to safeguard the general welfare of the village to such an extent that they would even "render a beating to 'inheritable' spirits" if these plagued the people (Faulkingham 1975: 40).

Although at the time of Faulkingham's research, the European colonizers had left Niger a decade earlier, their power lingered on. Transformed into spirits, the colonizers no longer took punitive action against the peasants but against the peasant's "inheritable" spirits. The struggle was thus continued in the spiritual realm. There, however, the spiritualized Europeans fought to the advantage of their human African followers, who sometimes were plagued by the spirits they inherited. A statement by one of Olivier de Sardan's Zerma interlocutors, made at about the same time as Faulkingham's observations, suggests that this was not an isolated occurrence. He said: "The Hauka are virtually French; ... [They] are against anything that could do harm to black people" (Boubakar Boureyma in Olivier de Sardan 1982: 196; my translation).

FAST-FORWARD: NIGERIA 1990S

As a generic term *Mushe* was still in use alongside *Babule* as a designation for the spirits I encountered in Kano during the 1990s. They appeared to be fully integrated into the pantheon of bori spirits, and as Besmer's (1983) data, collected between 1973 and 1974, suggests, this must have been the case for quite some time. Within the complex mythology of Kano bori, the Babule had developed multiple ties of kinship and joking relationships with other categories of spirits. What is more, the Babule had also accommodated some spirits of the older categories of spirits among their ranks, just as Africans had been conscripted into European armies during colonial times (Krings 1997). Although they were also called *Turawa* (Europeans), it became apparent during my conversations with their adepts that the main signifier of these spirits was no longer primarily their Europeanness but rather their "soldierliness." While military comportment has been a feature of Babule performances from the early days of their emergence, when soldiers were the only Europeans the Hausa knew, the relative eclipse of references to Europeanness in the bori of Kano points to a shift of the template on which the spirits were modeled. During the 1990s, this template was clearly the Nigerian military, and I assume this shift must have set in at least two decades earlier.

After the British colonizers left Nigeria in 1960, the country was governed by a succession of military regimes for most of the ensuing forty years. To a certain extent, it is safe to say that the Nigerian military inherited the "force" the early Babule adepts had seen in the colonial Europeans. During the Biafran War (1967–1970), the number of people in the armed forces soared from 10,000 to 250,000, leading to a heightened military presence and new military infrastructure, such as the building of barracks, throughout the country (Tyoden 1989). In the aftermath of the war, soldiers became role models of sorts for many young men. "The army's style of life . . . contains a strong emphasis on material consumption and its symbols. It is not uncommon to find that many officers own large and luxurious cars, large radiograms, and houses, and that they also consume a lot of alcohol and make little pretense over their delight in wine, women and songs" (Ukpabi 1976: 75–76). Popular cultural forms responded to the material wealth and power of the soldiers. Musicians chose impressive titles for themselves, such as "General" or "Brigadier," and members of youth gangs used nicknames like "Colonel" or "Commander" (75–76). Hausa musicians and their female dancers performed the *soja*-dance (soldier dance), which featured marching and parading dancers and musicians imitating military bugle tunes (Ames 1973).

Given the Nigerian public's fascination with all things military, it is not surprising that the images of the Babule spirits constructed by the bori adepts were also militaristic. In the bori mythology of the 1990s, the Babule lived in barracks, and their delight in "wine, women and songs" echoes the picture Sam Ukpabi has drawn of this borrowing of military elements into Nigerian popular culture. When the Babule mounted their "horses" during possession dances, they dressed in uniform (see figure 1.1) and ordered alcohol and cigarettes. Both substances also served as their sacrificial offerings. Moreover, they were believed to make their mediums rich and famous as long as the "horses" obeyed their rules. And it seemed to me that as the spirit mediums—many of them young men—came to resemble real-life soldiers, they became all the more appealing to women, who tended to be attracted to soldiers. Finally, some of the spirits' praise songs seemed to be highly influenced by the praise songs composed by Hausa singer-poets around 1968, which were intended for the federal troops fighting against the Biafran rebels (Krings 1997). Lyrics such as "Black ones, lads of the governor / You know how to dance, you know how to fight / Soldiers, rolling flight of the black-and-white crow / Everyone who sees your blackness / will also see your whiteness,"[4] harken back to the *wa'kar soja* (soldier song)

FIGURE 1.1

Bori medium, Lawan na Kawari, dressed in the uniform of Umaru, a spirit of the
Babule category, Kano, 1993. Photo by Esther Morgenthal.

of the famous singer 'Dan Maraya Jos, and reappear in the praise songs and
"epithets" (*kirari*) of the Babule spirits (Krings 1997: 85; see also Besmer
1983: 107; my translation).

An exploration of Hausa color symbolism may provide an even deeper
understanding of how the spirits were perceived in Kano during the 1990s.
Hausa color symbolism associates black with wilderness, death, illness,
and fright (Ryan 1976). Hence, calling the soldier-spirits "black ones" is a
reference to their frightening qualities. However, these qualities become
useful—and thus "white" and positive—if employed in a fight for a just
cause. The two-sided nature of the Babule spirits is aptly expressed by
the metaphor of the magpie's flight, which reveals the bird's white and
black feathers in quick succession. More than one association is likewise
made with the color "red" (*ja*), a color equally prominent among the
Babule—as reflected in their uniforms and sacrificial animals. Red carries
connotations of power, force, strength, and endurance. "Red is the most
ambiguous of the three colors; its associations are not easily classified.

In some contexts, red, red things, and redness appear to partake more of the associations of black, yet red is not necessarily associated with evil or with the socially undesirable. In a number of contexts *ja* tends to denote the powerful, either personal or spiritual. . . . Perhaps, then, this notion of power comes closest to explaining the Hausa connotations of *ja*" (Ryan 1976: 145). Here again, then, we rediscover the single quality the Babule/ Hauka have been associated with most—from the time of their earliest appearance back in colonial Niger in 1925—power or "force." Desired and feared at the same time, power is an ambiguous quality, and according to Pauline Ryan, both of these associations—power and ambiguity— converge in the Hausa conceptualization of the color red. Unlike the early adepts in Niger, however, the Babule mediums of Kano in the 1990s did not use this power for any particular purpose beyond the bori framework. Like any other category of spirits, the Babule were used for healing purposes and spiritual assistance, as well as for entertainment during public bori dances, which also served to advertise the efficacy of their human mediums. Moreover, the Babule had to share their mounts with several other spirits, often belonging to different categories, as each bori medium had more than just one spirit on his or her "head." Yet, since each spirit category was believed to specialize in a certain area or type of affliction, the Babule were most often sought after to remedy cases that were somehow connected to "things modern" (*abubuwan zamani*) or to witchcraft, the latter reflecting their specialization as witch hunters, the former their skill with things alien or nontraditional, such as the English language and modern schools.

A consultation that took place in February 1993 with the spirit Mai ya'ki illustrates how the Babule and their human clients interacted in Kano during the 1990s. The meeting occurred at the house of the bori medium Isa Mai Babule. Then about thirty-five years old, Isa belonged to a family that had produced several bori mediums. He dwelt in a section of his father's compound and "sat" for private consultations once a week. On such occasions, his wife assisted him as an intermediary while he himself embodied the spirits his clients came to consult. On that day, the first spirit to come was 'Dan Galadima, counted among the category of aristocratic spirits. When he left, Mai ya'ki, a Babule spirit whose name literally translates as the "Owner of War," took over. After putting on his uniform, aided by Isa's

wife, the spirit saluted and offered me a seat, and then he made himself
comfortable in a huge cushioned chair at the far front of the room. His
English was a bit rusty but still impressive and surely reflected the education his medium enjoyed at secondary school. After a short while, he asked
Isa's wife to bring in the first clients. The scene played out as follows:

> A woman and a young man enter. Mai ya'ki instructs them to sit down
> on a mat spread on the floor at some distance from his chair. The woman
> greets the spirit and I learn that she has visited him before. Her son, a lad
> of about 14 and his bad habits are causing her problems. She explains that
> he keeps bad company, smokes marihuana, and also enjoys gambling.
> Despite the medicine she got from Mai ya'ki on her last visit, and despite
> her sacrifice of a hen, her son's behavior has not improved. Mai ya'ki
> listens to her complaints, smiles mischievously, and finally orders the
> boy to come forward and sit down on the floor in front of him. The boy
> hesitates and casts his eyes downwards. Asked by the spirit if his mother
> is telling the truth, the boy confesses his misconduct and promises to bet-
> ter himself. The spirit warns him: "If you don't follow my orders you will
> see what happens!" I also become part of the Babule's rhetoric. While he
> converses in broken Hausa with his clients, he gives English summaries
> of their conversation. [Though I understand what is said in Hausa, the
> situation forces me to feign incomprehension.] The way he talks about
> the "spoiled behavior of Hausa youths" leaves little room for me to object
> and I respond in the affirmative. His verdict thus enforced by the second
> European present, he dismisses mother and son without prescribing yet
> another "medicine" (magani) and without requesting a sacrifice. (author's
> field notes, February 16, 1993)

Mai ya'ki's next clients were two young men:

> Listening to the conversation between Mai ya'ki and one of them, I learn
> that the latter's visit, too, is a return visit. He has consulted the spirit seven
> days earlier on behalf of his sister who is married and therefore cannot
> attend in person. The problem is that she lives in a polygynous household
> where her husband, influenced by his other wife, abuses her. The previous
> week, Mai ya'ki had prescribed a charm and requested a red-feathered
> rooster as sacrificial animal from the man's sister. Meanwhile, Isa has
> made the charm, which the spirit now hands to the man. He explains
> where and how the charm is to be buried and reassures the man that the
> woman's problems will vanish.
> The other man is a friend of the first. This is his first visit. He explains
> that he is a student at Kano Polytechnic College and that he is having

some difficulties at that school. Reading English textbooks is proving particularly challenging for him. His teachers, too, are unfair to him: although he goes to as much effort as his classmates, his grades are always worse than theirs. Mai ya'ki knows how to help. He will instruct his medium Isa to prepare a charm, which the student should bury under "the big kapok tree" at the school compound. That way, the teachers will become more favorably disposed to him. The student does not seem to know the tree and asks the spirit for its exact location. Mai ya'ki asks counter questions, which is typical of spirits, until the student names the place of "the" tree himself. On top of that, Mai ya'ki promises to provide a potion which the student is to drink before reading English textbooks. The student signals his appreciation and again explains how difficult he finds reading English. Mai ya'ki tells him the title of a textbook and asks the student to note it down and buy it. "It will improve your reading skills! And you may also buy fine English literature. Not just any trash, but something fine— like Chinua Achebe. Do you know Chinua Achebe?" The student confesses that he does not know that author. Mai ya'ki spells Achebe's name several times and tells the student to make a note of it. For his help, the spirit orders a red-feathered rooster as sacrifice for himself and a white-feathered hen for his mother (the Fulbe spirit Doguwa), and tells the student to bring the money for the two chickens when he returns to collect the charm and the medicine. The student accepts Mai ya'ki's request and promises to return next week. (author's field notes, February 16, 1993)

As no other visitors were waiting, the spirit prepared to leave. We shook hands, I bid him farewell, and his medium's wife helped to remove the uniform. He dismounted his medium through a series of gestures and movements somehow the reverse of those displayed during his mounting: energetically slapping his stomach several times with one hand, moaning with a deep rattling sound and foaming at the mouth, shouting his praise names, and suddenly becoming stiff—before sneezing three times and falling to the ground.

Apart from ordinary people, some Babule mediums, or rather their spirits, were said to also count among their clients Nigerian military men, some of whom, out of gratitude, gave Babule mediums parts of their uniforms, especially belts and boots. Many bori mediums believed that Nigerian soldiers were actually "working" with the Babule spirits—that is, offering them sacrifices to gain their assistance and protection. One of my interlocutors was even strongly convinced that someone like Lt. Gen. Joshua N. Dogonyaro, a prominent man in Babangida's military junta from 1985 to 1993, was in league with the spirit Mai ya'ki: "Dogonyaro, for example: since about 1970, when he would go to war, he worked with Mai ya'ki. When he put on his uniform, Mai ya'ki would mount his head and he would go to war. Others would shoot at him but always miss. Only he would shoot and hit the others. But it would not be him who would go to war but Mai ya'ki who would have taken possession of him and fight. Like this he was able to become famous and is now a powerful man in Nigeria. Mai ya'ki was the one who supported him" (Mohammadu Kwaki, Kano, author's field notes, February 11, 1993). The belief that the postcolonial soldiers actually "work" with spirits has been equally present in neighboring Niger. Paul Stoller (1995) has argued that Lt. Seyni Kountché, leader of Niger's military regime from 1974 to 1987, was a Hauka medium, as were some of his brothers-in-arms, and that in governing the country he had tapped into the Hauka aesthetic by "reappropriat[ing] the Hauka appropriation of the aesthetics of the French Colonial Army" (190). Whether this is true (Stoller does not reveal anywhere the basis for his assumption that Kountché was a Hauka medium), the popular belief that the lieutenant was such a medium suggests that, after all, there might be more to Finn Fuglestad's (1975) "theorie de la force" (213) regarding the early Babule/ Hauka mediums than his critic Jean-Pierre Olivier de Sardan (1993) might want to admit.

PASSIONES OF THE PAST IN THE TWENTY-FIRST CENTURY

Alterity may compel mimesis. Following Fritz Kramer (1993), who attributes the power to overwhelm to alterity—likening one's own body to that of an alien other might well be understood as a spontaneous physical reaction in the face of alterity. This must not necessarily imply possession-trance but rather may be conceived as occurring in many different contexts, from spontaneous everyday playful imitation to more stylized performances, such as dance and theater. However, mimesis has not been limited to situations of initial contact. Possession by spirits of Europeanness is something which occurred in many societies of colonial Africa and usually became manifest only decades after initial contact, mostly during the consolidation phases of European rule. As is suggested by the historical circumstances of the Babule's apparition, alterity must be experienced as the source of *passiones* in order to trigger mimetical reactions. Occurring within the framework of spirit possession, the apparition of the early Babule has to be considered nonintentional, based on a behavior that must be qualified as involuntary and nonpurposive, and that is also experienced as such by those who feel the compulsion to liken themselves to an other (locally conceptualized as a "spirit"). The apparitions, however, were then shaped in complex feedback processes among the spirits, while embodied by their mediums, and their human, nonpossessed interpreters. Babule rituals thus became arenas of bodily appropriation and "kinesthetic learning" (Masquelier 2001: 186) and were used to comprehend and literally grasp the power of the European other. As embodied pastiches of colonial Europeans, the spirits were molded after the very sources of the possessed's *passiones* and at the same time became their remedy, a means of resisting colonial rule and its effects on daily life. The very paradox that "contestation is intermixed with appropriation, and condemnation with identification" may be explained by the fact that the Babule adepts, just like the followers of many other revitalization movements, "appropriated icons of power they associated with military force and reforged them to serve their own interests and to articulate their local world with broader horizons" (Masquelier 2001: 173). Once the spirits had assumed shape and were given meaning, they could be used not only for social purposes but also for passing on to others and thus for transmission over space and time. The social purposes they served differed considerably, and so did the wider social acceptance beyond the limited numbers of their mediums and immediate followers. From a marginal cult geared toward the revitalization of local life in the early twentieth century, the veneration of the Babule developed into an almost central religion of the Nigerien diaspora in Ghana before losing that position again back in Niger and Nigeria because of its integration into the established cults of spirit possession. At the beginning of the twenty-first century, however, these cults have become more marginal than ever before due to the strong resistance to them by fundamentalist Islam.

In Nigeria, and perhaps also in Niger, the Babule are no longer limited to "embodying colonial memories" (Stoller 1995). As I have shown, the templates on which they are modeled have been expanded and at present also include postcolonial African military men, the *hommes de force* that ruled Nigeria (as well as Niger) for much of the second half of the twentieth century. Therefore, colonial *passiones* stirred by French officials such as Horace Croccichia, Victor Salaman, and their subordinates mingled in the apparition of the latter-day Babule with postcolonial *passiones* caused by Murtala Mohammed, Yakubu Gowon, Olusegun Obasanjo, Ibrahim Babangida (in Niger, Seyni Kountché), and their followers. These experiences with the mysterious and brutal quality of power have been stored and projected through the bodies of the possessed. Apart from power, what the Babule as embodied pastiches (neither originals nor copies, neither Africans nor Europeans) signify most is alterity. Having been different from other spirits and having inspired their followers to lead a life different from that of their immediate social others, they "embod[ied] difference that makes for many differences" (Stoller 1994: 646).

During my most recent visit to Kano, in June 2003, I again met the Wicked Major, Mai ya'ki, and Kafaran. This time I could meet them only in the privacy of some of my bori friends' houses. The spirits had not changed, but their social environment had. Public possession dances had almost ceased to exist. Many of the open spaces that had served as dance grounds in Kano's suburbs ten years earlier had been transformed into mosques. After the year 2000, with the establishment of the sharia legislature, the "religious police" ('yan hisba) harassed bori musicians, destroying their equipment on some occasions and beating the possessed. At the same time, a new type of curing ritual called *rukiyya* (Arabic for "healing"), which aims at exorcizing spirits (unlike the bori ritual, which focuses on incorporation and adorcism), had gained ground and provided an alternative to bori healing rituals. Rukiyya was considered more decent and Islamic by comparison. A few amusement quarters outside of Kano had become the only safe havens where bori dances could still be publicly staged under the watchful eye of the federal police that kept the 'yan hisba at bay. Ironically, then, the postcolonial successors of the colonial "native police," which the Babule adepts had set out to fight during the early days, now served as protectors to the Babule. But the religious shift was not the only reason for the relative absence of the Babule on the public stage. Once "an entertainment better than cinema" (Rouch 1978: 1007), the Babule had gotten competition from yet another, rather profane angle. The emergence of Hausa video films at the end of the 1990s had, by the year 2000, taken a firm grip on the imaginations of the average young city dweller and catered to the entertainment needs of the youth. Moreover, Hausa video films also provided those who dared to venture into the field of acting with a new framework for embodying difference. For the time being, the future of the Babule adepts was to remain open, but it seemed as if their significance, and likewise the prominence of live performance in Hausa popular culture, was diminishing at the beginning of the twenty-first century.

Lance Spearman

THE AFRICAN JAMES BOND

LANCE SPEARMAN, AKA The Spear, is a nattily dressed detective whose trademark is a fashionable straw hat, bow tie, and goatee. He likes cigars and scotch on the rocks, and is fond of beautiful women. From 1968 to about 1972, the crime-fighting adventures of "Africa's top crime buster," who had "a charming way with the girls" and "a deadly way with thugs," appeared weekly in *African Film,* a photo-novel magazine published by South African Drum Publications. Through the publisher's subsidiaries in Nairobi and Lagos, *African Film* had an almost Pan-African circulation, at least in Anglophone Africa, and was widely read in countries as diverse as Ghana, Kenya, Nigeria, Tanzania, Uganda, and Zambia.

By taking a closer look at *African Film,* this chapter draws attention to the photo novel, a genre and medium of African popular culture which, despite its wide historical circulation and immense popularity, tends to be largely overlooked in current discussions about African visual media. Although the African photo novel is still in circulation in various forms and countries, I am especially interested in its heyday, which was the late 1960s to the early 1970s. I suggest that at a time when African filmmaking was still a rather new and highly expensive venture, the photo novel—a kind of cinematic comic book—served as a surrogate for film. Probably no single title makes this argument more plausible than *African Film* magazine.

Devoted to the adventures of Lance Spearman, an African crime fighter inspired by the hard-boiled private eyes of American crime fiction and James Bond alike, the magazine introduced an African visual modernity and provided a stylish streetwise character with whom young urban Africans could readily identify (see figure 2.1). Unlike African celluloid filmmaking, which at the time was very much driven by the political zeal to decolonize the screens and the minds of African audiences, *African Film* had, by contrast, a commercial orientation. The photo novels were geared toward evoking pleasures and thrills in their viewer-readers as well as providing them with a template of modernity with which to identify. In their openness to borrowing from American and European media, and their transnational circulation, the photo novels of the late 1960s have much in common with current Nollywood video films. To a certain extent, then, the historical commercial South African photo novels of the late 1960s and early 1970s may well be understood as a forerunner to the contemporary phenomenon of Nollywood.

ROOTS AND ROUTES OF THE PHOTO NOVEL IN AFRICA

The photo novel first emerged in postwar Italy (called *fotoromanzo*) with mainly romantic content (Schimming 2002). As a medium, the photo novel seems to have a close relationship with film, and in fact it grew out of two early forms that remediated cinema: the graphic novel (which indicates a proximity to comic books) and pictorial summaries based on film stills with captions. Both forms appeared in Italian magazines during the 1930s as so-called *cineromanzi*. From early on, Italian photo novels served as stepping-stones into the film business; Sophia Loren, for example, started her career in the pages of *fotoromanzi* (Schimming 2002: 41–42). Lastly, the emergence of the photo novel in Italy and its ready adoption in neighboring France and Spain, as well as in Latin America, during the late 1940s and 1950s, has been interpreted as an indication of the form's functioning as a kind of surrogate cinema which catered to those who could not afford to go to movie theaters (Schimming 2002). While the explanatory power of this argument in terms of 1950s Europe

FIGURE 2.1

Advertisement from *African Film* magazine. Author's collection.

is doubtful, and the popularity of these early photo novels seems rather to have stemmed from the new form's transportability, which brought an equivalent of cinema much closer to its consumers, the idea of the photo novel as an ersatz cinema gains plausibility under conditions in which local film production was almost nonexistent, such as in sub-Saharan Africa of the 1960s.

The spread of the new generic form to sub-Saharan Africa had different roots and routes. Most likely, Francophone West Africa already witnessed the circulation of French photo novels (Nye 1977) either as part of women's magazines or as independent publications during the 1960s. In Senegal in the 1970s, popular women's magazines, such as *Amina, Bella,* and *Bingo,* devoted large sections to photo novels, which dealt with the complexities of gender relationships amid the rapidly changing conditions of urban Africa (Rejholec 1986: 366). During the 1960s, Italian photo-novel magazines translated into English entered the South African market, and from 1965 onward local South African photo novels, or "look-reads," firmly took root.[1] The first look-reads featured white characters, such as Captain Devil of the South African Secret Police, and were geared toward a white audience. At some point in the second half of the 1960s, Drum Publications, the publishing house of the famous *Drum* magazine, "decided to get in on the publishing boom and produce look-reads for Africans" (Meisler 1969: 80). By this time, *Drum* magazine's much-written-about golden age of the 1950s was long gone. With the tightening of apartheid rule, many of *Drum*'s former staff had been forced out of the country and the magazine had changed its face somewhat, more or less steering clear of investigative journalism and politics (Sampson 2005). Jim Bailey, the owner of Drum Publications, had been able to set up and maintain a distribution network for his magazine, with satellite offices in Accra, Lagos, and Nairobi, among other locations, which also provided content for the local issues of *Drum.* During the late 1960s, Bailey had also begun to expand the business of his publishing house beyond *Drum* magazine (Sutton 2006), and I assume that he published look-reads using an African cast with this expansion in mind. According to Jürgen Schadeberg (pers. comm., September 25, 2008), *Drum*'s now-famous photographer during its first decade, the magazine had already experimented with the photo novel format during the mid-1950s, in the form of two-page inserts, but ultimately dropped it. However, with the look-read boom of the 1960s, Drum Publications introduced at least three new magazines built solely around the photo-novel format.

In the beginning, Drum Publications experimented with a number of characters more or less modeled after famous characters from Western popular culture. There was the Son of Samson, an African superhero; Fearless Fang, a black Tarzan; The Stranger, a black Lone Ranger type of cowboy; and Lance Spearman, who turned out to be the most successful of the Drum characters. A black Tarzan and the jungle scenery in which these stories were set turned out to have been too close to the rural environment left behind by the young urban migrant that was the publisher's target audience. Then again, a superhero like the Son of Samson and a cowboy like The Stranger were just too far removed from everyday urban African life. These characters were therefore dropped around 1969.[2] In the early 1970s, *Sadness and Joy* was added, a magazine dedicated to photo novels with romantic content, which seems to have catered largely to a female audience.

In 1969, about twenty-five writers produced scripts for Drum Publications' look-reads. Most of them were Africans, some of them students at the University of Lesotho (Meisler 1969). They were paid the equivalent of sixty-five U.S. dollars for each story. According to Stanley Meisler, the scripts were edited in Johannesburg and then sent to Swaziland, where the actual shooting took place, and the strips were ultimately rushed to London for printing.[3] From there, the magazines were distributed throughout the former Anglophone colonies of West Africa, East Africa, and South Africa via the subsidiaries of Drum Publications. With a full-color cover, usually featuring a dramatic scene of the story, and thirty-one pages of black-and-white photographs, the technical quality of the look-reads was comparable to that of contemporary American or British comic books—their rivals on the African market. In East Africa and West Africa, they sold for one shilling apiece. The inside front and back covers as well as the backs of the magazines were used for advertisements (among other things, Bic pens, Bennett Airmail College, and Johnson insecticide) and the hawking of the company's other publications (YOU MUST READ DRUM / PEOPLE WHO THINK READ DRUM).

To ensure the circulation of a South African product in independent black African countries, most of which had begun to boycott the apartheid state, the same look-reads appeared under different names in and outside South Africa.[4] In addition, the West African and East African editions indicated "Drum Publications Nigeria Ltd." and "Drum Publications East Africa Ltd." as the respective publishers, as well as local personnel as editors. The content of these magazines, however, was essentially the same and all of it produced in South Africa. For the same reason, the editors in Johannesburg took the utmost care to delete all references to a South African environment, such as advertisements for South African beer and other boycotted products in Swazi towns where the look-reads where photographed (Meisler 1969). In 1969, *African Film* alone had a circulation of about 45,000 copies in East Africa, 100,000 in West Africa and 20,000 in South Africa, where it was published as *Spear* magazine (Meisler 1969).

Not much has been handed down about the cast of the look-reads. The man who acted as both Fearless Fang and The Stranger was a certain Alfred Holmes. Lance Spearman was portrayed by Joe Mkwanazi, who had been working as "a houseboy, scrubbing floors in an apartment in Durban for $35 a month and playing the piano in a night club for $1.50 a night, when a white photographer, Stanley N. Bunn, discovered him and decided he had the tough, sophisticated face needed for the role of Spear" (Meisler 1969: 81). For his incarnation of the African crime fighter, he earned 215 U.S. dollars a month—a very comfortable salary at the time.

LANCE SPEARMAN: AFRICA'S TOP CRIME BUSTER

Though Lance Spearman is somehow attached to the police of the fictional African state in which his adventures are set, it is never clear whether he is actually on the state's payroll or working as a freelancer. In his fight against crime, he is aided by Captain Victor, a police officer dressed in uniform; his female assistant, Sonia, who despite her elegant dresses and handbags, knows how to fight gangsters with well-placed karate kicks; and his little helper Lemmy, a cunning boy of about twelve years of age, whose bow tie already marks him out as Spear's successor (see figure 2.2). This firmly fixed set of protagonists (only Sonia disappears, about three years into the series) ensured both a high-recognition value for readers, a wide range of possible narrative arcs (Spear in peril,

FIGURE 2.2

The four crime busters in The Spear's office, *African Film* magazine (no. 124: 18).
Author's collection.

rescued by Lemmy; Sonia and Captain Vic kidnapped, rescued by Spear; and so on), and a male and female readership across at least two age groups with a strong sense of identification. Young Lemmy was the envy of many readers. One-time reader Tunde Giwa (2008) recalls: "When Spearman took on a young sidekick called Lemmy, many of us almost died of jealousy—we so wanted to be in his shoes."

Spear's enemies make up a wide range of evil characters, from ordinary thieves to power-hungry wannabe rulers of the world. There are professional masked gangsters like the Cats—a group of cat burglars all dressed in black, with eyeshades and claw gloves—who mysteriously cling to the highest wall of any building (nos. 130–133; 144–145; 164–165; see figure 2.3). Bald-headed Rabon Zollo, dressed in black with an eye-patch, is Spear's nemesis in the earlier episodes. He is succeeded by a panoply of evil characters, whose make-up and sinister plans are ever more fantastic with each new antagonist. There is Dr. Devil, dressed in a rubber Halloween mask and cape, who wants to rule the world (nos. 134–136); the one-eyed Hook-Hand Killer, who murders out of passion (nos. 172–173); and a syndicate boss, who uses the Earth Monster, a furry giant, to execute his will (nos. 181–185). The later episodes introduce a certain amount of science fiction in the form of mad professors such as Mad Doc, who has developed a special serum to shrink people (nos. 171–175); Professor Thor, who pos-

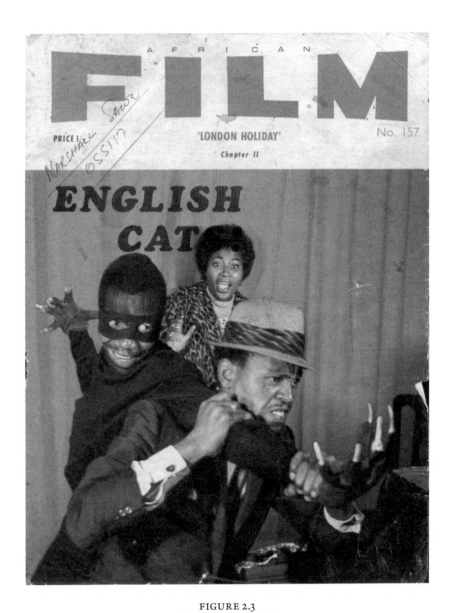

FIGURE 2.3

Cover of *African Film* magazine (no. 157). Author's collection.

sesses a brain machine which is able to read and transfer people's minds (nos. 150–152); and Professor Rubens, who succeeds in transplanting animal organs into humans, thus producing a werewolf (nos. 176–180). Each of these prominent antagonists have a number of hired thugs who regularly kidnap any of the four protagonists, allowing Spear and his friends to engage in a minimum of at least one fistfight per issue. As white faces were absent from the magazine, a black cast portrayed bad and good guys alike.

African Film magazine perfectly fits the category of the suspense novel within Tzvetan Todorov's typology of detective fiction. According to Todorov (1977: 50–51), this category sits between two other categories of crime fiction, the whodunit and the thriller, and combines their key properties: the mystery of the crime that has to be unraveled through a story of investigation, typical of the whodunit, and the emphasis on the present—on crime in the making—typical of the thriller. While the whodunit raises the reader's curiosity, the thriller aims at creating suspense. In *African Film,* mystery—the story of a past criminal event that has to be detected—is reduced to a mere point of departure while the main interest derives from the story set in the present, the plot which unfolds during Spear's investigations (see figure 2.4). This coincides with Todorov's (1977) observation that in the suspense novel, "the reader is interested not only by what has happened but also by what will happen next; he wonders as much about the future as about the past. The two types of interest are thus united here—there is the curiosity to learn how past events are to be explained; and there is also the suspense: what will happen to the main characters" (51)? As is typical of suspense novels, Spear and the other main characters are constantly risking their lives. Though tough and always proving victorious in the end, Spear is by no means immune from his adversaries' fists as the story unfolds. Often he comes out of a fight worse for wear, with severe bruises, aching limbs, and a black eye, and he has to be bandaged by his assistant Sonia. Apart from the plot, suspense is also created by clever employment of the specific properties of the photo-novel medium: the last images at the bottom of many right-hand pages serve as cliffhangers, keeping the reader engrossed and waiting with bated breath to see what will happen with the turning of the page. Most Spearman stories were stretched out over at least four issues of the magazine, which means that a suspenseful climax had to be created toward the end of all but

FIGURE 2.4

Cover of *African Film* magazine (no. 183). Author's collection.

the last issue—to keep readers buying the magazine. Thus, the last page of most issues carries an image of Spear or one of his friends in deep trouble and a caption stirring the imagination of the readers: "How can Spear save himself and Lemmy? How can anyone escape from this diabolical trap? Read the next exciting issue of 'Film' and find out" (no. 106).

The Spear templates are not difficult to make out. His style, dress, and habits seem inspired by James Bond, as already noted by contemporary observers (Meisler 1969); and one-time fans, too, remember him as the "African James Bond." Although there is surely a lot of truth in this observation, I suggest that the tone of the Lance Spearman series, both in terms of language and imagery, is quite deeply rooted in American crime fiction of the hard-boiled school. This may well have been mediated by Hollywood gangster movies of the 1940s and 1950s, or by the novels of James Hadley Chase, which have always been widely read in Africa. Though Chase himself was British, most of his thrillers are set in America. Influenced by Raymond Chandler and other writers of the hard-boiled school, he is said to have written his books with the help of American slang dictionaries. Some of the language of *African Film*—expressions such as "You dirty crime-busting punk," "She was a real doll; we got on like a house on fire," and the onomatopoeic "Phew! That was close!" mimicking a sigh of relief at a narrow escape—sound as if they came straight out of a Chase novel.

Already the *Drum* magazine writers of the 1950s were appropriating American crime thrillers and giving their short stories, set in the underworld of Johannesburg, a flavor of the hard-boiled school. In fact, this was in line with the style of the Johannesburg gangsters themselves who were avid followers of American B movies, which they used as inspiration for their personal names and gang monikers, as well as their language, the so-called *tsotsi taal* (Sampson 2005: 76–83). In the words of Lindy Stiebel (2002: 188): "The harsh world of the hard-boiled thriller requires special, tough skills to negotiate—it is the world of fast cars, fast dames, hot gangs and smart private eyes who aren't afraid to get their hands dirty; it's translatable to Sophiatown in the fifties, *Drum*'s world." Although Sophiatown had been bulldozed for more than ten years and the world of *Drum* had been buried with it when Lesotho students and others began to script the Spearman series at the end of the 1960s, the model of *Drum*'s short crime stories may not have been forgotten. A big difference between this earlier and highly politicized African genre and the photo novels, however, is the complete absence of the political in the photo novels. This is surely an effect of publishing under apartheid rule, which had firmly taken root in the 1960s when censors regularly scrutinized *Drum*. In *African Film*, the political is overwritten by the fantastical—and that is where James Bond and the fantastic world of espionage come in. Like James Bond, Lance Spearman has more than a few gimmicks at his disposal, such as a wristwatch walkie-talkie, a knife-flinging boot, and special cigars that contain either explosives or sleeping gas. The fantastic science fiction of the espionage film, however, is much more elaborate in the case of Spear's antagonists, who not only employ brain machines, shrinking serums, and other medical devices but also such fancy things as jet-powered wheel chairs and cars (in fact, a flying VW Beetle; see Meisler 1969).

Geared toward experiencing the pleasures of suspense, *African Film* seems apolitical at first glance. However, despite the announcement on every issue's last page that "all characters in this publication are fictitious," the magazine is deeply rooted in the wider political and social context of the production era. In *The Diamonds of Salamar* (no. 118), for example, the fictitious country of the Spearman adventures turns out to be one whose economy, which is largely based on diamond exports, is threatened because large amounts of precious stones (The Spear calls them "sparklers") are stolen. In this case, it is not difficult to make out South Africa—not to mention other African countries whose economies depended on the exploitation of mineral resources—as a frame of reference. The five-chapter series *The Power-Mad Tycoon* (nos. 122–126) introduces a power-hungry man who threatens the world with nuclear weapons he has stashed away on a lonely, uninhabited island. From this deserted location, he plans to stir up war between the East and the West and rule the world supreme. Although this plot could come straight out of a James Bond movie (even a submarine is part of the power-mad tycoon's plan), it nevertheless reflects the contemporaneity of the cold war. A similar plan to conquer the world is drafted by one of Spear's arch enemies, Dr. Devil, who enlists his henchmen by telling them: "Today all the big countries are trying to land a rocket on the moon"—a clear indication of this episode's production date, around 1969:

I will hi-jack these rockets by powerful radio control and send them crashing into the sea. / Then we will send our secret agents to give the governments of the different countries false information about the missing rockets. / They will suspect each other for hi-jacking their rockets and war will break out! / We will then move in and assassinate the leaders and take over. Each of you will be head of a country! (no. 117: 14–15)

Some of Lance Spearman's other adventures reference the era's prominent figures, such as British football legend Tony "Bomber" Brown, who lends his name to the underworld boss of the four-chapter story *The Spear Meets Bomber Brown* (nos. 102–105). And there is Ronald Biggs, the most prominent member of the British gang that pulled off the so-called Great Train Robbery in 1963. In *The Cats and £1,000,000* (nos. 164–166), "the Cats are loose again in England" and are after 1 million pounds "that is still outstanding from the Great Train Robbery" (no. 165: 1). Sometimes, Lance Spearman's investigations take him abroad and he visits European countries. In *The Spear Dices with Death* (no. 2: 20–21), he travels to Paris, and in *The Spear versus the Killer Crabs* (no. 19: 10–12), he boards a Lufthansa plane that takes him to Berlin. In *London Holiday* (nos. 156–157), he meets a long-haired black hippie who calls himself "Love," and in *Assignment Athens,* he chases the Cats in Greece (no. 166). This can be interpreted as an attempt to speak to the imagined reader's desire for the exotic. However, such exotic places could only be conjured up by using preexisting pictures of ordinary European street scenery or stock photos of specific landmarks, such as the Acropolis, the Moulin Rouge, or Checkpoint Charlie. These served as backdrops on top of which images of the actors were superimposed, with the resulting visuals being below the general quality of the magazine's artwork. One can only assume that it is for this reason that Lance Spearman was not sent on an even greater variety of overseas expeditions.

What is most striking about the imagery of *African Film* magazine is its almost entirely modern urban aesthetic. Outdoor sequences show neat buildings, sometimes several floors high, in addition to shops, sidewalks, well-paved streets, and models of the latest cars. Indoor sequences display modern, sometimes luxurious, interiors. There are tiled bathrooms, living rooms with coffee tables and easy chairs, bookshelves, and framed pictures on the walls. While Captain Vic's office is sparely furnished (just a desk with a nameplate and telephone), Spearman's office, which appears only in the earlier episodes, is straight out of a Hollywood B movie: venetian blinds on the window and a bottle of scotch in a drawer. Typical of this kind of scene, the detective is depicted relaxing casually in his chair—smoking a cheroot, his legs stretched out on the desk. The imagery of *African Film* is a celebration of an African modernity devoid of anything reminiscent of traditional Africa—in fact, only the characters who populate the streets and indoor settings give it an African sensibility. In *Gold Fever* (nos. 146–149), Lemmy and Spear travel to the countryside initially to go on a holiday (!). Driving through the hinterland, they discuss their destination as follows:

> (*Picture 1*) LEMMY: Where are we going Spear?
>
> SPEAR: It's an old mining town, and the mines have all closed down: Now it's just a settlement which caters [to] the farming people.
>
> (*Picture 2*) LEMMY: Aw! That doesn't sound exciting.
>
> SPEAR: Well, I want a rest.
>
> (*Picture 3*) SPEAR: There are still some of the old-timers around who haven't given up prospecting for gold, and it's quite a tourist attraction these days. We won't be bored.
>
> (no. 146: 4)

Throughout this episode—and it is one of the rare episodes that takes place outside of the city—rural African architecture is remarkably missing. The "farming people," too, are nowhere to be seen toiling the earth. Instead, the town has a black "Sheriff" whose clothing clearly echoes the Hollywood Western, and all of the "old-timers" are dressed in similar cowboy-style dress. An exchange between Lemmy and Spear, which takes place in a curio shop early in the same episode, may well be read as a meta-commentary on this absence of Africa in the whole of *African Film*; Lemmy marvels about some jewelry and says, "Gee! Spear, look at that. It's real African art." Spear gives him one of his typically laconic replies, saying, "Don't you believe it. It's either made in Birmingham or Hong Kong!" (no. 146: 5).

The world of Lance Spearman is a macho place, where young women are addressed as "dolls," are "pretty," and seem to be waiting only to be picked up by handsome men. This is where there is a merging of the contemporary African male attitudes toward women and the gender matrix observable within the two templates of *African Film* magazine—the contemporary espionage film and earlier American crime thrillers of the hard-boiled school. Still, Lance Spearman, who is always up for a romantic adventure, has probably more of James Bond's elegance and appetite for women than does Sam Spade or Philip Marlowe, both of whom harbor deep-seated ambivalent feelings toward the opposite sex. As in the James Bond movies, seductive women are collaborators of Spearman's antagonists, and even when he is fully aware of the role they are playing, Spear only rarely declines an invitation. Most often Spearman and a woman end up in her apartment. "You help yourself to a drink while I put on something more comfortable," she tells him before changing her clothes. And he might reply: "Gee . . . thanks, Doll." What follows, however, is never shown. Kissing is the utmost in terms of explicitness and only occurs occasionally.

But women may also turn out to be man-eaters in their own right, as *The Head Huntress* (no. 50: 1) demonstrates. This story opens with a bar scene, in which "Mister Munn E. Spinna, a rich married man," trips over his own sexual desire. "He sees a shapely doll with all the curves in the right places coming towards him. She gives him a big, friendly smile," which the reader cannot see because the actress is captured from the back, laying bare a substantial measure of her "curves" to the gaze of the presumably male reader. "Wow! That's what I call real sexy!" exclaims Mister Munn E. Spinna, and two pages later, he loses his head, quite literally, because Hilda, the headhuntress—a stylishly dressed woman—turns out to be avenging a racket that once destroyed her family and left her almost insane.

The only departure from these staples of female characterization in *African Film* is Sonia, Spearman's crime-fighting assistant. She always resists Spearman's advances and is not afraid to enter the fray and use her fists, if need be. In episode 128, for example, "Sonia gets into the mood" and butts into a fight Spearman is already engaged in. One of the thugs pushes her aside with typical male gusto, saying: "Out of the way, lady, this is a man's game." She replies: "Remember equal rights for women?" And as she punches him with a hard right in the next frame, she casually remarks: "This is one of them" (28). This sequence of just three frames is not only remarkable for its reference to the contemporary women's liberation move-

ment, and a modern African woman's claim to be part of it, but for its char-
acteristically ironic twist as well as the juxtaposition of text and images so
typical of the magazine (see figure 2.5). This is most frequently displayed in
the fighting sequences. Harsh violence is accompanied by a commentary
that seeks to establish the coolness with which the protagonists mete out
punishment—for it is always Spear and his friends who comment on their
own actions, the antagonists being granted only an occasional "Ooeff!" or
"Aarrg!" At the same time, our heroes turn karate kicks and upper cuts into
delightful comedy sketches. Spear plants a punch to a thug's face with the
announcement, "Have a knuckle sandwich" (no. 107: 10), and a few pages
later, he is in the air, knocking two guys out with a karate kick, letting them
know: "You guys look hungry. Have a meal" (no. 107: 23).

The fighting scenes are central to the elaborate imagery of *African Film*.
They convey a sense of action rarely found elsewhere in photo novels. This
is achieved by capturing actors as if in the middle of a dynamic move, from
camera angles usually associated with film. Sometimes speed lines, borrowed from comic books, are added. Frequent changes in point of view,
reverse shots, a meaningful variation of different camera distances (from
long shots to close-ups), and varying picture sizes per panel give *African
Film* its cinematic look and feel. Actors display vivid facial expressions.
This adds to the liveliness of the imagery and is distinct from the often
boring visual aesthetics of contemporary non-African photo novels, where
actors, even if engaged in lively conversation, are captured with sealed
lips, to appear as immaculate as possible. While images in European and
American photo novels have been analyzed as being only supportive to the
text-based narratives (Schimming 2002), images and texts are on a much
more equal footing in *African Film,* and in many sequences, especially the
fighting routines, images take the lead and would even work without accompanying texts. This is a remarkable development, which sets *African
Film* apart from the earlier European photo novel it was built on.

A PAN-AFRICAN FAN CULTURE

Most issues of *African Film* I could get my hands on carry a last page
with a portrait of Lance Spearman and a direct address to the magazine's

FIGURE 2.5

Fight sequence, *African Film* magazine (no. 128: 28). Author's collection.

readers: "If you are a Lance Spearman fan, cut out and save this portrait. Then write to: The Spear, P.O. Box 3372, Nairobi and ask to be enrolled as a member of the Spear Fan Club." In other issues, the final page shows lists of names and addresses of new fan club members from Kenya, Nigeria, Tanzania, and Uganda. The two such pages I have in my possession list ninety-one male names and only six female. Access to such fan mail would provide an ideal entry point for a discussion of the historical reception of the magazine. Since the offices of Drum Publications shut down long ago, these letters seem to have gone missing.

"No one, including *Drum* magazine, has done a market analysis," wrote Stanley Meisler in 1969 (81), "but anyone familiar with Africa can quickly deduce who the readers are." He suspects Spear's most avid fans to be "ordinary semi-educated young men . . . who have left the rural areas after a few years of schooling and come to the towns." This is because the magazine mirrors "their yearning, their uncertain identification with the fringes of Western culture, their need for fancy in a harsh urban world" (80). Following this observation, it is exactly because these high-spirited expectations of participating in the rich and sophisticated urban world rarely came true that the fictitious crime fighter gained such immense popularity. "Spear is their fancy come to life. He is the black man—smart, witty, tough—who rules the urban world they want to enter" (Meisler 1969: 81). There is surely some truth in this argument. But these readers were not the only ones by far. Reminiscences from one-time fans, which I gathered on the internet from different discussion groups and websites dedicated to African popular culture, lead me to suspect that the Drum look-reads also had a readership among young urban middle-class schoolchildren. A certain Counti from Nigeria, for instance, announces on the website Nigeria Village Square: "Me, I used to wait by the door for the vendor to bring my *Boom* every Monday and later, *African Film*. We devoured those things o" (January 1, 2009). Ibrahim Mkamba, who grew up in the small town of Kilosa, Tanzania, states: "A copy was sent to my dad every month. I really loved Spearman" (Mkamba 2008). And Vincent Kizza, who works as a liaison officer at the Uganda Parliamentary Office of Science and Technology, writes: "It is only now that I come across a discussion on Lance Spearman and Fearless Fang issues of which I would pay anything to get. Thinking about them makes me re-live my great childhood. By the way, were the characters themselves real??!! How I wish they were!" (chimurengalibrary.co.za, April 6, 2009). Obviously, such memories are shrouded in nostalgia, and such voices, invaluable as they may be, make up only a tiny fraction of the magazines' former readers, whose numbers must have reached upwards of 500,000 per week (based on the data provided by Meisler in 1969 and the fact that a single copy had more than just one reader).

In 2009, I was able to talk to about ten former Spearman fans in Tanzania who helped me get an idea of how and in what contexts *African Film* was consumed around 1970.[5] Most of them were in their teens when they encountered The Spear; only two were older than twenty years old. All of them had at least a secondary-school education and they read *African Film* during their school days. Judging by where they lived at the time, it becomes clear that the magazine penetrated far into the hinterland, beyond the major cities and towns. Only some were lucky enough to acquire their own copies, others had to borrow them. Some even had copies bought for them by parents wanting to enhance their children's English language skills. In the same vein, the proprietor of Drum Publications advertised *African Film* as educational material. "A message to all distributors and advertisers," printed in the second issue of the magazine, reads as follows:

> Far too many children come out of school and read little thereafter. So often the reading habit is lost and is never again recovered. . . . We hope with this magazine to cater [to] the lost readers. By giving them an exciting magazine made up with pictures in appealing form, the buyer is led to read and by this means is kept reading. Afterwards we hope he will move to buying newspapers, better quality magazines such as DRUM, and even books. But the first problem is to catch the otherwise lost literate and induce in him the reading habit. And so we supply him in this magazine with exciting serials after the style of films and television shows that he may see, executed in a style with which he can identify himself. Written in simple language, it will appeal to young and old, leading them by the hand into paths of greater literacy.

The young readers, of course, were looking for something else in *African Film*. "When you read Spearman it was actually as if you were watching a film," one interviewee said, and almost all agreed that the Tanzanian media landscape in about 1970 did not offer much for teenagers in terms of entertainment. Cinema was available only in the cities, and only to those who could afford it. Mobile cinema shows were held occasionally in rural areas. It was the action of the fighting scenes that was readily translated into the lives of the Spearman fans. Spear became a favorite nickname (one fan even told me about a seventy-year-old cousin still called Spear today), and the bad kids were called Zollo, after Spear's arch enemy. Spear's dress, especially hat and tie, was also copied. Only those who attended English schools were really able to follow the balloon texts. Most others had to make do with the pictures and the little they could grasp from the explanations of their peers who could read English. One fan, who grew up in the household of a primary-school teacher in the rural area around Mwanza, remembered that each month on payday the head of the household bought copies of *African Film* for himself. While the teacher was leafing through the magazines, he commented on them, talking to himself in Kisukuma, his native language. The children, who watched him from a distance, pricked up their ears lest they miss a word. As soon as the teacher was out of the house, they would gather up the copies and try to match what they had heard to what they saw in the magazines. Usually, heated debates about how to interpret certain sequences would follow until a consensus was established. *African Film* was so popular that it also found its way into the household of a more prominent "teacher"—President Julius Nyerere—where it was consumed by several of his seven children. Rose Nyerere, the youngest of the children, told me that it must have been her brothers who brought it into the house, though she also read it. In fact, she is the only female former reader I spoke to, and from her responses I assume that *African Film* must have been more popular among boys and young men than with girls.

Three longer essays written by former fans and published on different websites draw attention to the media-scapes the new generic form of the photo novel was placed in, and offer extremely valuable descriptions of Lance Spearman's popularity. In an essay which focuses on the social role of actors in current Tanzanian video films, for example, Ibrahim Mkamba recalls at length how, when he was a kid in 1960s Tanzania, he enjoyed the monthly mobile cinema shows that came to his rural hometown. He mentions Chaplin comedies and John Wayne Westerns, drawing a parallel between such films and the photo novels, especially between the figure of the cowboy and Lance Spearman:

> Because I loved film, I found myself a fan of Lance Spearman African detective picture magazines (Spear magazines) which were acted in Africa by Africans only. . . . Many people loved Spearman and there were some who called themselves that name. There were also those who imitated his yellowish-brown suit, and his wide hat, which was different from those of the cowboys. Some even started smoking by imitating him. He really loved cigars. He was an expert in using pistols, having a heavy blow like a stone! What people loved and respected about cowboys and Lance Spearman was the kind of job they did. They were the law's sideliners against criminals. (Mkamba 2008; translated from the Swahili by Vicensia Shule)

This is an interesting explanation of The Spear's popularity, probably partially inspired by the point this writer drives home. Mkamba argues that in contrast to cowboy films and Spear look-reads, current Tanzanian video films, which certainly depict their share of crime, do not actually portray characters who fight crime. Therefore, today's viewers might be more likely to relate to the criminal element in these films. This is a variant of a staple argument which frequently surfaces in debates about the negative social effects of all sorts of media, and ironically enough, it was applied forty years earlier by contemporary observers of the Spearman look-reads themselves. Stanley Meisler (1969) reports on a discourse at the time which held the look-reads accountable for an uptick in crime in the cities. The *East African Standard,* one of Kenya's leading newspapers, attacked the "violence and gangster dialogue of the Spear," already in 1968, and columnist John Elgon wrote: "Africans who desire a secret agent hero of their own, apparently considerable in number, deserve something better" (quoted in Meisler 1969: 83).

Reminiscing about her childhood in Nairobi, Kate Getao (2008) places the Drum look-reads into a wider context of an urban middle-class youth culture in which comic books played an important part. She remembers having the good fortune to receive a five-shilling allowance:

> With that amount of money, you could buy two comics, a bar of chocolate, a packet of liquorice all-sorts and have change to spare. . . . There were also "film strips" something that I have not seen for many years. These

had one-syllable names like "Boom" and "Film." They consisted of a
storyboard of black and white photographs with balloons for dialogue,
in other words, comics that used photographs instead of drawings. The
hero of Boom wore a leopard-skin thong and swung on trees, while the
hero of Film was improbably named "Lance Spearman" and was often
photographed leaping horizontally through the air to kick someone while
screaming "Aaaaargh! Take that!" . . . These comics and film strips were so
addictive that a collection of them gave one stature in the community. . . .
In those days, you could win friends and influence people by swapping
comics. I knew my relatives by what sort of comic collection they possessed, and never resisted visiting anyone who had a large pile of Boom or
Film stored under their bed.

In his critical essay "Black Like Us," Tunde Giwa (2008), himself a Nigerian and one-time fan of Lance Spearman, places the photo novels in the
same context. Additionally, he draws attention to the fact that comics sold
in Africa during the 1960s came from America and Europe, and therefore
were dominated by white characters, like Tintin, Thor, and the Marvel
superheroes. If Africans appeared at all, they did so only as extras, to add
a bit of exotic color to the landscape, against which the adventures of the
white main characters were set:

> Into this culturally colonised milieu came a new comic published by
> Drum Publications called *African Film* featuring Lance Spearman, a raff-
> ish and nattily-dressed black super cop with an ever-present Panama hat.
> And we all instantly fell deeply in love with him. No one forced Spearman
> on us. For the first time, we had a comic hero who was actually black
> like us. *African Film* was very different from other comics of the time.
> Not hand-drawn as other comics were, it was a photoplay magazine that
> used actual photographs of real black people with the dialog typed at the
> bottom of each panel. Located in an unnamed but strictly urban setting,
> Lance Spearman was cast as a black James Bond type.[6]

In search of explanations for The Spear's popularity across English-
speaking postcolonial Africa, it is perhaps important to remember that
the magazine came out at the end of a decade during which most former
colonies had gained their independence, sometimes, as in Kenya, only
after a severe struggle against the colonizers. This era of independence was
marked by nationalism and political and cultural attempts to shape a new
identity and gain a sense of self-confidence for the young nations. Within

this historical context, a multipurpose black super–crime fighter makes perfect sense. He not only contained crime within the fictitious nation his adventures were set in but was regularly assigned to defend it against aggressors from outside ("When the country's existence is threatened its leaders at once call in The Spear," announces the cover of issue no. 118). And as Africa's answer to James Bond and Marvel Comics' superheroes alike, Lance Spearman, who not only saved his nation but the whole world in many of his adventures, may have helped satisfy a deep-seated desire for equality within postcolonial African readers.

AFRICAN FILM'S LEGACY

The period from the late 1960s through the 1970s marked the heyday of the photo novel in Africa. The pioneering Drum look-reads served as templates for a number of local adaptations, often in vernacular languages. This is comparable to the pacesetting role of Nollywood, which during the latter part of the 1990s, spread across the continent, where it inspired several local film industries. Tanzanians could read their first Swahili photo novel in *Film Tanzania,* a magazine founded in 1969 by the Tanzanian writer and publisher Faraji H. H. Katambula, himself an avid follower of Lance Spearman.[7] During the 1970s, *Film Tanzania* came out every two weeks and had a circulation of 53,000 (Reuster-Jahn, forthcoming). It continued to be published, despite several interruptions, until 2006 (ending with issue no. 141).[8] *Swahili Film,* a sister magazine, was published by Katambula in Kenya. Finally, a magazine called *New Film Azania,* whose title indicates aspiring to a readership of a liberated South Africa, appeared in Tanzania in the early 1980s. Unlike *African Film,* these magazines were rather didactically oriented and featured stories dealing with ordinary people's everyday problems. In terms of quality and style, they were a far cry from the Drum look-reads. In Nigeria, however, the generic form was appropriated by drama groups of the Yoruba traveling theater tradition, who adapted their plays very successfully to the new medium. Famous company leaders, such as Hubert Ogunde, Oyin Adejobi, Kola Ogunmola, and others, had their plays reshot as "photo plays" and published by West African Book Publishers in Lagos.[9] These booklets, larger in size than the South African templates, provided the companies with a supplement to their income from stage performances and were in fact the first portable records of such plays available to a mass audience (prior to the printed photo plays, dramas had been broadcast on television; see Barber 2000, chapter 8). Founded in 1969, the Yoruba photo play magazine *Atoka*, which in each of its issues featured a play from a different theater company, survived well into the 1980s and went out of print only when stage drama declined and theater companies began to experiment with film and video (Barber 2000). While anonymous authors who were never mentioned in the magazines scripted Drum look-reads, Yoruba photo plays always printed the scriptwriter's name on the cover. The Nigerian photo plays must in fact be considered the first genuinely African photo novels: unlike *African Film*, which appropriated European and American templates, the Yoruba photo plays self-consciously display a very clear and specifically located African life-world—that of 1970s Nigerian Yorubaland, including its rich mythology and contemporary urban lore.

Despite the thrills and pleasures it conveys, the photo novel as a medium has almost ceased to exist in Africa today. Of the once-famous Drum Publications look-reads, only *True Love*, the South African version of Nigerian/Kenyan *Sadness and Joy*, is still published. Video, the medium that has made possible the reinvention of a truly popular African cinema, currently fills the space once occupied by the photo novel in the popular culture of urban Africa. Interestingly enough, in Tanzania, cultural producers have recently combined the two media by reinventing the format of the early *cineromanzi*. Some of the mushrooming tabloids include a page on which Nigerian and Tanzanian video films are recaptured, with video screen shots and pasted balloon dialogue in Swahili (see chapter 5). Within the realm of development communication, the photo novel also resurfaces here and there, albeit as a noncommercial "tool of communication." Various development agencies make use of the generic form to spread the topics on their agenda—for example, AIDS/HIV prevention, health education, and the empowerment of women—to clients imagined as being only barely able to read and thus receptive to an image-based form of communication.[10] Even the once-famous *Atoka* series seems to have been stripped of its initial entertainment value and remodeled into a tool for evangelism. Radio Abeokuta commissioned the first edition of a new Yoruba photo-play magazine called *Atoka Akewijesu,* which is written and directed by Adeleke Osindeko and performed by a group called Akewijesu Drama Ministry. This appropriation of a popular form by a religious (most likely Pentecostal) organization provides another possible parallel between the photo novel and Nollywood, since Pentecostal churches are among the leading producers of Nollywood films.

Though I have proposed to conceptualize the Drum Publications look-reads as distant forerunners of Nollywood videos, it is perhaps important to highlight some of the major differences as well. Unlike Nigerian video films, the South African look-reads never directly addressed the prevailing social, economic, or political conditions of the time, but opted for the fantastic, which the look-reads borrowed from European and American templates. Although Nigerian video films also owe a great deal to foreign media formats, such formats are employed as a kind of framework in which African stories are told, a process that may be understood as a re-mediation of either "traditional" or current urban lore, or a combination of the two. Nowhere does this become more obvious than in the Nollywood reformulation of the "traditional" African witch doctor as mad scientist (Wendl 2004b: 275–276). While *African Film* is full of mad scientists borrowed from genres of Western popular culture, Nollywood videos localize the figure of the mad scientist, recasting him as an African witch doctor. Similarly, although both the photo novel and Nollywood film revel in the display of modernity, Lance Spearman's modernity looks rather like that of Europe or America, while that of Nollywood is distinctly African.

The transnational and even Pan-African consumption of photo novels and Nollywood films is certainly the biggest similarity between the two genres, although what remains obscure is how successful Drum Publications look-reads were in crossing the Atlantic to Europe and America. Judging from the Nigerian editions' cover pricing of one shilling in the United Kingdom and twenty cents in the United States, the publishing house must have at least envisioned that the magazines could find readers in the African diaspora as well. Eventually, some copies must have made it even to the Caribbean: one of the internet discussions I monitored was initiated by a comic book fan. He wrote about a friend who grew up in the Caribbean reading Fearless Fang look-reads. Given the popularity of Nollywood videos in the Caribbean (Bryce 2013; Cartelli 2007), the plan to sell African photo-novel magazines outside of the continent was not totally unfounded. Perhaps the rise of television, especially of the related telenovela and daily soap formats, which during the late 1970s caused a decline in photo-novel consumption everywhere, prevented a thorough circulation of Spearman's adventures beyond Africa. "After he spent so many years enlivening my youth," writes Kate Getao (2008), "I wonder what happened to Lance Spearman. Did he retire, impoverished and unappreciated, into obscurity?" In a debate over memories of school days, which took place on Naijarules.com, the leading internet forum used by Nigerians living abroad, someone asked whether others remembered Lance Spearman. A certain Vince replied: "Do I remember SPEAR you ask? Man, LANCE SPEARMAN should be made into a movie for real" (February 16, 2004)! More than two years later someone writing under the pseudonym takestyle eventually came across this thread and replied: "I actually DID start writing a Lance Spearman screenplay a few years ago, but then I changed the character into an original creation because I wasn't sure what the situation was with the rights to the Spear character. I actually should look into that . . . because I think that movie SHOULD be made, if not by me then by someone else (but preferably by me)" (March 18, 2006).

POSTSCRIPT

In 2007, when I began researching the history of Lance Spearman and the other photo-novel heroes, hardly anything could be found about them on the internet. This has changed; during the past six years, a number of African bloggers have posted short essays about the African pulp fiction hero of the 1960s. Most of them draw on Stanley Meisler's article from 1969, which is now also accessible online. Others provide personal memories similar to those presented here.[11] I have shared scans of my own copies of *African Film* with a number of people in Africa, Europe, and the United States. Some of these scans now appear on Facebook, where a certain Kenney Kimeli from Kenya has created a Lance Spearman fan page.[12] Online since May 2012, and growing steadily, this page is a true catalyst for triggering memories of former *African Film* fans' reading experiences.

Some even post valuable information that allows a rare look behind the scenes of the photographed fiction. Thus, the story Subongo FX shares with other subscribers of the *African Film* Facebook page paints a rather miserable picture of the boy who impersonated Lemmy, and who, as the youngest of the characters, embodied the future of the fictitious world of *African Film* and that of its readers. His story goes like this:

> I remember my mother used to buy the Spearman comic when we lived in Zambia in the late 60's. In 1970 we moved to Swaziland. One day when we were shopping we saw Lemmy sitting on a street curb. All his [clothes] were rags and he looked very depressed. My mother and father gave him about 80 rand. He thanked us but still looked depressed. Then we found some rented accommodation with guess who? Sonia. My mother did not get on with her. I think my mother was trying to use her religion to make Sonia [feel] guilty about how Lemmy was treated. We all imagined they lived well from making money from the comic book sales. I think I had a crush on Sonia and I was really sad when we moved to new accommodation. . . . After meeting Sonia in Swaziland and realizing the comic books created a dog [eat] dog situation for the actors I felt pretty bad about the whole comic book thing. It was only then I realized that in all the episodes with Lemmy the poor guy always had the same [clothes]. He had the same [clothes] when we met him only they were now torn to pieces. His skin colour was very light. He most probably was of mixed race and probably got discrimination from both whites and blacks. (*African Film* magazine, Facebook, September 17, 2013)

Similar to ten years ago, ideas of how to create updated versions of The Spear continue to spread. Balogun Ojetade, for example, after discussing on his blog how *African Film* "presented a critique of colonialism," which is perhaps an overstatement, announces the upcoming publication (summer 2014) of his own photo novel, *The Siafu: Revolution.* "The Siafu is about escaped prisoner Jamil Brown, who suffers a virus-induced myostatin deficiency that gives him enhanced strength, speed and endurance. Jamil is hunted by his makers, while gathering others like him to help fight against the corrupt system that made him. For those of you who don't know, siafu are army ants that, while small, are powerful and—in large enough numbers—can bring down an elephant" (Ojetade 2013). This remix of motives from U.S. superhero narratives, African folklore, Afro-futurism, and postcolonial political sentiments is meant to be an expression of steam*funk.*

Ojetade is part of this literary movement, which was created by writers of African descent in about 2012 as a reaction to the "retro-futuristic" literary genre of steampunk, whose narratives, sometimes set in anachronistic Victorian environments, hitherto excluded black characters and experiences. The future will show what becomes of the figure of Lance Spearman, if appropriated by this latter-day blaxploitation genre.

Black Titanic

PIRATING THE WHITE STAR LINER

THIS CHAPTER FOCUSES on four African appropriations of the Hollywood movie *Titanic* (James Cameron, 1997), which at the time of its release in 1997, set a new benchmark for Hollywood filmmaking. It was the first film ever made whose budget reached an incredible 200 million U.S. dollars and whose box office receipts totaled 1.8 billion. Having won eleven Oscars, the movie still ranks among the three most successful films ever made (Parisi 1998: 223). Cameron's preoccupation with size (Keller 1999) echoes the nature of the historical R.M.S. *Titanic* itself, which like the movie, broke a number of records in terms of size, luxury, and cost at the time of her construction. The *Titanic*'s foundering on April 15, 1912, during her maiden voyage from Southampton, England, to New York City, turned the ship into a myth and, in a sense, made her "unsinkable" after all (Howells 1999). The film, unlike the historical ship, was not only kept afloat but even "floated triumphantly," wrote one of its American critics (Bernstein 1999: 16). That is perhaps something like the irony of history. Cameron's film has since become a signifier of success—in the Global North and no less in the Global South, as is aptly demonstrated by the examples I discuss in this chapter.

I argue that the four African appropriations—a Nigerian video remake, a Tanzanian comic book and Adventist choir's song, and a Congolese music video clip—are inspired by Cameron's movie and for at least three different reasons: the movie's very fame as the most successful film ever made; the melodramatic love story built around two lovers from different social classes; and the allegorical potential of the trope of the sinking ship, which actually transcends not only Cameron's film but, to a certain extent, also the myth of the *Titanic* itself. First and foremost, the four re-mediations try to capitalize on Cameron's success. Like most of the copies I discuss in this book, they are commodities, produced and distributed by African cottage culture industries. To boost their sales, and sometimes the ideologies or beliefs they promote, cultural producers tie their own products to a foreign "best seller," hoping their products will thus cash in on the popularity and fame of the original.

However, the copies discussed pirate the *Titanic* for more than just economic gain. Ships lend themselves to plays of thought and therefore make for excellent allegorical material. From the Bible's ark to Apollonius's *Argo,* Melville's *Pequod,* and Géricault's raft, watercraft have figured prominently in narratives and works of art throughout history. According to Michel Foucault (1986: 27), "the boat" has served Western civilization for a very long time not only as a powerful economical tool but also as the "greatest reserve of the imagination." Ships may come to symbolize whole societies, whose inherent social conflicts are embodied by the passengers aboard. But such vessels may as well take on the qualities of "heterotopias," spaces of otherness which are neither here nor there and thus serve as an ideal medium for utopian thought. Hence, Foucault (1986: 27) calls the ship "the heterotopia par excellence." Cameron's *Titanic* matches this tradition perfectly. The love story built around the two fictional characters of Rose and Jack is essentially utopian. It is a romance across the class divide—"Romeo and Juliet on the Titanic," as Cameron allegedly called his project during its initial stages (Bernstein 1999: 18). Moreover, Cameron's mise-en-scène for this romance is a melodrama that plays out openly the conflict between collective social norms and the individualistic antisocial force of love. It resonates perfectly with African audiences. Beginning with the Onitsha market literature of the 1950s (Obiechina 1973), popular genres all over Africa have reflected along similar lines on the social conflicts inherent to African modernities (Larkin 1997).

But it is not just this prominent feature—peculiar to Cameron's own *Titanic*—that we rediscover in at least two African copies. A number of other significations transcend Cameron's "original copy" and resort to much older adaptations. The interpretation of the tragedy as writing on the wall against hubris and naive belief in technical progress is one of them. Cameron alludes to this trope when he has Rose's fiancé boast: "God himself could not sink this ship." The trope of "speed and greed" is another one. It is prominent in many versions, including Cameron's, where White Star Line's managing director, Bruce Ismay, persuades Cpt. John Smith to accelerate in a bid to break a speed record, despite the dangers of navigating the North Atlantic. Moreover, the *Titanic* has long served as a symbol of a society marked by social inequality. This was already cast into the real ship's architecture with its sharp divisions among first, second, and third class, the latter being located in steerage. Cameron references this interpretation, too—most prominently perhaps in the sequences where the ship goes down and steerage passengers are forced to stay below deck while the more privileged board lifeboats.

The demise of the *Titanic* has been reworked in various media and genres throughout the twentieth century (Bergfelder and Street 2004; Biel 1997; Köster and Lischeid 1999). A historical event, meaningless alone, has thus been given new meaning time and time again, each treatment adapting the "raw material," as well as its former adaptations, to changing social, political, and economic contexts (Howells 1999: 4). Unlike James Cameron, African cultural producers have had only limited access, if any, to the vast archive of treatments about the White Star Liner's demise, the combination of which turned the historical event into a myth in Europe and America. Most seem to have encountered the *Titanic* myth initially through Cameron's film. They mediate a distant event of Euro-American history for African audiences by adapting and remediating a Hollywood movie. In this chapter I explore the meanings the *Titanic* myth—mediated through James Cameron's "original copy"—has acquired in its African versions.

A NIGERIAN VIDEO REMAKE

The Nigerian video remake *Masoyiyata/Titanic* (My darling/Titanic), directed by Farouk Ashu-Brown and released on vhs cassette in 2003, is particularly close to the Hollywood template.[1] The Nigerian video film-makers literally hard-copied a number of sequences from Cameron's movie and spliced them into their own video. This physical appropriation of original film material (from DVD) has to be seen as a creative device born of necessity; images of a foundering ocean liner would otherwise have been impossible to realize in northern Nigeria, where the average budget of a video film is less than the equivalent of 2,000 U.S. dollars. Ashu-Brown chose from among Cameron's *Titanic* wide-angle sequences—the passing ship, the boiler room, some of the sinking scenes—and combined these with indoor sequences shot from medium or close range in a Nigerian hotel. This gimmick not only proved useful in overcoming budgetary constraints but also aided in swapping out Cameron's passengers and crew. Because the all-white cast is almost invisible in the wide-angle shots, the ship could take on *Masoyiyata*'s all-African cast. Ashu-Brown's *Titanic* is therefore reborn as a Nigerian ship on its maiden voyage from Lagos to America. Despite the ship's change of course, the basic constellations of the plot remain the same. Aboard the vessel sailing toward its ultimate fate are Binta, Abdul, and Binta's fiancé, Zayyad—the Nigerian equivalents of Rose, Jack, and Caledon. Their ulterior motives, however, as well as the filmic articulation of these differ considerably from Cameron's "original copy."[2]

Masoyiyata displays several features typical of Hausa video films. Such movies are the products of Kanywood, one of Nigeria's regional video film industries, named after Kano, the commercial center of Nigeria's Hausaphone Muslim north and heart of this prolific video industry (which I explore in greater detail in chapter 4). *Masoyiyata* was shot in Hausa. The English subtitles, however, which were uncommon for Hausa videos at the time, suggest that Ashu-Brown had a broader audience in mind. The cast includes several prominent Hausa actors. The late Ahmed S. Nuhu, who was then one of Kanywood's most popular actors, plays Abdul, the Nigerian equivalent to Jack. The female lead, Binta, however, is played by newcomer Sadiya Abdu Rano; her fiancé, Zayyad, is portrayed by director Farouk Ashu-Brown himself, a newcomer as well. The two most prominent features that turn *Masoyiyata* into a Hausa video are its plot—built around the topic of arranged marriage and a girl's attempt to evade it—and the particular mise-en-scéne of song-and-dance intended to ratchet up a sense of the romantic.

Unlike Cameron's *Titanic,* in which "the (historical) ship is itself the main character" while the story about Rose and Jack is "only a fictionalised entry point for the audience to enter into the larger story of the ship" (Wolf 2004: 216), the Nigerian remake shines the spotlight on the love story. Hausa videos have a predilection for love stories. Often such plots develop against the backdrop of arranged or even forced marriages, a social practice still upheld by some parents in northern Nigeria, despite its considerable potential for conflict. In such video films, girl meets boy and they fall in love, only to discover that her parents intend to marry her off to another man. Cameron's *Titanic* with its love triangle of Rose, Jack, and Cal serves as the perfect template for a remake targeting as it does a local and largely female audience that expects a plot of similar constellations with almost every new release. The similarity of the main romantic story in Cameron's *Titanic* to local plot constellations, as well as its resonance with contemporary social reality, must have played into Ashu-Brown's decision to remake the multimillion-dollar Hollywood production under very different local conditions. Remaking, though, is a common practice in Kanywood. However, the films that serve as templates are usually popular Indian movies whose plots are almost invariably based on love triangles. They are used to articulate the conflicting experiences of individuals trapped between the forces of tradition and the liberating promises of modernity in a rapidly changing society. Hausa videos, in fact, can be said to have developed out of a long-standing appreciation for Indian films among Hausa audiences, an appreciation largely owed to these films' stark difference from Western productions, which do not echo Nigerian everyday life (Larkin 1997). In this respect, Cameron's *Titanic* is different. On account of a historical setting, Cameron is able to build the story of Rose and Jack around the tension of an arranged marriage—a story that would not have worked for Western audiences if it had been set in the present day. Hausa audiences, however, can relate to a girl like Rose who feels imprisoned by social norms that force her to unquestioningly obey her parents and to marry someone against her will. Her situation reflects contemporary social reality among the Hausa. Stories abound in northern Nigeria about girls who commit suicide by jumping into wells to escape forced marriages, just as Rose attempts to kill herself. Despite such general resonance, however, Ashu-Brown had to adapt the plot of *Titanic* considerably to its new social context of reception.

Aboard the Nigerian Titanic, Binta travels along with her parents. Unlike Rose, she is accompanied by both her mother and father. In a social context in which a bride has to be represented by a male relative, ideally her father, at her wedding, this makes perfect sense. While Rose's mother forces her daughter into the marriage to maintain the family's endangered elite status, Binta's parents are driven by concern for their daughter's well-being. In one sequence, Binta's father tries to persuade her by outlining the history of his own marriage, likewise arranged by elders. The sagacity of their choice of partner, he suggests, is borne out by the fact that he and Binta's mother lead a harmonious marital life. The Nigerian video is far from being a blatant critique of arranged marriages, and Binta's parents, in contrast to Rose's mother, are portrayed in a favorable light. The authority of elders remains untouched and unquestioned. For her part, Binta exhibits no signs of subverting Hausa norms of social conduct, either, showing the utmost respect for her parents. When her father talks to her, she casts down her eyes, listens silently, and does not answer back. Rose is quite the opposite. Cameron presents her as a prefeminist who rebels against social norms, ahead of her time, and argues with her elders—both with her mother and men the same age as her deceased father. Thanks to this characterization, a contemporary Western audience can identify with the leading lady of a period movie. Binta is granted nothing of that, and this is done precisely to allow conservative factions among Hausa audiences to sympathize with her. Hence, in *Masoyiyata*, Zayyad/Cal represents the only evil character, and Binta's parents take some of the blame for not realizing just how mean he is.

Zayyad is portrayed as a stereotypical *'dan mai ku'di,* a "rich man's son." His frequent code-switching between Hausa and English, his dress, and his Rasta hairdo mark him as someone who has been raised and schooled abroad, which is a common practice among Nigeria's elite class. Unlike Cal, Zayyad owns the *Titanic.* He inherited the ship from his deceased father who had it built. He is joined by his father's widow, a figure endowed with some of the characteristics of *Titanic*'s jovial rich man's widow, Molly Brown. A Nigerian "rich kid," which is actually no less of a stock character, replaces Cameron's Cal, the stereotypical personification of a prewar upper-class American bachelor. The Hausa popular imagination is ambivalent toward a *'dan mai ku'di,* who may be admired and envied for an affluence that affords him an easy lifestyle but who may also be regarded with suspicion for the potential breach of Hausa social norms implied by his Westernization. In *Masoyiyata,* this latter aspect combines with Zayyad's rude behavior toward Binta and therefore gives Zayyad an evil air. Evilness then becomes associated with the world outside Nigeria or, more precisely, America. Abdul, Zayyad's rival, is consequently portrayed as a country bumpkin—less sophisticated than globalized Zayyad and almost rustic in his manners—but of good character and with an unspoiled heart. *Titanic's* class distinction is translated topologically: a spoiled rich kid and globetrotter versus a poor young guy who has never left Nigeria. Since gambling is considered a sin among the Muslim Hausa and would have cast the character in a bad light, Abdul cannot win his ticket "in a lucky-handed poker," like Jack Dawson. A "lottery" has to serve this purpose—an allusion to the American Diversity Visa Lottery that offers up to 6,000 American immigrant visas (but without any financial support for traveling) each year to Nigerians who are otherwise ineligible.

Binta and Abdul express their love and yearning for each other in song-and-dance sequences. Such spectacular interruptions of the narrative are a stylistic device borrowed from Indian film and a common feature of Hausa videos. This musical approach seeks to bring social and religious acceptability to on-screen male-female romantic encounters that would otherwise be frowned upon if expressed diegetically (see chapter 4). Since these musical numbers are also important in selling a film, producers spend a considerable part of their budgets on the choreography in and editing of such sequences. *Masoyiyata* has three musical sequences. The first is a faint reference to *Titanic's* Irish dance party transposed from steerage to first class. In this rather unspectacular, almost diegetic sequence, Abdul shows up at Zayyad's party and sings a song to Binta. The second song-and-dance scene is considerably more elaborate and looks like a hybrid of Indian film and MTV video clip. Binta, clad in various costumes ranging from American college dress to Indian sari, is superimposed on changing backdrops—a waterfall, a beach, fireworks, a cloudy sky. The tune is borrowed from Céline Dion's song "My Heart Will Go On," whose melody appears in Cameron's *Titanic* as a musical theme for

Rose. In *Masoyiyata,* Dion's lyrics are replaced with semantically different lines in Hausa. The song's meaning changes. A touching remembrance of a passed-away lover becomes an elegy about Binta's dilemma of being caught up between her own desire and obeying her parents per society's norms. "Near, far, wherever you are, I believe that the heart does go on," is overwritten with: "Iyayena sun ce, sam, ba zan auri wanda na ke so ba" (My parents said, no way, I won't marry the one I love). Lyrical alterations similar to this one have a strong tradition in Hausa popular culture, from religious *bandiri* musicians, who turn Indian film songs into praise songs for the Prophet Muhammad (Larkin 2002), to the "playback" studio singers of Kanywood, who also frequently draw on Indian film songs for their own productions (Adamu 2007).

The third song-and-dance sequence, also less elaborate than the second one and also nearly diegetic, shows Binta and Abdul together, sharing the same visual space and singing about their love to the sound of a synthesizer: "Yare yarena masoyina, 'kauna gare ni" (Yeah yeah my lover, I am in love). This number has to be understood as an allusion to the original movie's lovemaking scene, in the cargo hold, that Ashu-Brown cannot show on a diegetic level as Cameron does. Instead Ashu-Brown shows the couple entering a room while the camera remains outside, a closed door filling the frame. When the couple reappears through the same door, they start singing and dancing. While such sequences are some of the most elaborate attempts at adapting Hollywood footage to local expectations of decency, other modifications can be observed as well. There is Cameron's "first kiss" at the bow of the ship, a sequence which has since become a romantic icon in Western popular culture. The kiss cannot be so much as hinted at in *Masoyiyata.* This is in a social environment where stones were thrown at the actress playing the female lead in the only movie that ever dared to show an attempted kiss (*Sauran 'kiris* [Almost], 2000). Likewise, Abdul cannot sketch Binta in the nude but must be content to capture her in full dress.

Unlike Cameron, whose film revels in historical detail, Ashu-Brown abstains from historicizing his setting with period-piece costumes and props. Since he, too, frames the main plot with Binta/Rose in flashback, this approach requires a certain degree of collaboration on the part of the audience (Kilian 2012). The viewers have to accept the filmmaker's proposition that what actually seems to be set in the present is meant to be taken as the distant past. But this is not the only "collaboration" Ashu-Brown enters into with his audience. I propose that his film cannot and is not intended to stand alone. It is a copy that deliberately evokes and also relies on its template. *Masoyiyata* itself suggests that its audience is familiar with Cameron's *Titanic*—the film presupposes this very knowledge on several levels. For example, *Masoyiyata*'s plot has many gaps; certain sequences are related to one another only if the spectator has Cameron's *Titanic* in mind, others are barely decodable by themselves and work only by evoking their equivalents in the absent original. In fact, the hard-copied *Titanic* footage that Ashu-Brown cut into his film constantly echoes the original.

Heike Behrend (2009: 233) argues that Ashu-Brown not only Africanized *Titanic* but also gave it an Afrocentric perspective. Five minutes into the film, a text insert reads: "This film is dedicated to all Africans who died when the real Titanic sank in 1929" (An sadaukar da wannan fim 'din da 'yan Afirkan da suka mutu a ainihin jirgin Taitanic da ya nitse a shekara ta 1929). According to Behrend, "This dedication strongly evokes the association of the Titanic with a slave ship and with the transatlantic slave trade in which millions of innocent Africans lost their lives." She continues, arguing that Cameron's *Titanic* has thus been "reformulated in a rather subversive way" and suggest that by drawing attention to the missing Africans aboard Cameron's *Titanic* and therefore criticizing his all-white perspective, the Nigerian movie reminds its viewers of the sacrifices Africans were forced to make for the sake of Euro-American capitalist gain. Ashu-Brown's dedication undoubtedly reveals disbelief in the historical accuracy of Cameron's movie and may have been inserted to correct what Ashu-Brown believed to be a historical fact. And indeed, contemporary African American observers of the *Titanic* tragedy have already criticized news coverage of the disaster because they found it hard to believe no black people were aboard the steamship (Biel 1997).[3] However, rather than fully agreeing with Behrend's interpretation of *Masoyiyata* as an Afrocentric critique of Cameron's *Titanic,* I argue that, on the contrary, the Nigerian video film shows strong evidence of being a pastiche, and as such may be understood as a "quasi-homage to and assimilation of a great master" (Hoesterey 2001: 4). *Titanic* won eleven Oscars and became a synonym for a new mastery of filmmaking. Its director, James

Cameron, became a famous figure of success. *Masoyiyata* may be read as Ashu-Brown's attempt to tie in with this achievement by imitating what *Titanic*'s success was founded on. This can been seen in the very title of the Hausa video. *Masoyiyata/Titanic* literally ties the two films together by placing them side by side. Furthermore, Sadiya Abdu Rano, who played Binta, is nicknamed "Céline Dion" on the official poster advertising the video (see figure 3.1). And as if directing wasn't enough to accomplish the "assimilation of a great master," Farouk Ashu-Brown played the role of Zayyad, thus associating himself—and his own real-life girlfriend, Sadiya Abdu Rano, who played Rose—with the Hollywood blockbuster in front of the camera as well.

Associating himself and his debut so closely with *the* quintessential Hollywood film of the era must be understood as a self-confident newcomer's attempt to make his presence felt on the local video-film scene in a big-time way and to make a name for himself right from the start. "This film makes a difference," declares Ashu-Brown proudly in the "Making

FIGURE 3.1

Advertisement for *Masoyiyata/Titanic* (2003) from *Fim* magazine.

of" track on the same VHS cassette. For local audiences and critics alike, however, his film—neither Hollywood, nor really Kanywood—was too much of a difference, and was not a success at all. "Just like the way the ship went down into the water, I felt the money for which I bought this film go down the drain" (from the Hausa; my translation), writes Abubakar I. Abdullahi in his critique posted at Finafinan_Hausa, a Yahoo! group dedicated to Hausa videos (August 21, 2003). Neither was the video appreciated as a critical response to Cameron's *Titanic,* nor as remarkable in any other way. "It seems that you alone enjoyed your cover version of Céline Dion's song, which, I must admit, almost caused the loss of my ears" (August 21, 2003). While the film flopped for many reasons, the fact that it was a remake prompted the most criticism. In 2003, when *Masoyiyata* came out, the practice of remaking had already been discussed very critically with regard to videos that borrowed their plots more or less straight from Indian movies. Critics usually complained about mixing "Hausa culture" with "Indian culture" that allegedly blighted local life. While these complaints pertained to Hausa videos in general (see chapter 4), they were even fiercer if the video in question turned out to be a remake and often went along with the allegation that the producer's only motivation was to make money without any creative effort. Since *Masoyiyata*—unlike other Hausa remakes—makes no attempt to hide that it is indeed a remake, the usual critics of "cross-cultural" copying were particularly harsh on its director. "Today we have someone who demonstrates to ordinary remakers that theirs is just a child's game (*wasa*), for his is a serious scrambling for money (*wasoso*)," says, Abdullahi, launching his critique, which he substantiates by pointing out that the filmmaker not only "stole" the title and the story but also pasted "more than 27 sequences" of the original into his own film. Referring to a Hausa proverb, he calls Ashu-Brown a "magpie which turns someone else's offspring into its own" (Hankaka—mai da 'dan wani naka; August 21, 2003).

A TANZANIAN GRAPHIC NOVEL

In Tanzania, Cameron's *Titanic* was appropriated by comic artist Joshua Amandus Mtani, who turned the movie into a graphic novel titled

Mkasa wa mapenzi ndani Titanic (A romantic tragedy on the Titanic). Tanzania has a very lively tradition of comic art in Swahili, its national language. While early productions date back to the 1950s (Beez 2009), the genre continued to develop mainly as short comic strips in newspapers after independence and throughout Tanzania's socialist era. Following the liberalization of the economy and the introduction of the multiparty system in 1986, *katuni,* as comics are called in Swahili, began to proliferate considerably (Packalén 2009). The 1990s witnessed a huge number of new publications, and comics were no longer limited to cartoon pages of newspapers but filled the pages of humorous magazines and funny tabloids launched at the beginning and the end of the decade, respectively. In addition, comic artists began to publish their work independently as small booklets (Packalén 2009).

Mtani, born in 1973, belongs to Tanzania's third generation of comic artists. When he began working on his graphic novel *Mkasa wa mapenzi* in 1998, he was a political science student at the University of Dar es Salaam and earned his living as a part-time cartoonist for a number of Kiswahili newspapers. At first, he adapted the movie to the format of a comic strip that was printed in *Alasiri,* one of the daily papers he was working for. However, he stopped the strip after only ten episodes and—encouraged by readers—developed a book-length project instead. It took him about eight months to finish the drawings and turn Cameron's movie into a graphic novel. His initial plan was to divide it into a series of sixteen booklets, each with a color cover (see, e.g., figure 3.2) and about thirty-two pages of black-and-white drawings. The first volume of his series appeared in the year 2000, with a circulation of 3,000. It was sold in Tanzania's main cities—Dar es Salaam, Mwanza, Arusha, and Moshi. At that time, the supply of new comic publications was higher than the demand, and many of those initially planned as a series never made it to a second volume. Despite the fact that he was able to make a moderate profit from his first volume, Mtani had expected much higher returns and dreamed of laying the foundation for his own publishing company. Needless to say, he was disappointed and postponed the publication of the remaining volumes—a decision he was later to regret after gaining more experience in the media industry (Beez 2007). It was not until August 2006 that he recommenced publication of *Mkasa wa mapenzi,* not in the form of booklets, however,

FIGURE 3.2

Cover image for one of the unpublished volumes of *Mkasa wa mapenzi ndani ya Titanic,* by Joshua Amandus Mtani. Courtesy of the artist.

but cut up into short episodes, each filling a page of *Maisha,* the weekly paper whose editor-in-chief he had meanwhile become.[4]

Mtani's graphic novel shares a number of features with the Nigerian video adaptation. Like Ashu-Brown, Mtani puts the love story center stage, Africanizes the characters, and inserts himself into the action. Cameron's Jack characterized as a talented but poor young artist must have functioned as a personal lead-in for Mtani, an artist with meager earnings who identified with the fictional character. Hence, his Jack's physical features closely resemble Mtani's own. Like the Nigerian director, Mtani is interested both in Cameron's film as such and in associating himself and his product with it. His interest in the real historical tragedy, however, seems to be far more pronounced than that of his Nigerian counterpart. Thus, his *Titanic* does not change course like the Nigerian steamer does, his main characters are dressed in historical clothes, and he takes great pains to give correct dates and place names and to explain certain details he assumes his readers are unfamiliar with. According to Mtani, his intention was to educate Tanzanians about the real historical event.[5] While "teaching through art" is a well-established trope in Tanzania—a trope that likens artists to teachers and draws its power from the model of Tanzania's most prominent "teacher," former president Julius Nyerere, revered today as *mwalimu* (teacher)—it certainly reflects Mtani's own interest in the historical event. In interviews with Jigal Beez and Claudia Böhme, the comic artist recalls his captivation with Cameron's movie when he first saw it at a friend's house in 1998. Taking it to be purely fictitious initially, he became even more excited when he learned that it was based on a true story. His interest sparked, he began searching for background information on the internet that he would later share with his readers. In the first volume of his *Mkasa wa mapenzi,* he provides a written account of Robert Ballard's deep-sea exploration of the *Titanic* wreck, and on the first page of volume 2, he announces: "This pictorial story is drawn from the film that starred Leonardo DiCaprio and Kate Winslet as Jack and Rose. Nevertheless, in this book Amandus Mtani gives you the actual details of the accident with the help of the internet." Sometimes his mediating voice can be heard in the middle of a sequence and he explains, both in pictures and writing, something he assumes his readers may otherwise find difficult to understand. An image of two sailors in the lookout, for example, is supplemented by a schematic sketch depicting the location of the crow's nest on the mast (vol. 7: 4). When the ship is about to hit the iceberg, he inserts a panel with a sketch of an iceberg and explains the nature of this phenomenon in a caption (vol. 7: 25).

Turning a sound film into a graphic novel is akin to turning moving images into stills, as well as dialogue into writing. In terms of images, Mtani stays remarkably close to Cameron's film. This is due to what he calls "pause-and-sketch," a technique he developed in transferring (video) film images into his sketchbook: he would sit down in front of his VCR in search of key scenes and, when he found one, he would press the pause button to halt the video film and copy from the screen. Hence, a film frame that corresponds to almost every panel of the graphic novel can be found (Beez 2007). I suggest that this relative closeness to Cameron's "original copy" is both indicative of Mtani's captivation and is an attempt at maximum authenticity. The latter suggests that the artist buys into Cameron's creative mixing of historical events with fiction and assumes that the story of Rose and Jack, though reenacted by Hollywood actors, actually happened on the historical voyage and that Cameron's film is the closest possible account of this relationship. Certain passages in the graphic novel even suggest that Mtani reads the framing narrative of Cameron's *Titanic*—the deep-sea exploration and elderly Rose telling her story to the team of treasure hunters—as nonfictional footage (which in part it is). In this regard, the summaries he provides in each of his booklets are revealing. The first page of volume 4 reads: "Just as in the previous book, the main character in this big disaster and tragedy, Rose, who at the point when the film was produced was over 90 years old (she is now dead), continues to narrate the story, picking it up at the point where they are out on the ship kissing" (vol. 4: 1). That he Africanizes the characters must not necessarily contradict his attempt to provide an account of the tragedy that is as authentic as possible. Mtani himself explained this as a tool of mediation, a necessary means to help his readers identify with the characters in his comic and bring the distant historical event closer to his present audience. I suggest that this change on the visual level has to be conceptualized as equivalent to the use of Swahili on the textual level. Both are instances of translation and therefore make it easier to infer meaning from a past event which is distant for African readers in many respects.

Mtani's faithfulness to Cameron's film has a considerable effect on the way he organizes his graphic novel. Most panels have the rectangular shape of a television screen, which leaves almost no room for more than two panels on each page. Rarely is a page filled with a single panel alone or with three panels. This gives Mtani's work a rather static appearance. Moreover, since he took only limited license to create his own images, it is almost impossible to grasp the plot from the pictures and the speech bubbles alone, in contrast to many other comics in Tanzania and elsewhere. What governs the story, in fact, is the written narrative that runs throughout the sixteen volumes at the top of each panel. Like Cameron's film, the elderly Rose narrates the story in first person singular. The major part of the graphic novel is marked as a visualization of Rose's memory, something Mtani makes visible on a formal level when he draws the frame lines of these memory panels with little edges and dents, alluding to old manuscript pages or photo prints that have changed hands many times. Even the panels that depict the narrative frame of Rose's memory— elderly Rose telling her story to the team of treasure hunters, which is kept formally distinct by straight frame lines—are linked by a running text told in third person by an absent narrator. As written texts, both types of narrative serve the same purpose; they bridge the "gutter," as comic theorists call the empty space between panels (McCloud 1994: 66), and thus help the reader to connect the various pictures with one another. Mtani's work leaves less room for readers to participate actively than other comics, which invite their readers to use their imaginations to fill the gutter. Thanks to the written narratives, however, his graphic novel works even for readers who have not seen the film. This is a major difference compared with the Nigerian remake, which as I have argued, takes it for granted that the audience is familiar with Cameron's *Titanic*.

Nevertheless, Mtani references the film frequently. This is done noticeably in the first volume of his series, which features a full-page photo of Céline Dion with a caption explaining that her song served as part of the soundtrack for the film, a page with the lyrics from "My Heart Will Go On," and a color photo of Kate Winslet and Leonardo DiCaprio on the back cover. Likewise, in his rendition of the "first kiss" at the bow of the ship, Mtani references the soundtrack and urges his readers to participate actively: "My brother, reader, at that time the song *My heart will go on* is heard, and if you like you can sing along" (vol. 3: 31). And as if to lay open how faithfully he copies the movie, he inserts a film still of this iconic scene next to his adaptation of it (vol. 3: 32; see figures 3.3 and 3.4).

Even in terms of the more explicit romantic scenes between Rose and Jack, Mtani stays faithful to his template. This is remarkably different from the Nigerian video film and suggests a social context that is slightly more liberal about depicting nudity. When Jack draws Rose naked, Mtani even adds considerable eroticism, showing Rose in a transparent negligee before she undresses. Compared to the length of the equivalent sequence in the movie, Mtani devotes more space to showing her in the nude. Compared to so-called *Katuni za mapenzi*, a Tanzanian genre of "love comics" with explicit imagery, however, Mtani's nude scene is rather modest. Since this genre was prolific when Mtani drew his *Mkasa wa mapenzi*, his modesty has to be viewed as a conscious decision, and in an interview with Beez (2007) he indeed criticizes such comics for seeking merely to titillate while lacking any educational value. According to Mtani, comic art, like any other art, should entertain *and* educate. With regard to his *Titanic* adaptation, I suggest that similar to James Cameron, Mtani uses the love story as an entertaining lead-in to the historical tragedy, and it is this educational story he really wants to tell.

Mtani's interest in the historical event may well be explained by the close parallels between the *Titanic*'s demise and a local tragedy of comparable dimension that occurred on Lake Victoria only a year before Cameron's film was released, a tragedy which foreign observers almost immediately labeled "Tanzania's 'Titanic' disaster" (Britain-Tanzania Society 1996: 13). In the early hours of May 21, 1996, the M.V. *Bukoba* ferry capsized about thirty minutes offshore from Mwanza, the country's second largest city and Amandus Mtani's hometown. There were an estimated 800 passengers aboard, almost double the steamer's capacity. Overloading and improper storage of cargo, in combination with a long-ignored stability problem, were later identified as the main causes of the disaster. The capsized vessel had remained floating on the surface for more than half a day. Inexperienced rescue teams cut a hole into the hull to free surviving passengers still trapped inside. As a result, the air that had kept the hull afloat was released, causing the ship to go down (Britain-Tanzania

FIGURE 3.3

Page from *Mkasa wa mapenzi ndani ya Titanic*, by Joshua Amandus Mtani
(vol. 3, unpublished): (1) "Close your eyes now, Rose. . . ." (2) "We were leaning
on the big ship *Titanic*. For me it was a spiritual experience. *My brother, at
that time the song 'My Heart Will Go On' is heard, and if you like, you can sing
along." (3) "All that time the ship was swaying very fast that night. . . ." Courtesy
of the artist.

FIGURE 3.4

Page from *Mkasa wa mapenzi ndani ya Titanic*, by Joshua Amandus Mtani (vol. 3, unpublished): (1) "I opened my eyes and felt as if I was flying in the air. . . . It was a dance. Jack turned me around gently and our tongues met and . . . weee!" (2) "Mmmmmh! Mmmwa!" (3) "I love you Jack. . . ." (4) "And that was the last day for the *Titanic* to see the sunlight." (5) "My dear reader, don't feel too tired to follow this story in the next book. —Mtani." Courtesy of the artist.

Society 1996, 1997). Only 120 out of an estimated 800 passengers survived. The sheer magnitude of the lives lost plunged Tanzanians into a state of shock for days. President Benjamin Mkapa declared three days of national mourning and ordered all entertainment and sporting activities to be suspended. Newspapers were full of tragic stories about people who had lost their entire families and listed schoolchildren, church choirs, and businessmen among the drowned. Sympathetic readers composed poems to express their grief (Beez 2007). Rumors and press reports about the tragedy's causes immediately focused on human error. In his song "MV Bukoba," popular musician Justin Kalikawe accused corrupt officials (of Tanzania Railways, whose marine division operated the vessel) of intentionally overloading the ship for personal gain, putting the passengers' lives at risk (Beez 2007). As a matter of fact, negligence—overloading for personal gain, in the case of the M.V. *Bukoba,* and seeking the glory that comes with breaking a speed record (the trope of "speed and greed" presented in Cameron's *Titanic*)—is what makes the two distinct events, or rather their mediatizations, comparable beyond the mere parallelism of two ships sinking with huge numbers of passengers aboard.

In the first volume of his *Mkasa wa mapenzi,* Mtani evokes the comparability of the two disasters. Before he actually starts with the transposition of Cameron's film, he provides a three-page "factual" account of the historical event in nine panels. These panels are dominated by drawings of the *Titanic* and her demise from various perspectives (pages 6–8). On page 9, another capsized ship can be seen and bold letters announce "The last night of the MV Bukoba."[6] This turns out to be an advertisement for a graphic novel about the tragic demise of the M.V. *Bukoba* that Mtani had planned to work out but actually never finished. The written teaser clarifies his intention to use Cameron's *Titanic* as a template: "Be prepared to read this exciting book. It is an exciting love story based on a true event. It is the story of the horrible accident of the MV Bukoba. Don't miss this captivating story by J.A.L. Mtani!" Although Mtani never pursued this idea any further than a first storyboard (Beez 2007), others did: in 2007, a group of actors from Mwanza produced the video film *Majonzi* (Grief). The video tells a love story set against the tragic M.V. *Bukoba* shipwreck on Lake Victoria.

A TANZANIAN ADVENTIST CHOIR'S SONG

The M.V. *Bukoba* tragedy of 1996 may also have provided part of the context in which local audiences received the Nyasho Kwaya's "Titanic" song even before it was recorded and distributed more widely in 2000. After all, Musoma, home of the Kamunyonge Seventh-day Adventist Church with which the choir is associated, is on the shores of Lake Victoria, too, and only a four-hour journey from Mwanza. However, as choir members told me in 2009, the song was written much earlier, probably even before the choir was formed in 1994. It goes back to the choir's founder, the late Kilion Otuk Angoche, who introduced the song to the Nyasho Kwaya's repertoire. If this is true, and I have no reason to doubt the veracity of my source, it means that Cameron's *Titanic* cannot be the template of the song. A primary school teacher by profession, Angoche must have come across the myth of the *Titanic* through some other source, perhaps some publication or the sermon of a traveling preacher who may have used the tragedy as a parable.[7] Even though the song itself was not inspired by the Hollywood movie, Cameron's *Titanic* and the interest it stirred must have played some role in the choir's decision to record the song in 2000. The church elders told me that the recording was not only meant to spread Adventist belief but to raise funds as well.

Both *kwaya* (choir) music and its taping and sale of audiocassettes began to flourish in the 1990s. According to Gregory Barz (2003), who conducted research on urban kwaya music in 1994, modern choir music is a blend of indigenous Tanzanian musical traditions and the dominant Western hymnody practiced in African Christian churches of various denominations for the greater part of the twentieth century. It is also characterized by the use of electric musical instruments, most notably guitars and keyboards, to accompany the singers. The Nyasho Kwaya's "Titanic" reflects this trend. On the tape recorded in a Nairobi studio, a synthesizer that produces electric-guitar and organ sounds accompanies the thirty-one members of the choir. In terms of chord sequence, instrumental and chorus melody, as well as vocal rhythm, the song displays the typical features of kwaya music, too (Katharina Aue, email, April 5, 2007). Thus, the Nyasho Kwaya choir, which has since produced five more volumes of its repertoire and was about to record two more when I talked to choir members in 2009, has to be viewed as part of a larger tradition of popularized church music. According to Barz (2003), Tanzanian kwaya groups produce *kandas,* as audiocassettes are called in Swahili, for a number of reasons:

> First and foremost is the preservation and documentation of musical repertoires. . . . *Kwaya* members and the congregations they minister want to listen to their *kwaya's* hit tunes when they return home. In addition, *kwayas* also use their *kandas* as fundraisers to promote the activities of the *kwaya.* Probably most significant for many members of *kwayas* is the role *kandas* assume in the evangelizing effort of the church. The current popularization of *kwaya* music has enabled *kwayas* to "send their messages" beyond their home communities to a greater population. (127)

A good-quality cassette of a choir's repertoire becomes the source of considerable prestige, both for the choir and the church with which it is associated. On its return home from the recording session in Nairobi, the Nyasho Kwaya brought back a master tape and 200 audio-cassette copies, which were subsequently sold among church members and friends around Musoma. Inspired by the successful sale of that first collection of cassettes, the choir approached GMC, a Dar es Salaam–based distributor, to market its album nationwide. Since this cassette would now have to compete with the huge number of kwaya tapes in music stores, the choir needed a cover that would attract attention. The cassette, which contains twelve songs, was named *Titanic.* Its cover was dominated by a still from Cameron's film—a long shot of the *Titanic* under full steam—which was taken from the internet by a pastor who was on friendly terms with the choir and helped design the jacket (see figure 3.5). The title and cover made the cassette stand out nicely from the mass of kwaya tapes, whose jackets typically sport images of the choirs and their instruments (Barz 2003). Above all, it tied in very well with the keen interest in the myth of the *Titanic,* which Cameron's film had sparked in Tanzania around 2000. It is therefore safe to assume that although the Hollywood movie did not serve as the inspirational source for the song, it certainly helped boost sales of the cassette and send the choir's message to a larger audience.[8]

The Nyasho Kwaya song turns the story of the *Titanic* into a parable about the end of the world, according to Adventist conviction. The generic form of the parable invokes church sermons and the preaching of Jesus

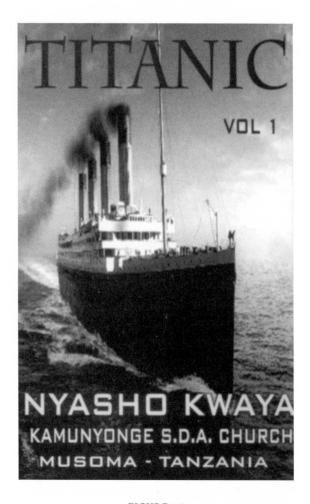

FIGURE 3.5

Audiocassette cover art for Nyasho Kwaya's *Titanic* (2000).

Christ, as imparted by the Bible. The very form in which it is presented legitimizes the song's message. The simile of the ship that sank despite a common belief that it was unsinkable lends credibility to Adventist eschatology. The passengers on the *Titanic* are likened to the inhabitants of a world who live as if the world would last forever: "On the journey they got drunk to celebrate because Titanic / cannot sink." The song admonishes those who have yet to bear witness to the Adventist creed. "And so it was lies and stupidity / There is nothing that has a beginning but has no end," intones the choir, taking the listener aboard the *Titanic* as she sails toward her ultimate destiny. The last lines of the song ensure that the parable's message gets through to the audience: "And now our world is the Titanic about to sink, it is true / My friend / And even if people find it hard to accept that the world is ending / It is true / The world is going to sink / And human beings are going to perish."

Na kumbe ilikuwa uwongo na upuzi	And so it was lies and stupidity
Hakuna chenye mwanzo ambacho hakina mwisho	There is nothing that has a beginning but has no end
Hakuna chenye mwanzo ambacho hakina mwisho	There is nothing that has a beginning but has no end
Wanadamu walitengeneza meli hiyo kubwa ya Titaniki	Human beings built that big ship called Titanic
Waliamini na kutumaini kwamba meli hiyo si ya kuzama	They believed and hoped that it was not a ship that could sink
Na kumbe ilikuwa uwongo na upuzi	And so it was lies and stupidity
Hakuna chenye mwanzo ambacho hakina mwisho	There is nothing that has a beginning but has no end
Hakuna chenye mwanzo ambacho hakina mwisho	There is nothing that has a beginning but has no end
Na kwenye meli yao Titaniki safari ilianza kwa furaha	And aboard the ship Titanic the journey started happily
Walisafiri kwenda Amerikani wakitokea nchi za Ulaya	The passengers were travelling to America from European countries
Safari ilianza kuvuka pazifiki	The journey started to cross the Pacific
Meli hiyo Titaniki kweli iliwapendeza	And the ship Titanic really pleased them
Meli hiyo Titaniki kweli iliwapendeza	And the ship Titanic really pleased them
Wasafiri wote walikuwa na furaha na matumaini ya kwamba wangefika	All the passengers were happy and hoped to arrive

Salama	Safely
Waliposafiri walikunywa na kulewa kushangilia ya kwamba Titaniki	On the journey they got drunk to celebrate because the Titanic
Haizami	Cannot sink
Na kumbe mbele yao kulikuwa na wa hatari ya kutisha	And then ahead of them was dreadful danger
Na kumbe mbele yao kulikuwa na wa hatari ya kutisha	And then ahead of them was dreadful danger
Na kumbe mbele yao kulikuwa na wa hatari ya kutisha	And then ahead of them was dreadful danger
Na kumbe mbele yao kulikuwa na wa hatari ya kutisha	And then ahead of them was dreadful danger
Walipoona ya kwamba mbele yao kuna hatari	When they saw that ahead of them was danger
Nahodha na wasafiri hawakujali hilo	The captain and the passengers were not bothered
Walisema: Titaniki	They said: the Titanic
Haizami	Cannot sink
Waligonga mwamba, bum, na meli ilizama	They hit a rock, bang!, and the ship sank
Titanic kweli ilizama, na watu pia waliangamia	The Titanic truly sank and the passengers drowned, too
Titanic kweli ilizama, na watu pia waliangamia	The Titanic truly sank and the passengers drowned, too
Titanic kweli ilizama, na watu pia waliangamia	The Titanic truly sank and the passengers drowned, too
Na sasa dunia yetu ndio Titaniki inakaribia kuzama, ni hakika	And now our world is the Titanic about to sink, it is true
Mwenzangu	My friend
Hata kama watu ni wagumu kukubali kwamba dunia yaisha Mwisho wake	And even if people find it hard to accept that the world is ending
Ni hakika	It is true
Dunia yaenda kuzama	The world is going to sink
Na watu waenda kuangamia	And human beings are going to perish

| Na watu waenda kuangamia | And human beings are going to perish |
| Na watu waenda kuangamia | And human beings are going to perish[9] |

The references to the end of the world—likewise found in several of the eleven other songs on the tape, such as *Dunia yafika mwisho* (The world has come to an end), *Sasa ni wakati* (Now is the time), and *Zipo ishara nyingi* (There are many signs)—make up the Adventist core of the song. Seventh-day Adventism, so-called after its observance of Saturday, the original Judeo-Christian seventh day of the week, as the day of rest and worship, is rooted in nineteenth-century North American Protestant revivalism. It emphasizes the imminent return of Jesus Christ and considers itself to be a "remnant"—"a movement consisting of God's faithful end-time people called out of 'every nation, tribe, language and people' (Revelation 14:6)" (Höschele 2007: 1). Adventist missionary activity, which resulted in the church's arrival in Tanganyika in 1903, has been driven by the central motive of "warning the world" of God's impending judgment. The Nyasho Kwaya song shows that the denominational task, which around 1900 was defined "as conveying the 'last message' to the perishing human race" (Höschele 2007: 28), was still intact by the year 2000. Since German missionaries founded the Majita mission station in 1909, the Adventist doctrine has gained considerable ground in Tanzanian territory, and the northeastern part of the lake region has become a particular stronghold in the process.

Stefan Höschele (2007), who published a detailed study on the history of Adventism in Tanzania, mentions two types of reasoning within Adventist missionary activity: while many believed that Christ's Second Coming depended on the successful accomplishment of the task at hand, others were convinced "that the end was so impending that they had to snatch away perishing souls from the grasp of the evil one" (440). The latter conviction may have laid the foundation for an "apocalyptical mood" among Tanzanian Adventists expressed in an "enormous" quantity of statements throughout the history of Tanzanian Adventism (438–439). Adventism at large inherited this kind of belief from the North American Millerite movement, whose end-of-days speculations and prophetic calculations climaxed in 1844. In light of present-day apocalyptic belief, it is perhaps no coincidence that the Nyasho choir recorded its tape in 2000. As early as the 1960s, important Tanzanian church leaders referred to a belief about the near termination of history that, according to the late-nineteenth-century writings of the church's founding prophet, Ellen G. White, was believed to last for only 6,000 years. Writing in 1972, one of Tanzania's church leaders made his own calculations and expected the year 2000 to mark the end of history. As the year came closer, quite a number of Tanzanian Adventists believed that all those who until then had not "accepted the Sabbath" would "receive the mark of the beast" (Höschele 2007: 447–448).

During our conversation at the church, one member of the choir said he believed that there was something special about the "Titanic" song. He had noticed that wherever the choir performed, the audience's attentiveness would be most intense while listening to this particular song, but he could not explain why. I suggest the explanation for the audience's reaction is multifaceted. First of all, the song tells a story. This sets it apart from many other kwaya songs, whose lyrics are built around standard phrases in praise of the lord and other Biblical figures (cf. Barz 2003). Moreover, the story is dramatic. The listener's curiosity is piqued from the opening verse, which suggests that the tale to be related will not end happily. Listeners are thus keen to find out how a "journey [that] started happily" turns tragic. In addition, the lyrics are dramatized through a very skillful musical arrangement. Its overall pattern is the alternation of voice types across verses, so that female and high-pitched male voices combine to sing one verse, male bass voices the next, and so on. The first two verses sung by the bass voices are accompanied by higher, humming female voices. This gives the song a joyful, light-hearted timbre. The ship is built and leaves Europe for America in expectation of a happy voyage. The verses that follow build up suspense. This is achieved through switching the alternation of the voice types into a call-and-response pattern, in which verses sung by the bass voices ("All the passengers were happy and hoped to arrive . . .") are completed by the chorus of the high and middle voices (". . . Safely"). The song's climax is marked by a dramatic slow-down in tempo: "When they saw that ahead of them was danger / The captain and the passengers were not bothered / They said: the T-i-t-a-n-i-c [pause] / C-a-n-n-o-t s-i-n-k."

Stressing the hubris of the captain and passengers and thus marking this climactic aspect, and not the sinking of the ship as one might expect, is in line with the Adventist message: it is not the end of days as such that needs to be emphasized but rather the imminence of the Last Days—there are many signs which need only be interpreted correctly. Accordingly, the sinking of the ship is performed less dramatically. Another rising tempo is this time marked by a break in the musical accompaniment, which returns only in the following verse. Finally, the intermediality may also account for the song's popularity. Given the circulation of Cameron's movie on pirated cassette and disc, many of the song's listeners must have been familiar with the story told by the lyrics. This means that people who watched the Hollywood movie almost certainly saw images of Cameron's *Titanic* in their mind's eye while listening to the song.

A CONGOLESE MUSIC VIDEO CLIP

The last appropriation I discuss is a song and video clip called *Titanic,* by Wenge BCBG, a band from the Democratic Republic of the Congo whose acronymic epithet, BCBG—an abbreviation of the French *bon chic, bon genre* (good style, good attitude)—is a self-ascription of sorts, and conveys certain kind of chic that has become synonymous with Wenge. The group has been at the forefront of a new generation of popular urban musicians since the 1990s (White 2008: 50). The song is part of the album of the same title that was released in 1998. As is common for Congolese music, this album was produced and recorded in Paris. The music video, however, was realized by Shabani Records, a company based in Kinshasa, the capital city of the Democratic Republic of the Congo. In 2006, a street-side vendor on Nairobi's River Road sold me a pirated copy of the video. Back in my hotel room, I was riveted by the enigmatic images that appeared on the screen when I slipped the VCD[10] into the drive of my laptop. Only later on, after talking to fans of Congolese music and to colleagues familiar with Congolese ethnography, did the images begin to make sense.[11]

The clip consists of two parts: a supporting intro and the music video itself. The intro begins with the credits ("Simon Music—SIPE / presente / Wenge BCBG / dans / Titanic"), which are copied on top of translucent-white negative-film images that show a running film projector intercut with the sight of a spectator sitting in front of a movie screen. In combination with the underlying sound—a windlike roaring that rises and ebbs, accompanied by a woman's screams—these images make cinema appear as an enchanting technology somehow associated with the spiritual realm. The prelude ends with a cut to a running film projector in full color, and we are shown an African audience watching Cameron's *Titanic*. Hard-copied footage from Cameron's film is cut into the clip in a fashion similar to the Nigerian remake. Here, however, it is combined with images of a young boy who first sits among the audience and then leaves the cinema at the dramatic climax of the film—when the ship breaks apart. As if in a trance, he goes to a mansion with a swimming pool. Film-image flashbacks—intercut footage from Cameron's movie—persistently haunt him. He folds a paper boat, sets it afloat in the pool, and then unexpectedly dives into the water, as if chasing after it. A last flashback of a drowning passenger from Cameron's *Titanic* seems to foreshadow the boy's fate. The intro ends with a hard cut to *Titanic*'s roaring horn, which pulls the viewer into the music video itself.

The intro serves as paratext to the music video insofar as it reflects on both the medium of film in general and the African audience watching James Cameron's movie in particular. Global media may have unexpected effects on local audiences, and the story of the drowning boy may, at first glance, appear as part of a discourse on the dangers, moral and otherwise, of cinema, which supposedly causes young moviegoers to identify with characters and situations in the film that might put the spectators themselves at risk. Along with the music video itself, however, I suggest that the intro's allusion to film as a spiritual technology and to water as the substance that constitutes a type of boundary, separating the realm of the living from that of the dead in Congolese cosmology (MacGaffey 1983: 126–127), are key to understanding the intro. In this light, the projection of Cameron's film can be interpreted as a call by spiritual forces belonging to a parallel "other" world. Access to this world is through water, and the boy who is drawn into the water enters this world through the pool. The abysmal waters cross-fade on an underwater shot of a drowning passenger from Cameron's movie. The music video following this intro is an illustration of the boy's dreamlike vision of the spiritual realm. A brief look at the history of the band gives us some further clues to validate such an interpretation.

Jean-Bedel M'piana, Noël Ngiama Werrason, and several other musicians founded Wenge Musica in the late 1980s. During its first ten years, the band witnessed several splits; a common occurrence in the Congolese music world. These breaks are referred to as "splintering" by Bob White (2008: 195). The most important split occurred in 1997, when Werrason struck out alone. Taking a few band members with him and gathering additional young talent, he called his new band Wenge Musica Maison Mère. M'piana and the majority of the original band that stayed behind became "Wenge BCBG," attaching the former moniker of Wenge Musica to their name. Werrason's band, which began as a splinter group, soon became a proper rival band, challenging M'piana and Wenge BCBG (Tsambu Bulu 2004). Congolese music has a strong tradition of rivalry and competition, which is often played out through the lyrics and symbolic registers in its songs. The release of Wenge BCBG's album *Titanic* has to be understood in this light. The CD cover shows an image of M'piana and the band depicted as survivors in life buoys—the sinking ship in the background (see figure 3.6). The epithet under the band's name reads "Les anges adorables" (The adorable angels). According to White, the audiences in Kinshasa understood the message clearly: "The 'original' Wenge was a sinking ship, and M'piana and his allies were the only true survivors" (2008: 252). In the song, M'piana laments the split in veiled language, blaming Werrason without mentioning his name.

Botala ndenge Titanic eza' koinda	See how the Titanic is sinking
Boluka basauvetage, ah	Look for the lifejackets
Bakadia bazinda	The devils shall drown
Baange babika	The angels shall be saved
Aha, Titanic, eh	Oh, Titanic
. . .	. . .
Bana mama dila	My brothers and sisters are crying
Bana nkento dila	Girls are crying
Bayakala dila dila	Boys are crying
Bana mama dila	My brothers and sisters are crying
. . .	. . .

FIGURE 3.6

DVD cover art for Wenge BCBG's *Titanic* (1998).

Yo yongana ngambo mama	You cause me problems
Tala nga nakudila	See how I am crying
Lelo olali wapi?	Where did you sleep last night?
Awa makambo kuna makambo	Problems here and problems there
Biso tosuki wapi?	Where did we end up?[12]

Werrason promptly reacted to this provocation by releasing the album *Force d'intervention rapide* (1998). This title, borrowed from military language, made it quite clear that Werrason's new band, Wenge Musica Maison Mère, was ready to take up the challenge.

The *Titanic* music video suggests M'piana and his band are the only survivors of the tragedy and therefore the true heirs to Wenge Musica's legacy. Their survival is in fact encoded as a spiritual resurrection, combining symbolical references derived from both local cosmology and Christianity. At the beginning, we see footage from Cameron's film—the *Titanic* about to disappear beneath the sea and underwater shots of sinking bodies. In front of these images, a band member dances and addresses the viewers, saying: "See how the Titanic is sinking." With the next few lines of the song, we see an image of a choppy sea (in fact, the one from Cameron's *Titanic,* showing the swirl after the ship has disappeared into the sea). Synchronized with the song's lyrics "the angels shall be saved," three translucent-white columns emerge from the sea, symbolizing the surviving spirits of the three musicians who make up Wenge BCBG.[13] Next we see female dancers dressed in white head-to-ankle body suits—an allusion to the spirits of the dead, who are associated with the color white in Congolese cosmology. We also see translucent images of the three musicians. They are superimposed on to images of the *Titanic* and its wreckage under water. The video suggests an analogy of "survival and resurrection" between those who drowned during the *Titanic* disaster and the three band members. Both return in a different form—the dead, according to Congolese cosmology, as newborns of future generations after their journey through the waters, and the three members of the old band as the newly formed Wenge BCBG. This interpretation is based on the work of Wyatt MacGaffey (1968), who summarizes Congolese cosmological beliefs as follows: "This world is the realm of the living who are black. The spirits of the other world are white. They are the dead, but also the generations to come; the fathers, but also the children."

It also seems significant that the video clip was released following Wenge BCBG's successful European tour. In traditional Congolese belief, Europe (*mputu* in Kikongo), the land that lies beyond the ocean, is sometimes associated with the spiritual realm of the dead (MacGaffey 1968: 174). At the same time, Europe is a place where migrants may eventually return as rich and powerful, akin to the spirits of the ancestors who return from the world of the dead. Wenge BCBG indeed returned from Europe with aspirations to wealth and success. During the celebration of "la descente"— a ritualized form of arrival from Paris or Brussels which constitutes an important part of the Congolese "cult of elegance" (*la sape*) (MacGaffey and Bazenguissa-Ganga 2000)—M'piana and his band mates were met by enthusiastic fans who welcomed them in Kinshasa on November 18, 1999, with a boat mounted on a truck—an obvious reference to the *Titanic.*[14]

THE UNSINKABLE SHIP

My exploration of the four copies of the *Titanic* suggests that the producers' motivations for appropriating the myth and Cameron's version of it must be understood on at least two different levels: content and marketing. In terms of content, two of the four examples—the Nigerian video remake and the Tanzanian comic book—are particularly close to Cameron's film. The Nigerian remake shows a keen interest in the social relations of Cameron's plot, especially the love story, and adapts these for Hausa audiences. It is less interested in the catastrophe of the sinking ship. The Tanzanian comic book, though surely not indifferent to the romantic plot elements, is particularly interested in the historical tragedy and takes Cameron's movie as an authentic account of the catastrophe. The artist aims to educate his readers about the historical event. Therefore, he stays as faithful as possible to his template, tracing images directly from the screen and creating sketches for nearly each of his panels. In doing so, he mimics Cameron's attempt at re-creating images of the *Titanic* as authentically as possible. The remediation as a comic book turns the *Titanic* tragedy—mediated by Cameron's film—into a didactic tale. Giving his characters an African appearance has to be understood as a visual translation on the part of the artist. The comic book's significance for local audiences is the trope of "speed and greed," which connects the historical demise of the R.M.S. *Titanic* in the North Atlantic to the more recent shipwreck of the M.V. *Bukoba* on Lake Victoria.

The two other copies draw more on the allegorical potential of the *Titanic* myth than on Cameron's particular version of it. The Tanzanian song and the Congolese music video lack any reference to Cameron's romantic couple. Instead, the emphasis is on the ship's journey and its ultimate fate. However, pirated images of Cameron's *Titanic* are present in each. By drawing on the *Titanic*'s allegorical potential, the Tanzanian choir and the Congolese band connect to a well-established tradition in American and European interpretations of the disaster throughout the twentieth century. The Adventist parable is especially close to religious interpretations of the tragedy as a divine message, which were propagated in the United States. Writing in 1912, Alma White, founder of the Pentecostal church Pillar of Fire, interpreted the tragedy as "God's handwriting on the wall, foretelling the doom of those who are given to greed and pleasure in a world cursed by sin," which she also observed in the "profanation of the Sabbath by dancing, game playing, and other amusements among the first-cabin passengers" (in Biel 1997: 97–98). The popular song "Down with the Old Canoe," performed by folk musicians Howard and Dorsey Dixon and recorded in 1938 (although the song is much older), takes this line of interpretation a step further. It construes the *Titanic* as a symbol of hubris and compares the ship's journey to an individual's journey through life, one that can only be saved if guided by Jesus Christ (Biel 1997). This allegory is remarkably close to the Nyasho choir's *Titanic* parable. However, the *Titanic* has not only served as a metaphor in religious readings. In political discourse and literary works with political intentions, the sinking of the presumably unsinkable ship has also been used to symbolize the expected demise of whole societies, political systems, and even Western civilization and modernity as such. Hans Magnus Enzensberger's poem *Der Untergang der Titanic: Eine Komödie* (The sinking of the Titanic: A comedy), published in 1978, is a complex example of such a reading. In this book-sized poem, the ocean liner symbolizes capitalist society about to hit the revolutionary socialist iceberg and, paradoxically, also Germany's New Left, itself doomed to submersion (King 2004). Enzensberger, himself a prominent figure of that political movement, disembarks and survives its wreckage. The Congolese band's equating of the ship with a former mother band, whose foundering is survived by the three members of the new band, parallels such metaphorical usage. The Congolese and the Tanzanian examples show that ships—sinking ships, to be precise—are good to think with, and that the potential of the *Titanic* myth as metaphorical material is no longer limited to Western cultural production. It has since spread to Africa as well. Cameron's movie has certainly been instrumental in this, but—as the Nyasho choir's example proves—not as the only source.

On the level of marketing, the attempt to share the fame of the original they invoke and capitalize on its success is common to all four copies. This makes perfect sense within the commercial logic of culture industries. In America, Europe, and beyond, the success of Cameron's film has spawned a flood of *Titanic*-related merchandise, from the usual "making-of" books and soundtrack CDs to T-shirts, posters, stickers, coffee mugs, exhibitions, and even theme parks (Studlar and Sandler 1999). All of these operate on the logic of "copy and contact," where the copy is meant to draw on the power of the original. The four African copies, products of cottage culture industries, operate on the same logic. A major difference, however, is that they do so without compensating Twentieth Century Fox, the company that owns the copyright. Needless to say, this strategy is not always successful. If the product is far below local quality standards, as was the case

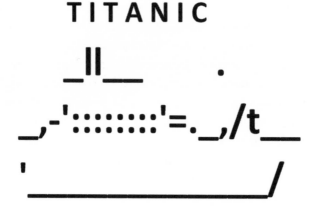

TITANIC

Meli hii ikuvushe hadi mwaka 2008, Mungu akuzidishie baraka! Wish u happy new year

FIGURE 3.7

Text message from Tanzania: "May this ship carry you safely to the year 2008, may God bless you!" Courtesy of Claudia Böhme. Message would have originally been displayed on a 2.8-by-2.3-centimeter cell-phone screen.

with the Nigerian video remake, even the invocation of an international best seller does not boost its sales.

The tag *Titanic* and the iconic images copied from Cameron's movie onto the cover of an African comic book, a CD, and an audio and a videocassette is meant to attract potential consumers. The products and their producers are therefore associated with an event of world history, promising their consumers contact with a life-world far beyond the local. The ubiquitous presence of the *Titanic* label in Dar es Salaam, for example, where video shops, cell-phone centers, and city buses are named after the ship, not to mention self-help books for the love lorn and even plastic bags carrying its image, suggests that *Titanic* has developed into a signifier, evoking associations of globalism and success (via the global success of Cameron's movie) and of romance and glamor (via Cameron's romantic plot)—perhaps even of endurance and stability—for the steamship is now truly unsinkable thanks to its myriad mediatizations almost one hundred years after its wreckage in the North Atlantic. Paradoxically, a nautical tragedy has been turned into a symbol of everything but catastrophe. How else can we interpret a text message from Dar es Salaam, wishing its addressee a happy new year in the name of the *Titanic*? (See figure 3.7.) And how else can we understand newspaper reports about the biggest boat ever built on a Senegalese wharf (Sagna 2006a), a wooden vessel 24 meters in length and 4 meters wide, constructed in the town of Rufisque in June 2006? Purportedly, it was meant to take African emigrants across the Atlantic to America. By November 2006, before officials stepped in, its builder had already earned a small fortune, equivalent to 55,000 U.S. dollars, by selling tickets to about one hundred people desperate enough to leave the continent, despite the risk (Sagna 2006b); the boat's name was *Titanic*.

4

Vice and Videos

KANYWOOD UNDER DURESS

IN MARCH 2005, an ultraorthodox Muslim group organized a public burning of hundreds of videotapes to protest an awards ceremony for Hausa video film stars, to be held in Bauchi state, in northern Nigeria. In his speech, the leader of the group justified the symbolic act as pious: "We are gathered here to repent to Allah and to demonstrate our disgust at all those sinners, immoral people and hooligans who broadcast sins, and who are trying to do the same in our part of Nigeria. We are gathered to burn these video tapes, set them on fire because they are paths to hell-fire" (quoted in Adamu 2007: 90). The public burning of videotapes, carried out repeatedly in the ensuing years, was the most visible sign of the public controversy that surrounded moral corruption and the alleged un-Islamic nature of Hausa video films in northern Nigeria. This chapter traces the history of that controversy in the city of Kano, the center of a Hausa video film industry dubbed Kanywood.

Early on, many Hausa video films were inspired by Indian movies. The most evident marker of this inspiration was the frequent use of song-and-dance sequences in Hausa videos. This stylistic device in particular— showing women and men dancing together, singing about their love and yearning for one another—sparked public debate. Against the backdrop of religious revival, epitomized by the reintroduction of sharia law into the legislation of Kano state in 2001, and advocating an Islamic purification of local cultural practice, conservative factions of society eyed films suspiciously that overtly mediate between a local and a foreign life-world. After all, such movies establish contact between things that according to the religiously inspired cultural policy, are better kept apart, such as unmarried women and men, or Hausa and Indian "culture." In the critics' eyes, blueprints of other possible lives, as provided by Hausa video films, threaten the moral upbringing of young people, and therefore need to be kept in check or even forbidden. Since the evolution of Kanywood is intimately linked to the proliferation of video technology, the controversy over Hausa video films exemplifies the challenges cultural globalization and the proliferation of small media technologies may pose to Muslim societies in Africa and beyond. While the young especially value the creative, communicative, and economic possibilities digital media provide, others condemned these phenomena as the devil's work. "With video technology," Abubakar Rabo (2008), the former director general of the Kano State Censorship Board, said, "the devil has been piped into the home and corruption is only a click away."

I have organized my discussion of "Kanywood under Duress" more or less chronologically. It covers a time span of roughly a decade (2001–2011). The first section sets in with the reintroduction of sharia law and the implementation of censorship in Kano state in 2001. This is followed by an exploration of the relationship of Hausa videos to Bollywood films by analyzing *Khusufi* (2003), a Hausa video "remake" of the Indian film *Taal* (1999). Then I discuss how in around 2003, Hausa filmmakers, in reaction to censorship and a growing critique of their films, reinvented filmmaking as a kind of preaching. Later on they resorted to the standard crowd-pleasing song-and-dance formula, using footage of girls in tight-fitting Western-style clothing. The last section starts with the Hiyana sex scandal of 2007, a turning point in the short history of Kanywood that was followed by a ban on video production for six months, the emigration of leading production companies to neighboring states, and the reorganization of the Kano State Censorship Board. Director General Rabo began to hunt down filmmakers in an operation he labeled "Fire for Fire." This last section ends with Rabo's own fall in 2010 and his loss of power in 2011 due to a change in state government.

MORAL PANICS, SHARIA, AND CENSORSHIP

Following Nigeria's transition from military rule to an elected civilian government in 1999, many of its northern states introduced sharia law into their legislatures. The divine law was commonly expected to be a catalyst for a much broader push for moral reorientation and religious reversion (Last 2000). A "religious police" force (*hisbah*) was formed. Its task was—and still is—the eradication of cultural practices considered to be contrary to Islamic doctrine, regardless of whether these practices are of local traditional origin (such as musical performances and spirit possession dances, for example) or associated with a brand of modernity modeled on the West. The attempts at religious reorientation led to an increased scrutiny of female bodily comportment, dress, and mobility. Among the first changes to be effected after the introduction of the sharia was gender-segregated public transport, so as to forestall joint bus rides by men and women. In public, women were expected to cover as much of their bodies as possible. The radicalness with which the female body was turned into an index for the moral condition of society at large added a new dimension to older ideas about the female body as the primary domain for the articulation of notions about religious piety, morality, and respectability.[1] Hausa videos, which brought men and women in ever-closer contact in daring song-and-dance sequences and featured actresses dressed in tight-fitting apparel, deviated vastly from the new paradigm of religious reversion:

> For the sake of Allah, actors, you should remember Allah! Remember the religion of Islam! Girls in particular should stop exposing their bodies in films. They should remember that the female body ought to be covered completely; but instead they clothe themselves in blouses and trousers, and smooth out their hair as if they were Europeans—such attire is not in line with the Muslim tradition. Thus, you should stop this, as your behavior bothers us because you, too, are Muslims as we are. Be cautious in filmmaking in order to avoid offending God Almighty. (Bamalli, Muhammad, and Namaibindiga, "Letter to the editor," in *Fim* 9, 2000: 4; my translation)

Right from the beginning, the public debate about video films was dominated by metaphors of cleansing, which go well with the paradigm of religious and cultural purity associated with the religious reversion project. Videos were said to pollute "Hausa culture" and to "poison" their viewers, who were conceptualized as passive recipients and easy prey to the manipulative potential of video images. "Before Hausa films arrived," writes a concerned school headmaster in a letter to *Fim* magazine, "we didn't see our children and siblings wear American and Western dresses. Girls always copy the dresses of the film stars. These films destroy our children's moral upbringing, and they prevent our children from attending school" (quoted in Adamu 2007: 89).

Following the official introduction of sharia law in Kano state in December 2000, filmmakers faced a difficult and uncertain situation: a potential ban on video production. A total ban—as called for by fundamentalist clerics—would have meant the loss of income for thousands of young men and women employed in the industry. Such a move would certainly have given rise to a severe political crisis. Therefore, the Kano state government, together with liberal religious scholars and leading video filmmakers, advocated an Islamic reorientation through censorship (Abdulkareem Mohammed, president of the Motion Pictures Practitioners Association of Nigeria, personal interview, March 17, 2003; Ali Bature, Kano State History and Culture Bureau, personal interview, March 19, 2003). Pending the implementation of a new censorship law and the subsequent establishment of the Kano State Censorship Board in March 2001, video production and distribution were banned for four months. When the board came up with its guidelines, it became clear that the censors would closely scrutinize particularly mixed gender song-and-dance sequences as well as female bodily comportment. Although these sequences were produced as spectacular "showstoppers" (Rubin 1993)—that is, interruptions of the narrative that serve to demonstrate characters' dreams and desires—local critics maintained that women and men dancing together and singing about their love and longing for one another would be inappropriate in "Hausa culture." Another argument that surfaced hinted at the roots of Bollywood's song-and-dance routines in Hindu religious worship, which according to the critics turned Hausa filmmakers who "copied" these routines into advocates of idolatry. The then executive secretary of the Kano State Censorship Board, Abdulkadir A. Kurawa, explains as follows:

> The government did not ban songs. You can sing. Even in Hausa culture there is singing and dancing, but moderately. What the government did say is: you cannot have male and female dancing of this kind, dancing that is being shown in our movies. That kind of dancing where you see a lady half naked dancing with her breasts shaking—it's not allowed. . . . So the government said: no male and female dancing of such kind—useless dancing I am talking about. If you do that in your film, we will ask you to remove that. (personal interview, February 4, 2003)

Censorship was considered "sanitization," aiming at eradicating alien cultural elements from Hausa video films. Besides film content, it was also the practice of video production as such that caused considerable doubt among conservative Muslims. Kanywood offered nubile girls many opportunities to become financially independent of their parents, not only as actresses or studio singers but also as scriptwriters, caterers, and costume and makeup designers. Public opinion was at odds with this deviation from traditional female roles. To prevent them from entering into illicit sexual relationships, girls were (and still are) expected to marry at an early age. If a girl attends secondary school, her parents expect her to marry as soon as she graduates. Unmarried girls and divorced women working in the industry earned a living wage, which allowed them to prolong their adolescence and unmarried period of life, respectively. Their economic independence and interaction with men on the film sets—that is, in nonpublic and therefore socially uncontrolled spaces—as well as their exposure in video films meant that these girls and women were likened to *karuwai,* "free women," or prostitutes.

Under the conditions of sharia law, movie shoots often took place in secluded locations and became imbued with heterotopian qualities. They constituted the quintessential "other spaces" (Foucault 1986) where constraints that governed male-female interaction in everyday life lost their validity. To shoot their films, well-to-do admirers of their craft often provided the film crews with whole houses. Others rented hotel suites for a few days and turned them into film sets. When I went on location in April 2003 with a Kano-based producer who was shooting in a hotel in Jos (see figure 4.1), the cheerful atmosphere that the film crew created on and off set struck me in particular. Male and female crew members were constantly teasing one another, engaging in sexual innuendo. During the

FIGURE 4.1

On the set of *Salam Salam*, Jos, 2003. Photo by the author.

five days of the shoot, the crew developed an in-group lingo, using words
with subtly erotic meaning. Although such behavior was certainly beyond
what parents and custodians of the girls and young women involved in
film production would have tolerated, the reality of film sets was definitely
not as full of vice as the rumors suggested. One evening, Binta, a divorcée
who earned some money from acting in minor roles and catering for the
crew, mimicked a mobile phone conversation with her uncle: "Yes, surely,
men and women are sleeping in separate rooms," she told her fictive uncle,
and: "Yes uncle, we also won't forget to say our prayers five times a day."

LOCALIZING BOLLYWOOD

During the 1990s, Hausa video films developed out of stage drama
and TV serials. The commercial success of the early films attracted young
cultural entrepreneurs who had backgrounds in the Hausa market literature movement (*littatafan soyayya*, literally: "love books"). This move-

ment had begun to flourish a couple of years earlier (Furniss 2003). The romantic melodrama is the dominant genre in Hausa videos. Inspired by Indian films, which have been part and parcel of Hausa popular culture for several decades (Larkin 1997), young filmmakers borrowed the foreign concepts of romance and love-marriage and contrasted them in their plots with the traditional concept of arranged marriage, where parents choose the marital partners for their children. "Thus, Hausa videos depict open, teasing relationships between lovers who share emotional time together, spend leisure time walking with one another, and declare their love openly, all of which, in many ways, were foreign to Hausa gender relations," summarizes Brian Larkin (2008: 204). In line with Abdalla Uba Adamu (2007, 2010, 2012) and Larkin (1997, 2008), who have written extensively on Hausa videos, I suggest that one way of approaching these movies is to see them as transcultural transpositions of Indian films. By adapting Indian films to the social context of their own society, Hausa filmmakers localized Bollywood. *Khusufi* (Eclipse, 2003), a video film directed by Ali Nuhu, who is also Kanywood's most prominent male actor, and sometimes referred to as the Nigerian Shah Rukh Khan, may serve to highlight the process of localization (see figure 4.2). Its plot develops around the unlikely love story between a rich man's son and the daughter of a rural cattle breeder who achieves stardom as a studio singer in the local video film industry. Though *Khusufi* is not a straight remake, it certainly draws inspiration for its plot, characters, and key scenes from the Indian movie *Taal* (1999). In an interview, scriptwriter Abubakar Baballe Hayatu, a close friend of *Khusufi*'s director, explains the relationship between Hausa videos and Indian films:

> The difference between Indian culture and our own is only on the surface.... Together with Ali Nuhu we watch Indian movies and then think about what we would have to change so that the average Hausa will respond to it by saying, "Yes, this is part of our culture" and not "For God's sake, this is not our culture." Everything is adapted to such an extent that it is in line with our culture. Sequences that do not violate our culture or religion will remain unchanged. (Hayatu in *Fim* 11, 2002: 47; my translation)

The Indian template *Taal* is a movie typical of Bollywood's masala genre (having a mix of movie styles), with a very prominent cast, spectacular

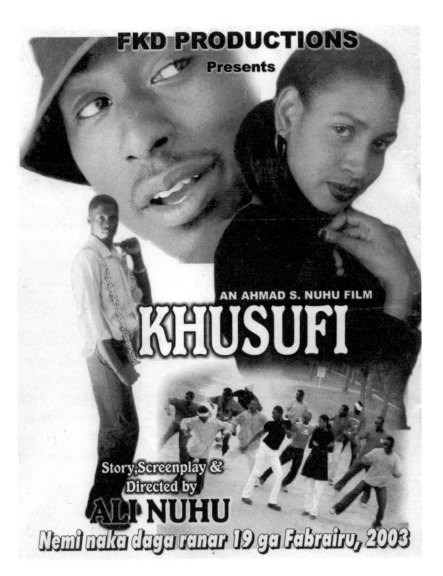

FIGURE 4.2

Advertisement for the video *Khusufi* (2003) from *Fim* magazine.

showstoppers, and music composed by the popular composer A. R. Rahman. The film's lovers meet in the countryside, where Mansi (Aishwarya Rai) lives with her father, a poor musician, and Manav (Akshaye Khanna), the London-raised son of an Indian tycoon, spends his holidays in his father's manor. Despite the class difference, Manav's father befriends Mansi's—yet for selfish reasons, as it turns out later. After Manav, who has promised to wed Mansi, leaves for Mumbai, Mansi persuades her reluctant father to travel to Mumbai, too. They are met with hostility at the house of Manav's father. Manav's paternal aunt verbally assaults Mansi's father, calling him a dog and a pimp. Deeply hurt and suddenly realizing that his new "friend" has betrayed his trust, Mansi's father slaps Manav's father. The two lovers side with their respective fathers. Eventually, the lovers split up. Reconciliation takes place only after another one and a half hours, when Mansi is on the verge of marrying the music producer who meanwhile has fostered her career as an internationally acclaimed singer. But Manav finally triumphs in his desperate bid to win her back, and they wed.

With its opening sequence shot in Jidda, *Khusufi* foregrounds the cosmopolitan ties of its male protagonist, something to which *Taal* merely alludes. Khalid (Ahmed S. Nuhu) is the son of a rich Kano-based merchant. After finishing school in Saudi Arabia, he returns to Nigeria. Back home, he visits his father's country house, where he "discovers" Hajjo (Maijidda Ibrahim) and immediately falls in love with her. Like Manav in *Taal*, Khalid hides out and starts taking snapshots of the village girl, using a small handheld camera. His voyeuristic gaze, amplified by the camera, turns into that of the spectator. The lovers' first encounter takes the form of a song-and-dance sequence. In this musical number, Hajjo is dressed in traditional Fulbe attire; this is a far cry from the tight West-style garb on display in other Hausa films, which had been deemed scandalous. However, in *Khusufi* it is not so much the dress but the suggestive movement of the girl's upper body, gliding back and forth in slow motion, and the camerawork focusing on her bosom, that caused controversy. Reverse footage of Khalid, who snaps pictures of Hajjo while she is dancing, continuously suggests that the viewer sees Hajjo as an object of Khalid's (and the viewer's) desire.

While earlier Hausa films would likely introduce a second suitor at this point, favored by the girl's parents and therefore an obstacle to the

lovers' relationship, *Khusufi* builds up tension through the conflict between the couple's fathers. Although this conflict is set off in a sequence
modeled on *Taal*'s slapping scene, the social background of the characters
involved is different. At this point, localization goes beyond the surface
level. *Taal*'s class divide is translated into ethnic terms. Hajjo is the daughter of a Fulbe cattle breeder, Khalid the son of a Kanuri businessman.
In northern Nigeria, these ethnic groups are linked through a ritualized
joking relationship, which means that the two families are much closer
to each other than the couples' families in the Indian movie. Musicians
belong to a castelike endogamous group in northern Nigeria; a marriage
between the daughter of a musician and the son of a businessman—like
in *Taal*—would thus have been unthinkable, and perhaps also undesirable, for a Hausa audience. Moreover, since the two fathers in *Khusufi* are
childhood friends and *auren zumunci*—meaning, the marriage of children
from two families that are on friendly terms with each other—is highly
valued, Khalid and Hajjo are each other's preferential marriage partners.
Hence, in *Khusufi* the "unruly emotion" of love, which in other Hausa
films is often portrayed as "somewhat out of control" and "frequently in
tension with the wider social order" (Larkin 2008: 205), is neutralized by
traditional values: boy meets girl and even custom would sanction their
marriage. However, things get complicated when Hajjo and her father
meet Khalid's stepmother. A transposition of Manav's vicious aunt, this
woman is portrayed as an envious and selfish wife who fears that her step-
son's marriage will deprive her of her husband's riches. The stepmother is
overtly hostile when she meets Hajjo's father, calling him a dog. When he
retaliates by calling her a prostitute, her husband—his former childhood
friend—steps in and insults him as well, thereby betraying their friendship; this provokes Hajjo's father into slapping him across the face. As in
Taal, the two lovers side with their respective fathers, which leaves them
no other option but to break up. In this narrative twist, the young lovers
show their parents great respect, highlighting the fact that many Hausa
videos—despite the challenges they pose for their critics—still try to
negotiate between traditional values and modern desires.

While Hajjo puts all her energies into her singing career in the video
industry, Khalid apologizes for his stepmother's rude behavior and tries to
win back Hajjo's love. At this point, part one of the movie ends abruptly,

which is not uncommon for Hausa videos, and leaves the question of rec-onciliation open-ended for part two. In this second part, *Khusufi* diverges from *Taal*. While the Indian movie tracks Mansi's career and introduces a second suitor (her manager), the Hausa video is keen on castigating those who have done wrong and thus keeps to a Kanywood narrative conven-tion. Khalid's father loses all his money and even has to sell his house, to Hajjo's father, who allows him to remain there. In this way, Kahlid's father is taught the value of friendship. In keeping with the presence of a certain measure of misogyny in many Kanywood films, Khalid's stepmother is portrayed as the root of all evil. On learning that her husband is about to run out of money, she steals a large sum of cash from him. However, the friend whom she entrusts with the money betrays her. She ends up divorced and empty-handed—unlike Khalid's father, who is lucky enough to regain part of his wealth. In the end, all obstacles to the union of Khalid and Hajjo are smoothed out, and they finally wed.

Taal contains a self-reflexive, critical metanarrative on the production practices of the Indian music industry, which is closely linked to Bolly-wood filmmaking. Inspired by the possibility of film reflecting upon its own conditions of production, Ali Nuhu seized this opportunity and used *Khusufi* to address the critical issue of female careers in Kanywood. Al-though the Cinderella-like career that depicts a village girl becoming a famous studio singer is unlikely, many young female video film fans were willing to try their luck in Kanywood. In 2003, there were many rumors about runaway girls who joined "the industry" without their parents' consent. The case of the fictitious Hajjo is different. She is encouraged by Khalid to chance her luck as a playback studio singer. Though at first reluctant, her father eventually agrees to take her to the city. A scene in the film shows the studio owner, who agrees to sign Hajjo only after her father has given his written consent. By emphasizing that unmarried girls can only embark on a Kanywood career with parental consent, Ali Nuhu uses his movie to dispel the myth of Kanywood as a safe haven for run-away girls. The few shots of Hajjo in the recording cabin serve not only as diegetic intro to the film's most spectacular song-and-dance sequence but also provide glimpses behind the scenes of filmmaking.

For the critics of Hausa videos, *Khusufi* was just another Kanywood movie with typical shortcomings, including its failure to promote "Hausa culture." Rabee'u Bebeji's (2003) detailed critique of the film, published in *Fim* magazine, focuses on the three staple strands of critique common at the time: the use of "song-and-dance sequences" (*rawa da wa'ka*), the "copying" of "foreign movies" (*wanki*) and therefore of alien customs, and the predominance of "love" (*soyayya*) as a central element of the plot:

> Like I have said many times before, song and dance is not part of our cul-
> ture; it's a custom of idolaters, and it does not fit in with our culture. For
> that reason, I think it would be good to stop dancing and singing in our
> films.... Again, I wish to caution Ali Nuhu about the films he is making. It
> would be truly appropriate if he started making films that show our pure
> Hausa traditions, instead of contenting himself with imitating others or
> the traditions of others. It would be great if Ali and his kind began to make
> films we could be proud of, films that could help us in the moral upbring-
> ing of our younger brothers, children and wives, and even ourselves. I
> would love to see [FKD Productions] abandon [their predilection for]
> Hindu traditions and instead turn to our own, as they did [in *Khusufi*]
> with those of the Fulbe and the Kanuri. (42; my translation)

The sequence showing Hajjo in her rural home is actually the only scene Bebeji finds remarkable. It seems to suit the critic just fine that the Fulbe in this sequence have little in common with those living in present-day rural Nigeria and are instead related to the noble savages staged in the folkloristic performances of the Kano State History and Culture Bureau. He goes on to demand that the filmmakers stop making movies about love because such films "spoil children" and "teach them how to say 'I love you'" at much too early an age. Though he claims that "*Khusufi* has almost no message," he has to admit that "the film still teaches some things, such as the importance of trustworthiness, friendship, and respect for elders." Bebeji (2003: 43) is quick to diminish this positive evaluation, however, by adding wryly: "It also teaches dancing and singing and how to dress up as a real 'Nigga.'"

FILMMAKING AS PREACHING

Despite Ali Nuhu's statement a few months prior that he would not "stop imitating Indian films,"[2] the constant critique from people like Bebeji did not go unheard. To appease their critics and to justify the moral legitimacy of their video films, some filmmakers began to recast their work in religious terms, as "admonition" (*fa'dakarwa*) or "preaching" (*wa'azi*), and publicly likened themselves to religious teachers. Filmmakers now claimed to help *malamai* (religious learned men) to teach morals (cf. Krings 2008). The terminology of *wa'azi* and *fa'dakarwa* is significant in this context. Both terms have religious connotations, but at the time under discussion, they were generally used to provide a moral justification for any kind of cultural activity. Writing books and performing music, for instance, were re-labeled in a similar fashion (Abdalla Uba Adamu, email, June 21, 2007). *Wa'azi* (sermon, preaching, warning), much more than *fa'dakarwa* (admonishing, drawing attention to ill-considered behavior), connotes religious authority because it uses quotations from the Koran to support its arguments. *Wa'z,* which is the Arabic root of the Hausa term *wa'azi,* is a genre of Islamic preaching that comes closest to religious agitation. Though part of Nigeria's Islamic vocabulary for a long time, *wa'azi* of late has been more closely associated with northern Nigeria's Wahhabi-inspired reform movements, based on ultraconservative Sunni Islam. The most popular of these is the Jamâ'at Izâlat al-Bid'a wa Iqâmat as-Sunna (Society for the Removal of Innovation and Reinstatement of Tradition), founded by Abubakar Gumi in 1978, better known under the Hausa acronym of 'yan Izala (followers of Izala; Kane 2003; Loimeier 1997).

Izala, as well as other reform groups, such as Sheik Aminudeen Abubakar's Daawa and Sheik Ibrahim Al-Zakzaky's Ikhwan, which were founded in the late 1970s on university campuses, used small, cassette-based media to spread their messages. Though most filmmakers do not belong to any of these religious groups, it is the reformists' strategy of preaching through cassette technology that was at the bottom of the filmmakers' claim to preach through films. The mere use of the same technology, however, is not enough to make feature films comparable to *wa'azi.* Video filmmakers were therefore at pains to deduce the legitimacy of their craft from religious sources, such as the Hadith or Koran. A paper presented by producer, director, and actor Hamisu Lamido Iyan-Tama at the First International Conference on Hausa Films, which took place in Kano in 2003, is instructive in this context. Titled "Matsayin Fina-Finan Hausa a Musulunci" (The place of Hausa films in Islam), the paper is built on the rhetorical form of *wa'azi*. Its author tries to address both the religious critics of video filmmaking and his fellow video filmmakers (Iyan-Tama 2004). While he admonishes his cohorts to produce work with a moral message and abstain from mixed-gender singing and dancing, he goes after his critics with their own weapons—that is, with quotations from the Koran—and thus demonstrates, *en passant*, the legitimacy of the video filmmakers' claim that they are comparable to religious teachers.

With regard to the content of Hausa videos, many participants at the same conference voiced the opinion that video films should, to count as "legitimate" (*halak*) before Islamic law, represent the culture and religious constitution of the Muslim north (Yusha'u 2004), and as such propagate Islamic reform within and outside northern Nigeria. Such calls also came from video film fans, who referred to the example of Christian video films from southern Nigeria when "calling on [northern] filmmakers . . . to show their love for Islam and to make films that demonstrate the wonderful power of the Qur'an" (Tanko 2000: 10–11; my translation). Although there were Hausa videos with religious subtexts prior to the implementation of the sharia and censorship, it was this religious intervention that worked as a catalyst and gave rise to full-blown religious video films.

Most often set in a precolonial, mythical past, these films feature story lines about Muslim heroes who conquer pagan tribes and subsequently convert them to Islam. The first film to be released was *Shaheed* (The martyr, 2002/2003), although the foundations of the genre seem to have been laid by director and scriptwriter Dan Azumi Baba, who had begun to shoot his film *Judah!* (2003) much earlier. Unlike *Judah!*—which is built around a story about a faithful Muslim falling in love with Judah, a pagan princess—*Shaheed* is more puritanically oriented and avoids the romantic pitfalls of the average Hausa video. Directed by the late Zikiflu Moham-med, who was also an actor, *Shaheed* was produced by a production com-pany closely associated with the Ikhwan brotherhood. Sheik Ibrahim Al-Zakzaky, leader of this so-called Shiite brotherhood, openly advocates the use of video films to propagate his group's religious stance—one that has long pursued the transformation of Nigeria into an orthodox theocracy modeled on the Islamic Republic of Iran. Through his personal contacts with Iran, Al-Zakzaky was undoubtedly well aware of the revolutionary potential of small media such as audio- and videocassettes (Sreberny-Mohammadi and Mohammadi 1994).[3]

Shaheed idealizes the figure of the martyr who dies for the cause of his religion during his efforts at proselytizing. While on his mission to free a tribe of unbelievers from their submission to bloodthirsty idols and lead them onto the path of a just and merciful God, a Muslim villager dies the heroic death of a true believer. His selfless sacrifice is rewarded by his immediate ascension into paradise and, since it serves as proof of the superiority of his faith, prompts a young pagan warrior to convert. Before the neophyte can win his fellow tribesmen over to Islam, he has to overcome the opposition of the pagan king. In a showdown between convert and king, the convert shows his willingness to die for his new religion as the first martyr did. Facing the king, who is pointing a spear at him, the convert tells the king that he will only be able to kill him, the convert, if God Almighty permits: "If you want to kill me, you have to say, 'In the name of Allah.'" At first the king appears speechless and unable to move his spear, but then he reluctantly utters the phrase and subsequently kills the convert. A fade shows the immediate ascension of the convert's soul into paradise. In a blue sky appear the translucent images of the first martyr and a girl holding a bowl of fruit—probably one of the many virgins who inhabit the Muslim paradise. Together they welcome the second martyr. Down on earth, the pagans are impressed by the martyr's bravery, desert their king, mass-convert to Islam, and destroy their idols.

To render visible what their Muslim audiences always knew but were never able to see—the "wonderful power of the Qur'an" (as demanded by the video film fan quoted previously)—filmmakers employed special effects, ranging from simple jump cuts to blue-screen montages. In *Shaheed* the future convert has to fight a bush monster. About to be killed by the creature, he remembers a Muslim prayer he has heard before, says the words, and throws a stone at the monster. The stone turns into a grenade and sets the monster on fire. Deeply impressed by this miracle, the pagan is ready to convert. The power of prayer is made visible in a similar manner in *Judah!* The video's Muslim hero is captured and put in chains by pagan warriors. When he prays, his bonds miraculously turn into dry leaves. Another sequence of *Judah!* shows a girl fleeing a bunch of warriors, who is able to climb up to the sky after beseeching Allah.

Shaheed and *Judah!* both feature religious showstoppers. *Shaheed* has three song-and-dance routines showing women and men dressed in proper white Muslim garments, chanting in praise of the martyr, and begging Allah to have mercy on him. The religious legitimacy of these sequences is stressed by the use of the *bandir* drum, which is associated with Sufi Islam and therefore has religious connotations. *Judah!* has a song-and-dance sequence (though dance is rather reduced to walking) in which the Muslim hero, Anwar, manages to get the pagan heroine, Judah, to open up her heart not only to his love but also to the love of his religion: "Judah, stop worshiping this idol / Come, let us worship Allah / I am following Him / If you will also follow Him / I will surely marry you / Believe that Allah is the One and Only / Don't say there are two [Gods] / Stop this worship even if it is your custom / If you will follow Him / Allah will never leave you / Repent! Allah is forgiving / And He is beneficent / He forgives us our sins / He is your Creator / And He will surely not ignore you" (my translation).

Another religiously inspired type of showstopper is modeled on religious sermons and reflects the reformulation of filmmaking as preaching. These showstoppers interrupt the narrative flow with lengthy, didactic monologues. A sequence of *Shaheed* may serve to illustrate this point: after the first neophyte has succeeded in converting several of his fellow tribesmen to Islam, the pagan king responds by putting up a fight. On receiving news of these events, the imam of the Muslim community calls on his followers one night. The scene focuses on the figure of the imam who is captured in medium-close and close shots as he delivers a sermon. Inserts of footage showing members of his intra-filmic audience listening to him serve to draw video film viewers into the scene. The viewers thus become part of the imam's congregation, and what he preaches to them applies equally to those sitting in front of the screen. The imam opens with a lengthy prayer in Arabic and then goes on to tell his followers that since their brothers in faith are under duress, it is their duty to come to their brothers' rescue, even if they are few in number and lack weapons. By referring to the Battle of Badr, which is mentioned in the Koran (3:123–125) and was the first battle victoriously fought against the army of the idolatrous Meccans by Mohammed and his small number of followers, the imam explicates that true believers and those who fight for the cause of Islam will always be assured of Allah's miraculous help. During his sermon, he frequently quotes from the Koran in Arabic. These verses from the Koran usually follow and legitimize a statement, and are translated into Hausa immediately after they are spoken. The imam ends his sermon by stressing Allah's promise that those who die during jihad will enter paradise immediately without having their good and bad deeds weighed against each other. Finally, the imam and his audience shout *Allahu akbar!* and the sequence ends. What is significant about this particular showstopper is that diegetic references are made only at the beginning. Since the major part of this four-and-a-half-minute sequence remains free of references to the filmic narrative, the viewer is encouraged to transfer the meanings of this sermon to any extra-filmic context he deems fit.

MORE DANCING GIRLS, MORE TIGHT DRESSES

The *wa'azi* conversion genre was only short-lived. The video films were not successful enough to encourage Hausa filmmakers to continue producing them. In his monthly column in *Fim* magazine, Dan Azumi Baba—the director and producer of *Judah!*—relates the frustrating experience of having invested almost one million naira (about 7,000 U.S. dollars at the time) into a religious film that flopped (cited in Adamu 2008). Likewise, films without song-and-dance sequences, which some filmmakers attempted, proved far less successful than those still featuring such showstoppers.

In 2003, the video market crashed. Too many newcomers had dabbled in film production; as a result, the total number of films released by Kanywood each week had climbed to about seven. Since more films in a limited market meant fewer returns for each, a number of production companies had to stop doing business. According to Abdalla Uba Adamu (2008), this development marks a crucial moment in the history of Hausa video film, for it was at this juncture that a number of video film dealers, whose task had formerly been limited to duplicating and selling the movies, assumed the role of producer as well. With a keen knowledge of the types of films that would sell, these dealer-producers invested only in those movies that promised returns, leaving less room for anything beyond the mainstream formulas of comedies and romances. The remaining independent producers did the same. Hence, the films tended to focus increasingly on attraction and spectacle and vigorously brought back the song-and-dance routines that were crucial to selling movies. Promotional film trailers, which are fed into the market a couple of months before a film's release, began to consist almost entirely of such showstoppers. On top of that, they displayed the stars in spectacular dresses modeled on styles of the West, which became an equally important factor in drawing audiences.

The fact that such elements remained crucial for Hausa videos despite censorship can be accounted for by the policy of the Kano State Censorship Board at that time, which left plenty of room for negotiation between filmmakers and their censors. As Adamu (2004) suggests, the board was expert at exploring all sorts of "ways of generating revenue for the Kano State Government through the various fees it charge[d] filmmakers for almost all aspects of film production (licensing, censoring, screening, distribution)," and according to rumors, the board was not above raising fees to line the censors' private pockets (55–56). In a press interview, the executive secretary of the board, Abulkadir A. Kurawa, defended his office's work by pointing a finger at the filmmakers:

> What the law enables us to do is to make corrections. Most of the films with singing and dancing have thus been censored. We have asked them to effect corrections. But because of their sheer indiscipline, irresponsibility and stubbornness, they always release the unedited version of the films. There is little we can do about this because we don't have enough equipment and personnel to monitor the market. (quoted in Adamu 2004: 56)

The filmmakers, however, justified the production of films lacking sharia compliancy by referring to their audiences. As filmmaker Dan Azumi Baba points out, the video industry is a market-driven business, and must therefore keep a keen eye on consumer preferences: "The Hausa viewing audience contributes significantly to encouraging us to adopt Westernization in Hausa films. This they do through refusal to buy films that do not have these elements, because despite all their criticisms, they still rush out to buy these films" (quoted in Adamu 2007: 90). In a similar fashion Mansura Isa, an actress famous for her suggestive dance style, comments on the reason for the inclusion of song-and-dance routines:

> It's modernity. . . . The audience likes the way we get down in the films.
> If not, they would not buy them. If a film is to show all the girls in hijab
> [Islamic dress] and not getting down, I swear, the film will flop. . . . But if
> you make a trailer of a film showing nubile girls dancing and getting down,
> the audience will whoop with approval; yet those who abuse us are those
> who will go to the market and buy the films. (quoted in Adamu 2007: 93)

Some of the films produced in 2004 and 2005 mirror this double moral
standard referred to by Mansura Isa. *Gidauniya* (2004) is a particularly apt
example of the moral ambiguity of such films. The movie's cover catches
the eye by depicting three actresses in more or less tight-fitting, and thus
provocative, dresses. At the same time, however, its plot mimics the public
discourse on the transgression of female propriety by women who wear
such clothes. Hence, the film's images and its overall message contradict each other. One sequence is particularly revealing: Amira (Maryam
Abubakar), the main character, visits her elder sister (Jamila Haruna),
together with two of her female college friends (Farida Jalal and Rukaiyya
Umar). All three of them are clad in apparel associated with the West. As
an additional marker of their deviation from a Hausa way of life, the girls
greet Amira's elder sister in English: "Hi, Auntie, how are you?" The sister,
herself dressed in local attire, shakes her head in disapproval, and speaking in Hausa, points to the first girl: "Get up, let me see your dress!" The
girl smiles, stands up, and obviously comfortable in her rather tight-fitting
blouse, slowly turns around, presenting her dress to Amira's sister—and
the spectators alike—as if on a catwalk. Amira, dressed in jeans and a
snug top, and her other friend, who sports straightened, uncovered hair,
are asked to do the same. "Now, for God's sake and for the sake of the
Prophet, what do you think you look like?" asks the sister. The girls answer
in unison: "Like cool ones!" When she realizes that the girls are far from
ashamed, she starts admonishing them: "As children of Muslim parents,
you walk around all the time with this type of dress: no shawl, no scarf."
Two of the girls protest, pointing to their "scarves" (which look more like
fashionable fish nets and are therefore more revealing than concealing),
and then blame the third girl, who is wearing no scarf whatsoever, for
arousing "Auntie's" disapproval. "If you, as Muslims, continue to wear
such dresses," Amira's sister continues, "you are neither cool, nor warm,
but hot [as hell fire]! By God, if you don't stop wearing such clothes, who

will rescue you on the very day when you enter the hereafter looking like the English or the Germans? It befits everyone to follow the traditions of his/her own people!" The girls reply in English again, saying, "Thank you, Auntie!" and giggle carelessly when she leaves.

This is the last of three admonitions the girls receive from different people during the first ten minutes of the film. They do not accept the advice, however, and Amira is made to pay the price for this. With her revealing clothes, Amira unknowingly arouses the desire of her elder sister's husband, who plans to kill his wife in order to marry Amira. In pointing to Amira and her seductive style of dress as the root of all evil, *Gidauniya* is in line with the misogynist tendency of many Kanywood films. On the level of its plot, the film seems to teach morals and caution against the social dangers of clothes that reveal too much of the female body. On the visual level, however, this very deviance is celebrated through camera work and acting style. This discrepancy of textual and visual messages constitutes a double bind. It comes as no surprise that films such as *Gidauniya* prompted even more complaints about the nature of Kanywood movies.

In March 2005, the directorate of the Kano state governor's "Program for Societal Reorientation," founded in September 2004 under the label A Daidaita Sahu (Let's Realign Our Steps), addressed the film-viewing public through an open letter in *Fim* magazine. In this letter, Bala A. Muhammad (2005), director general of A Daidaita Sahu, commends the many complaints his office receives from people who voice their discontent with the "dresses the woman who appear in such films are wearing," the "lack of meaningful messages of some films," and the song and dance "absolutely unknown to Hausa traditions." He continues:

> The office of A Daidaita Sahu is equally concerned about these things and tries its best to work toward a change of such matters by interrogating those government agencies that are burdened with the task of enforcing change. But before one will be able to say that everything has been remedied, the first step we should undertake to remedy this matter is to shun this type of film and to evade all those who prepare them. (3; my translation)

The double moral standard typical of the discourse about Hausa films at the time was certainly not lost on the director of Kano state's new "Program for Societal Reorientation." Although his office began to investigate how the Censorship Board performed its task as well as to commission a number of writers and filmmakers to produce suitable scripts, and even finance the production of sharia-compliant films itself, the program's impact on Kanywood remained marginal for the time being. This was despite the Censorship Board's May 2005 ban on mixed-gender dancing and the wearing of tight-fitting clothes by actresses with straightened, uncovered hair in films produced in Kano (Adamu 2008: 14). Also effective from May 2005, and likewise without any significant effect on Kanywood during the following two years, were the guidelines proclaimed by the Kwamitin Ladabtarwa da Daidaita Sahu (Disciplinary and Moral Alignment Committee), newly founded by the Kano State Filmmakers Association. As Adamu (2008) points out, these guidelines remained recommendations without any mechanism for enforcement. Moreover, constituting something like a code of conduct for actors, directors, and other filmmaking personnel, the ban addressed the social practices surrounding film production rather than the content of the films as such.

A SCANDAL AND ITS AFTERMATH

Although always on the verge of being banned, Kanywood filmmakers had managed to sustain their industry until August 2007, when a private, pornographic cell-phone clip was leaked to the public. The clip of about eight minutes shows actress Maryam Usman, commonly known by her stage name Maryam Hiyana—after the title of her breakthrough film, *Hiyana* (2006)—having sex with her boyfriend, a Lagos-based Hausa businessman. Despite the fact that the clip was of a strictly private nature, taken by the boyfriend with his cell phone and never meant to be circulated (it was made public almost two years later), it served the critics of Kanywood as ultimate evidence of the industry's alleged immorality. Since 2000, rumors had been spreading about "blue films" sooner or later to be produced in Kano; now the subject matter of such rumors seemed to have materialized. All in the span of a few days, the clip was uploaded on the internet, passed on from handset to handset, and literally downloaded by hundreds of thousands of people. The public outcry focused on the girl, blaming her alone, despite the fact that two people could be seen in the clip and that it was her boyfriend who had captured the amorous scene on his cell phone. The video was discussed in a session of the Kano State House of Assembly, and "Maryam [was] roundly condemned" ('Yarshila 2007). Likewise, the chief imam of Zamfara state called for a ban on cell phones for girls and expressed the opinion that possession of cell phones by girls "is leading to a total collapse of morals" (quoted in 'Yarshila).

The fact that it was not a properly produced and edited film but a cell-phone clip of very poor technical quality, and linked to the video film industry only through the woman seen in the clip, was of little help to the members of the Kanywood film industry, who were held collectively responsible for the immoral act one of them had committed. Although leading Kano filmmakers reacted immediately, announcing a three-month moratorium on film production (beginning on August 13, 2007) and expelling seventeen industry members (mostly actresses) notorious for their immoral behavior, they were unable to prevent an official ban on film-making, however, which the Kano State Government imposed (Sheme 2007a). In an open letter dated August 16, 2007, A Daidaita Sahu called the attempts of the Kano State Filmmakers Association at self-regulation insufficient and advised filmmakers to stop shooting for a full year to gain enough time to set up solid rules and regulations for sharia-compliant filmmaking. Consequently, the three-year celebration of A Daidaita Sahu's founding, which took place in Kano on September 11, 2007, featured a public immolation of Hausa video films. This demonstrative act was presided over by the emir of Kano, the grand khadi of Kano State, the majority leader of the Kano State House of Assembly, and an assistant to the Kano state governor (Sheme 2007b).

The Task Force Committee on the Sanitization of the Film Industry was formed, and the directorate of the Censorship Board was exchanged. When the new director, Abubakar Rabo, formerly deputy commander of the *hisbah* (religious police), announced on September 21, 2007, the conditions for future filmmaking which the board had drawn up (Sheme 2007c), it became clear that the control of Hausa video filmmaking was about to become far more rigid than ever before. The new guidelines included compulsory registration of film production companies and any individual involved in the industry (producers, directors, scriptwriters, actors, and production and postproduction workers), as well as the approval of scripts and locations by the censors before shooting. As a prerequisite for registration, a film company was expected to have a minimum of 2.5 million naira (20,000 U.S. dollars at the time) as working capital, professional equipment (a detailed list of which was published by the board), and a "crowd-free office environment" (Kano's Censorship Laws 2008). As to the regulations for individuals, it is worth quoting the "General Guidelines for General Registration of Film Operators" at some length:

> 1. A film operative must possess "O" Level Certificate or its equivalent (Additional qualification is an added advantage). 2. Director/Producer must possess a Diploma or Certificate in the field of production from a recognized institution. 3. A film operative must avoid any act capable of polluting public morals. 4. A film operative must observe and respect religion, culture and public interest. . . . 7. Female artiste, musician and lyricist must be under the care of her husband, parent or guardian (Not independent as the case may be). . . . 13. Singing and dancing has been cancelled in Hausa films. 14. Producer must discourage free mingling of opposite sexes for the whole night during production. 15. An artiste must be mentally and of sound moral behavior.[4] (Kano's Censorship Laws 2008)

The rationale behind the requirement of individual registration was later explained by the board's new director as a measure "to avoid people of questionable character, drug addicts, paedophiles, alcoholics, cultists and robbers hiding under the guilds to pass on their corrupt morals to younger people" (Rabo 2008). The Censorship Board's new no-nonsense policy of "cleaning up" Kanywood was labeled "Fire for Fire." The meaning of this dawned on the filmmakers when in September 2007, the director, actor, and singer Adam A. Zango was sentenced to three months in prison and slapped with a fine of 100,000 naira (about 800 U.S. dollars) for the release of an uncensored album of music video clips (McCain 2013: 232). Officially, he was charged with breaking the ban on video production and distribution and for circulating an uncensored video. One particular song titled "Bahaushiya" (Hausa woman), however, seems to have been the unofficial reason for Zango's conviction. The judge said the video clip, in which three women dancing in an erotic non-Hausa dance style and Zango himself performing with them, was obscene and brought disgrace on the honor of Hausa women. The judge's decree meant he concurred with the Censorship Board's director, who said that the video clip "portrayed nudity to a certain degree" and that "the type of dressing and dancing . . . contravenes the teachings of Islam and Hausa culture as well" (Ibrahim 2007a).

As a consequence, major Kanywood production companies moved their businesses to neighboring states, mostly Kaduna and Abuja, and began to reorganize the industry from there (Ibrahim 2007b). Films were shot outside Kano state, the rushes taken to Kano—where postproduction could still be done—and the finished product was then taken outside the state again for distribution. To avoid conflicts with the Kano State Censorship Board, films produced in this manner got a sticker reading "Not for sale in Kano" (McCain 2013: 233). When the ban was lifted on February 12, 2008, many filmmakers, including Sa'idu Gwanja, chairman of the Filmmakers' Association, found the board's new registration guidelines far "too stringent to be complied with easily" (quoted in Ibrahim 2008). Most were reluctant to register immediately, probably hoping that the new guidelines would somehow ease in the future. Throughout 2008 and 2009, however, the Kano State Censorship Board, through Director Abubakar Rabo, called on filmmakers to "consider the Board as their partner in progress, but not as their enemy," did everything to prove that it intended to live up to its task "to bring sanity into Kanywood" (quoted in Ibrahim 2008). Police raids of industry-related offices, studios, and shops as well as a series of arrests and hasty trials at a so-called mobile court—established especially for the purposes of the Censorship Board—turned Rabo and the filmmakers into fierce adversaries. In 2008 alone, about a thousand people, mostly youth, were arrested and often convicted within an hour without legal representation (McCain, Hausawa, and Alkanawy 2009). Among them were also two of the industry's most prominent figures: producer, director, and actor Hamisu Lamido Iyan-Tama and comedian Rabilu Musa Danlasan. Iyan-Tama was arrested in May 2008 and was accused of running his company without renewing its registration and releasing his film *Tsintsiya* (2008) in Kano state without the approval of the Censorship Board. Ironically, a few days earlier the film—a transposition of the American musical *West Side Story,* sponsored by the American Embassy—had won the award for best film in the category of "Social Issue" at the Zuma Film Festival in Abuja. In Kano, a copy of the film fell into the hands of the Censorship Board during a raid on a video shop.

Despite the fact that the film was not for sale in Kano, and even though Iyan-Tama was able to prove that his company's registration was up to date, he had to spend several weeks in custody. In January 2009, he was finally sentenced to three months without bail and could either pay a fine of 300,000 naira (2,200 U.S. dollars) or serve an additional twelve months in prison (McCain, Hausawa, and Alkanawy 2009; Sheme 2009a).[5] In October 2008, Kanywood's most popular comedian, Rabilu Musa Danlasan (aka Ibro) and his sidekick, Lawal Alhassan Kaura, were charged for showing indecent dancing in two of their video films (*Ibro Aloko* and *Ibro K'auran Mata*) and for allegedly running a film production company without registration. They denied the charges, and although both films had been released prior to the implementation of the new censorship guidelines, Ibro and Kaura were sentenced to two months in prison without bail (McCain, Hausawa, and Alkanawy 2009; Sanusi 2008).

The "travesty of justice" (Sheme 2009b) carried out in the name of religion and culture by Abubakar Rabo, his staff, and Magistrate Mukhtar Ahmed, who presided over the mobile court (and whose competence was later publicly questioned by the Kano state attorney general), led many to suspect that Rabo—and perhaps even some people higher up the political ladder—used the opportunity offered by the censorship law to settle old scores with their political enemies among the filmmakers. Sani Mu'azu, president of the Motion Pictures Practitioners Association of Nigeria (MOPPAN), suspected that Iyan-Tama had become a victim of his political activities. As a candidate for the governorship of Kano state in the 2007 gubernatorial elections, Iyan-Tama had vociferously targeted the Shekarau administration's lack of openness and, according to Mu'azu, was now forced to pay the price for it: the "Kano Censors Board is just being used to get through a script written from the Government House" (quoted in McCain 2009). The conviction of comedian Ibro would fit the same pattern. His film *Ibro Aloko* featured a satirical song that made fun of a certain kind of striped robe worn by the Kano state governor, Ibrahim Shekarau. Ibro was arrested on October 6, 2008, after a mob of protesters, frustrated with Shekarau's administration, pelted the governor with stones. The incident took place in September 2008, at the end of the last Eid-el-fitr prayer, a public event celebrated at the emir's palace in Kano. The crowd sang the satirical song from *Ibro Aloko* as they threw stones at the governor, who was wearing the same striped garment described by the lyrics (Sanusi 2008).

Faced with harassment by the censors whose dubious actions seemed to be backed by the state government, Kanywood practitioners began to fight back. More than once MOPPAN and individual filmmakers sued the chief censor, Abubakar Rabo, for defamation: in August 2009, for example, Rabo was sued in a sharia court in Kano after calling filmmakers "a bunch of homosexuals and lesbians" in a radio interview (Sheme 2009c); and in July 2010, he was sued in a magistrate court in Kaduna after accusing Hausa filmmakers, in a television interview, of producing pornographic movies and calling upon the citizens of Kaduna to chase them out of the state (Sheme 2010). Although summoned by the courts, Rabo never appeared before any judge. Instead, the intimidation of Kanywood practitioners by the Censorship Board's task force, raids on shops and offices, and arrests and convictions by the board's mobile court continued.

Kanywood singers and composers fought back, using their music as weapons. Adam A. Zango, Rabo's first victim, took revenge with his music video *Oyoyo* (2008), in which he calls on God to deal with those who jailed him (McCain 2013). The video shows him in a prison environment "pumping iron" with fellow inmates. Members of a group headed by Aminu Ala jointly produced the song "Hasbunallahu" (2009). The title refers to a well-known Islamic prayer which is used to implore God's help in troubled times. In the song, "God is exhorted to destroy the enemies of the artists, who are opposed to their art and the people" (Liman 2010: 56). Other musicians turned to irony. Rapper Ziriums (Nazir Hausawa) addressed the government restrictions on singing and dancing in Kano in his song "Girgiza kai" (Shake your head, 2008): "Hey, don't dance, you know they banned it / The governor of our city here. He banned it / If you hear a good beat, just shake your head" (quoted in McCain 2010a). Although the Censorship Board dragged Aminu Ala and some of his fellow musicians involved in the production of "Hasbunallahu" before its mobile court (Sheme 2009c, 2009d) and banned the song along with ten others, it became famous and spread from handset to handset.

The battle between the censors and the filmmakers took an unexpected turn when Abubakar Rabo became involved in his very own sex scandal. On August 22, 2010, the police in Kano arrested him after a late-night car chase. During the chase, he knocked down a motorcyclist, and when the police finally apprehended Rabo, they found a teenage girl in the backseat of his car. Out on bail, he left for Saudi Arabia the very next day to perform the lesser hajj, a series of virtuous acts recommended during Ramadan (Abdulaziz 2010; Aliyu 2010). According to Adamu, the Islamic establishment rallied in support of Rabo, one imam even saying in his Friday sermon that Rabo should be excused because he "was human" (Abdalla Uba Adamu, email, May 18, 2011). Although the case was dropped, allegations of an illicit relationship with the girl persisted. Rabo's power further declined when Kano state got a new government following the gubernatorial elections in April 2011. Compared with the former governor, Ibrahim Shekarau, who entertained close ties to the religious establishment, newly elected Rabi'u Musa Kwankwaso, who had already run the state from 1999 to 2003, was known to be less strict in religious matters (see figure 4.3). In November 2011, the director general of the Kano State Censorship Board was replaced and a number of filmmakers, among them Rabilu Musa Danlasan, who had been imprisoned by the former director general, were given

FIGURE 4.3

New hopes for Kanywood after the gubernatorial elections in Kano state, 2011.
Courtesy of *Daily Trust.*

seats on the board, explains Carmen McCain (2013), further elucidating
the unlikely goings-on between politics and filmmaking in the following:

> The events had a mixed-up poetic justice that seemed to come straight out
> of a Hausa film: the governor who first banned film in Kano came back
> promising the salvation of the film industry; the censor appointed after a
> sex scandal to "sanitize" a film industry was disgraced by his own sex scan-
> dal; an actor imprisoned by the censors board was appointed to the board
> in the next political tenure. A public discourse that idealized politicians'
> promises to use Islamic law to protect culture moved toward indignation
> over how those same politicians abused Shari'a to hide their own corrup-
> tion. (236)

A CONTESTED TASTE OF DIFFERENCE

Video technology provided Hausa cultural entrepreneurs with a tool
to develop and shape their fantasies of what localized versions of other
possible lives would look like. In terms of form and content, these versions
were strongly influenced by Indian films, which had brought northern
Nigerian audiences into contact with visions of a "parallel modernity"
(Larkin 1997) since the 1960s. For many years, Indian films were valued
for their very difference from Hollywood productions and their proximity to local experience. In light of the trope of "contact and copy," it is
significant that the critical debate began only when self and other became
intertwined through localized copies of Bollywood movies. Indian films
as such were not considered problematic, for they were thought to portray "Indian culture"; yet their appropriation and localization by Hausa
authors and filmmakers sparked considerable controversy. Mere contact
with other possible lives, as portrayed in foreign media, was not necessarily disturbing. Copying them, however, could prompt a debate. In this
sense, it is also significant that for the better part of the censorship debate,
pirated copies of foreign films (from Hollywood, Bollywood, Hong Kong,
and southern Nigeria) were left untouched by the censors and remained
on sale in Kano video shops, despite the fact that many featured far more
female (and male) nudity than Hausa videos; this fact was considered
particularly unjust by Kanywood filmmakers, who kept arguing that their

films were actually counteracting the influence of foreign films that contained scenes far worse than their own.

Despite the many challenges, or perhaps even because of them, the video filmmakers have displayed a remarkable sense of unity and a spirit of cooperation throughout the almost twenty years since video filmmaking began in northern Nigeria. Most of them consider themselves devout Muslims and Hausa. Nevertheless, during the past ten years, a certain discourse surfaced within and outside the industry, questioning the "Hausaness" of a number of those involved in filmmaking. The rationale behind this was to marginalize those dancing in a particularly indecent manner or wearing particularly obscene clothes (in and off film) as immigrants with different ethnic backgrounds or as children of immigrants who lacked the typical "Hausa mind-set." This logic included a certain amount of scapegoating, as it associated everything considered undesirable about Kanywood with alleged internal strangers, often referred to as "nonethnic" Hausa. Luckily enough, this discourse seemed to have died down before it could unfold its socially explosive potential. Interestingly, this discourse was based on "the prison house of culture" model which would not allow individuals to act beyond the norms of their "culture" (cf. Çaglar 1990). This, however, is exactly what happened during the past twenty years of Kanywood's short history. Inspired by foreign media, young people explored the taste of cultural difference and what it would mean to be modern and Hausa and modern and Muslim. The video medium gave them the opportunity to disseminate these explorations. Since the films transgressed social norms, they became the focus of heated debate. It would be wrong, however, to view Kanywood filmmakers as radicals. Prior to the censorship crisis in the wake of the Hiyana scandal, they more or less tried to accommodate their critics. They experimented with new, religiously inspired genres, even dropping the much-debated song-and-dance sequences and the theme of love in a couple of films produced between 2002 and 2003. While the standard formula returned as a response to audience preference, the ongoing public controversy and the censorship rules still left their mark on the subsequent videos. Filmmakers therefore tended to incorporate more images signifying local "culture" (*Khusufi*'s Fulbe, for example), introduced current debates into their films (such as the controversy in *Gidauniya* over dresses in the style of the West),

frequently reduced the dancing in showstopper sequences to a mere shaking of the head, and introduced many more girls wearing hijabs than ever
before. Even after 2007, the film industry demonstrated its willingness to
cooperate with the new censorship regime, and only when the Censorship Board's actions became unbearable and the board seemed intent
on the destruction of the industry, did Kanywood filmmakers begin to
fight back.

5

Dar 2 Lagos

NOLLYWOOD IN TANZANIA

NOLLYWOOD FILMS HAVE left the narrow confines of domestic consumption in their country of origin and are currently watched by diverse audiences throughout many parts of Africa (Krings and Okome 2013a). When I first went to Dar es Salaam on a short reconnaissance trip in March 2006, I was fascinated by the enormous presence of Nigerian video films in this East African city. They were sold on cassettes and discs in shops and by street vendors, rented out in video rental stores, broadcast on several TV stations, and advertised at the doorways to video parlors. Given the fact that many Tanzanians do not speak English and must have had difficulty following the dialogue, I thought of returning a year later to ascertain what Tanzanian spectators were gleaning from Nigerian video films. When I returned in August 2007, however, the demand for Nigerian films had declined dramatically, to the extent that they were almost nonexistent in the shops and video parlors. Meanwhile, local video film production had tripled its output. As they had the advantage of being produced in Swahili, these films quickly took a leading position in the market for "African films," which had hitherto been dominated by Nigerian video films. Suddenly finding myself dealing with what seemed a historical phenomenon and having difficulty discussing films that had lost their audiences, I became interested in the short history of Nigerian video film in Tanzania and in the traces Nollywood videos had left in Tanzanian cultural production more generally. I was also curious about Bongo movies in particular (as the films produced by the emerging Dar es Salaam–based video film industry are called—after a nickname for the city).

New local forms of media production in Tanzania have used Nigerian video films as "scripts," drawing on them to varying degrees. Earlier forms, such as photo novels, essentially a "remediation" (Bolter and Grusin 2000) of videos (based on screen shots, with Swahili in speech bubbles) or VHS cassettes that present audio dubbing, into Swahili, were attempts at translating and thus making Nigerian video films more accessible to Tanzanian audiences. Other forms of localization, such as those observed in Bongo movies, aim rather at appropriating the "aura" of Nigerian video film. In a bid to cash in on Nollywood's fame, a number of local video producers have adopted a Nigerian video film style or, in the case of one producer, established direct contact with Nigeria and started producing films featuring Nigerian actors and directors. On the basis of several examples, I shall demonstrate how these processes of adaptation work and how specific tropes—motives and plots—are translated between Nigeria and Tanzania.

NIGERIAN FILMS IN TANZANIA

Nollywood videos only began circulating widely in Tanzania in 2000. Early distribution relied solely on pirated material, and this had not changed much in 2007, when I gathered the data for this chapter. Only one distributor was legally importing Nigerian films on VCD—Mtitu Game, who owned and still owns the film production company Game 1st Quality. During the heyday of his import business, Game received consignments of up to 3,000 VCDs by air from Nigeria each week. They were sold not only in Tanzania but also bought by traders from Zambia, Mozambique, and the Democratic Republic of the Congo. As Mtitu Game told me, he reduced the volume of his imports only in 2006, partly because of inflation and a hike in the Tanzanian import tax, and partly because the demand for Nigerian videos declined as the local video industry expanded (personal interview, August 8 and 31, 2007).

In 2007, Nigerian videos were rarely sold as single copies but as collections of up to eight films on a single DVD (at a price of 4,500 shillings or 3.85 U.S. dollars—the same price as a genuine copy of a single Nollywood film in Game's shop). These collections carry hyperbolic names, such as *Nigerian Box Office, Nollywood Bestseller, The Best Nigerian Movie Collection*, or simply *Africa Movie Collection*. Given the delicate nature of this business, relying as it did on pirated material, I was unable to find out by whom and where these DVDs were produced, despite the fact that they had allegedly been pouring into the market since 2006. Some suspected dubious Chinese or Indian businessmen, who also provided the *machinga* (street vendors) with a constant supply of pirated Hollywood and Hong Kong movies. Others suspected Tanzanians with international business contacts in Singapore or China, where these DVDs were believed to be produced. Whoever fabricated them certainly were industrious and also had a fine sense of humor: all the covers carry the logos typical of genuine DVDs, such as the "Dolby" and "dts Digital Surround" labels (which, given the sound quality of both the pirated copies and the originals, is frankly laughable); the back covers usually announce subtitles in "1. English, 2. Chinese, 3. Bahasa, 4. Portuguese," and have a warning against piracy: "Criminal copy right infringements is investigated by the FBI and may constitute a felony with a maximum penalty of upfive [*sic*] in prison and/or a $250,000 fine." Also, whoever produced these DVDs had some expertise in Nollywood films; some movie collections are not randomly organized but compiled by either genre or actor. Other collections are devoted to movies dealing with the occult and romance (*The Best Occaultic* [*sic*] *Movies, Nigerian Love Collection*); one DVD even juxtaposes two genres: *Epic vs. Comedy*.

Nigerian video films were broadcast by two private television stations—ITV (Sundays at 12:30, 21:15) and Star TV (Saturdays at 22:30, and Sundays at 14:00). On both channels, Pepsi-Cola sponsored the respective program slots, meaning that there were several interruptions to advertise the soft drink. State broadcaster TVT also aired Nigerian films for about four months in 2005 (cut up into 30-minute weekly segments) but decided to stop after receiving too many complaints from viewers about the heavy dosage of Pentecostal content in the films. As a national television station, TVT was obviously expected not to show an inclination toward any particular religious doctrine (Umari Semindu of TVT, personal interview, September 3, 2007).

One of the first Nigerian films to arrive in Tanzania seems to have been *Suicide Mission* (1998), which was on the lips of almost everyone I interviewed. Another film many people must have seen is *Billionaires Club* (2003). Both are typical variations of two well-known Nollywood plots. *Suicide Mission* is about an innocent family man who falls prey to an evil woman. Austin (Richard Mofe-Damijo) becomes the victim of Monique (Regina Askia), who acquires her secret powers through witchcraft. In the end, the inevitable pastor appears and saves the day. *Billionaires Club* (along with its two sequels—all starring Pete Edochie and Kanayo O. Kanayo) is a rather late variant of the wealth-through-secret-cult story, where Zed (Tony Umez), a poor pharmacist, offers to sacrifice his child and his wife to the billionaire's cult to get rich quick, only to discover later that he is haunted by the spirit of his dead wife and members of the club who insist on even more sacrifices.

Films displaying occult economies were of great interest in Tanzania. It is a country in which a series of ritual murders involving the trade in human body parts (especially skin) has shocked its citizens since 1999 (Sanders 2001). The most popular explanation for the success of Nollywood films in Tanzania was that Nigerian films, considered "African" films, reflect the social and cultural realities of everyday Tanzanian life. Nigerian films were hailed for their "Africanness," which means, essentially, black characters on screen in settings similar to the Tanzanian environment (although the huge mansions and luxury cars make a difference and later become *the* marker for Nollywood-like iconography of a particular Bongo movies brand). Screen characters were expected to deal with problems similar to those of their Tanzanian audiences. People were fascinated (and thrilled) by the special effects, which render visible witchcraft, something they—though they believed in its existence—had never been able to *see* before (e.g., *Suicide Mission* has a double of Zed trapped in a bottle, and other films show men being turned into animals). Videos in the romance genre, with their various and well-established plots, were also popular: lovers who meet with resistance from their parents (*True Love*, 2003), suffer at the hands of their stepparents (*Pains of Love*, 2003; *Super Love*, 2003), or are betrayed by a jealous friend who turns evil (*Christ in Me*, 2003).

Nigerian films made their entrance into local video parlors and living rooms as novelties and were met with great acclaim. In the beginning, images of the occult, luxury cars, huge mansions, and a wealthy lifestyle had served as attractions and helped non-English speakers endure the incomprehensible, lengthy dialogues, but ultimately these flashy images would not be enough. Therefore, during the heyday of Nollywood's popularity in Tanzania, in 2003, local cultural producers began experimenting with the remediation of Nollywood films by tackling the biggest obstacle to their local reception: the English language. Adding commentary and translations in Swahili, they drew on older media genres, such as the photo novel and oral narrative.

FILLING IN THE GAPS: VIDEO FILM AS PHOTO NOVEL

Photo novels were introduced to Tanzania during the late 1960s, when South African Drum Publications came up with so-called look-reads—photographed stories with an African cast. The most famous of these magazines was *African Film*, which featured the adventures of Lance Spearman and had a circulation of forty-five thousand in East Africa alone (see chapter 2). Tanzanians would read their first Swahili photo novel in *Film Tanzania*, a magazine founded in 1969. As the titles of the magazines suggest, the photo novel served as a substitute for film, which until the introduction of video technology, was too expensive to be realized on a greater scale.[1] The medium was quite well established when Sultan Tamba, a well-known novelist, video filmmaker, and columnist, took a Nigerian video film and made it into a serialized photo novel, which appeared in *Sani* in November 2003. Moreover, since the tabloid is famous for its comics, Tamba could count on a sophisticated readership that knew how to read "sequential art" (Eisner 1990).

For his experiment, Tamba chose *Omereme* (2002), a village-based film about a polygynous Igbo household. The central figure is Mama Nnamdi, who feels disrespected by her husband and his two other wives. With the aid of a secret female cult, she acquires deadly powers and kills the members of her household and the village, until the preacher son of one of her husband's other wives discovers what she has done and saves the family. As a video filmmaker, Tamba prefers making films about village life (depicting so-called traditional culture), and this must be one of the reasons why he chose a film with a village setting for his experiment. Not only does *Omereme* contain a couple of occult scenes to dazzle viewers, it also has the potential to become a didactic piece about the hazards of polygamy. The introduction to the first episode of the photo novel reads: "Polygamous life is difficult and full of problems. A beautiful film, loved by many viewers, [it shows that] polygamy breeds horrible actions including witchcraft and other malicious deeds. Have a look at this life in the Swahili translation."

Space is for a photo novel what time is for film, which means that this particular medium needs space for a story to progress. Given the spatial limitation of one page per issue, Tamba had to choose the images carefully and adjust them to suit the new medium. Medium and close-up shots proved more suitable than long shots (lest the reader require a magnifying glass). Each episode contains up to twelve rectangular images, arranged in three rows. Panel size is critical in photo novels and graphic novels alike. Size can signify the length of an action depicted in a panel, and panel frames are important for creating the gutter—the empty space between panels. This space leaves room for the reader's imagination. The reader is more active in completing the story as it proceeds from panel to panel than film viewers watching a movie (McCloud 1994). For the *Omereme* adaptation, this means the reader is liberated from the confines of the video medium (with its constant flow of images) and space is literally opened up for the imaginative transfer of the Nigerian story to the Tanzanian reader's own social and cultural experience. The reader draws on this experience to fill in the space between the panels and complete the story.

Of course, readers are also guided by the texts accompanying the images, and without which the panels would not constitute a story. Three types of voices appear in writing: a narrator's (usually at the top of the panel in a rectangular insert), and either the characters' speech (in the first episode inside bubbles, later in rectangles) or their thoughts (marked by small bubbles leading to the text). A textual comparison of original and copy makes it obvious that Tamba creates his own story. What he does is a twofold adaptation of the template. First, he adapts it to the format of the transcribing medium. He does this by adding a narrator's voice, which comments on and contextualizes the images. And he invents characters' thoughts (though there are almost no inner voices in the film) to give insight into their inner feelings. Second, he de-localizes the content to facilitate the reader's transfer of the foreign story to his or her own cultural realm. The following example demonstrates how a typical reference to the southern Nigerian life-world—the dish called "bitter leaf soup"—is erased as a result of the adaptation process (see figure 5.1, which shows panels 3 and 4):

FIGURE 5.1

Page from *Omereme* (2003), a Swahili photo novel based on the Nigerian video film of the same name. Courtesy of the newspaper *Sani*.

Video Film

(Shot: Husband tastes Mama Nnamdi's food and grimaces in disgust)

(Shot: Mama Nnamdi and co-wife) MAMA NNAMDI: It's bitter leaf [soup].

(Shot: Husband) HUSBAND: I know, but it's too bitter.

(Shot: Mama Nnamdi and co-wife) MAMA NNAMDI: That's so that it will wash your mouth.

Photo Novel

(Panel: Close-up of husband eating) TEXT 1—NARRATOR: The husband tasted the food of one of the wives! He did not like it, then of another ... TEXT 2—THOUGHTS OF HUSBAND: Aaah! She cooks such a bad food. No, I cannot eat it. I cannot continue eating it, I'll get a stomachache!

(Panel: Mama Nnamdi and co-wife) TEXT 1—MAMA NNAMDI: This is what I have prepared! The one that you love! TEXT 2—THOUGHTS OF CO-WIFE: Uh! Look how she is boasting!

While the viewer-reader of the photo novel gains some kind of translation (in fact an interpretation of the Nigerian original by Sultan Tamba) and a greater chance to transfer the story to his own cultural realm, he also misses out on a number of the template's qualities. Unlike the viewer-listener of the video film, he gets only black-and-white pictures, has to wait a full week before the story continues, and exchanges static for moving images and silence for sound. Above all, he must be able to read! Each medium has its own intrinsic qualities. Remediation not only affects the content but also changes the ways of accessing it. The remediation of *Omereme* alters the form, time, and setting of its consumption: from a communal viewing and listening experience—in a public video parlor or with friends and family members in front of a private television screen—to an individual, silent viewing and reading experience.

Ultimately, *Omereme* spanned twenty-five issues of *Sani* before the photo novel, and remediation of the video film, was complete. According to Sultan Tamba, the newspaper decided against any further remediation of Nigerian films due to a low readership (personal interview, March 25, 2006). In 2007, *Sani* staff informed me that remediation was stopped for fear of the legal consequences, as the newspaper had not resolved copyright issues with the Nigerian producers. The form continued to exist, however, in the weekly *Kiu Movie Magic,* although only locally produced video films (understood as free promotion) were being remediated.

TURNING RICE INTO *PILAU:* THE ART OF DUBBING

Another way to localize foreign films is through dubbing. In Tanzania, this form of remediation dates way back, prior to the advent of video film. An early forerunner was the colonial cinema narrator who interpreted the film live while standing next to the screen. This form of remediation has survived in Kenya and Uganda, where so-called veejays (video jockeys) do live commentary on foreign films shown in local video parlors (Krings 2009). In Tanzania, live interpretation was also practiced in the past but seems to have been completely replaced by its mediatized variant of "dubbed" vHs cassettes. The development of this adaptation is closely linked to a single person: Cpt. Derek Gaspar Mukandala, who until recently had a virtual monopoly on dubbing foreign films into Kiswahili on vHs.[2]

Born in the Bukoba District on the shores of Lake Victoria fifty-five years ago, Mukandala has dubbed more than 1,000 films in his career so far. These works are mostly American and Chinese action movies but also include about ninety Nigerian films and a number of Indian productions. Before he started dubbing on vHs in 1996, he had almost two decades of experience as a live narrator, running his own mobile cinema show (personal interview, September 8, 2007). Although Mukandala calls his work *tafsiri* (translation)—and when we chatted in English, he said "dubbing"—what he actually does is much more than mere dubbing. Mukandala is simultaneously an interpreter, a translator, and a voice mime. This means that he offers his audience more than the simple illusion of foreign film characters speaking Swahili. Technically speaking, he switches constantly between voice-over translation of dialogue and commentary, using an audio mixer to add his soundtrack to the "original" video, whereby he constantly fades in an out (sometimes after every sentence) to preserve as much of the original soundtrack as possible. As a translator, he interprets the dialogue, changing his voice according to the gender and age of the screen characters, thus imitating voices of women and men, young and old. As commentator, he takes on the role of a narrator who interprets those actions and images he thinks his audience cannot understand. He is thus a guide through foreign audiovisual terrain.

The following examples from Mukandala's narration of *Super Love* (2003) highlight some of the peculiarities of his art. *Super Love* is a Cinderella story set in rural Igboland, involving a prince called Obinna (Ramsey Nouah Jr.), who has returned from abroad and—despite being introduced to many other women—falls in love with Amaka (Genevieve Nnaji), a poor girl who is suffering at the hands of her stepfather (Pete Edochie). On every tape, Mukandala starts by introducing himself and locates for the audience where the the film comes from (sometimes even undertaking an imaginative journey from Dar es Salaam to the place where the film was shot). Accompanied by the opening credits of the film, he says:

> My beloved viewers, my beloved relatives, Captain Derek Mukandala
> Lufufu who is available at Aggrey Street, Kariakoo, in the center of Dar
> es Salaam city, brings to you one good film from the nation of Nigeria in
> this season of 2004—from the nation of Nigeria which is ruled by Gen.
> Obasanjo. (0:00:26–50)

This is followed by an introduction to the plot:

> Our film begins at a time when young Obinna returns from Europe,
> where he went to study. Obinna was a prince, as it is normal in a family of
> the chief. If your son is from that family, you are supposed to prepare his
> future. Among the things you should prepare for him is a girl to marry.
> And that should be arranged while the girl is still very young. Therefore,
> even three-year-old girls are prepared early for their marriage to the son of
> a chief. This is what happened in this place. (0:00:51–01:55)

In order to bridge the distance between the strange and the familiar, Mukandala makes explicit comparisons, helping his audience transfer the meaning of the film to the audience's own cultural realm. In the following example, Mukandala comments on a scene in which young women dance to different drum beats, using Tanzanian names to refer to the Nigerian tunes:

> The beautiful girls who wanted to become the wife of the chief's son
> were passing in front of the chief one by one in order to get a chance. The
> tune that was beaten in that place is *Chunda doka*. This dance of *Chunda*

doka is very famous in different places in Nigeria and in other areas like
Tanzania and Uganda. . . . Now they changed the type of dancing to
Ekadiya, the dance of the Wahima, where you are supposed to dance very
slowly twisting [the hips]. This dance is not different from the one which is
danced by the tribes of Rwanda and Burundi. It is danced by the Watutsi.
(0:40:15–42:28)

Some scenes—even though they are self-evident—are flavored with Mukandala's comments, which give the effect of making the pictures talk. The
following is an example of such a comment on shots of Amaka, collecting firewood in the forest, and Obinna, who is looking for her. When the
dialogue starts, Mukandala stops speaking as a narrator and switches to
imitate the voices of Amaka and Obinna, whereby the original dialogue
remains partially audible. The alternation of original dialogue and inserted translation makes Mukandala's voice sound as though it is echoing
the characters' voices:

In the morning Amaka went straight to the forest to cut firewood. As
usual for her, she was singing her sad songs; sad songs about her hard life
due to her being an orphan without support from anyone. Obinna failed
to stop his desire. In the morning when the sun rose, he also went to the
forest in order to listen to the voice of Amaka.

OBINNA: Hey, don't run away! Why are you running away?

AMAKA: Because you are a prince.

OBINNA: Yes, I am the son of the king, and you are the woman I love.

AMAKA: No that is impossible, I don't match your status.

(0:49:09–50:45)

Mukandala's exuberant commentary also produces what at first glance
looks like redundancy. After all, the phrase "Amaka went straight to the
forest to cut firewood" provides almost as much information as the images,
which actually show Amaka collecting wood. According to Walter Ong
(2010: 40), redundancy and repetition are fundamental characteristics of
oral thought and speech. "Redundancy, repetition of the just-said, keeps
both speaker and hearer surely on the track. . . . In oral delivery, though
a pause may be effective, hesitation is always disabling. Hence it is better
to repeat something, artfully if possible, rather than simply stop speaking

while fishing for the next idea. Oral cultures encourage fluency, fulsomeness, volubility." While the kind of redundancy Ong refers to exists in Mukandala's performances—the repetition of phrases while looking for the right words to continue the story—if we consider the performance context of video narration, redundancy dissolves when it takes the form of images combining with the narrator's commentary. Video parlors are usually equipped with ordinary television sets only—tiny screens in front of several rows of wooden benches packed with spectators. Hence, most viewers are sitting too far away from the screen to be able to see the film in any detail. The narrator—irrespective of whether he is performing live or his voice is coming from a dubbed cassette in the video recorder linked to the television set—provides a remedy to the visual constraints of the video parlor. His remediation, the rendition from visual to acoustic signs, makes it possible to enjoy a film without actually watching it. As a general effect, the narrator's commentaries and translations cause the images to lose their governing, storytelling function. Mukandala's voice takes the upper hand over the preexisting moving images, which turn into mere illustrations of his oral performance. The hierarchy of foreign original and local copy is thus reversed.

At the end of the film, images of Obinna and Amaka, who are married amid the cheers of an onlooking crowd of villagers, give Mukandala enough time to deliver a moral message to his audience—a plea against forced marriage. As a practicing Christian, he picks up on the insert, "In God we trust," which follows the final images of the film, translating and elaborating on it:

> *Mzee* Peter Edochie and his two daughters were arrested and jailed. The king sentenced them to twelve years in prison. Baby Amaka got her sweetheart easily. Remember, Amaka wasn't in a beauty contest. But Obinna loved her soul. And this is good for a boy or a girl, to choose a sweetheart to love. And this will be true love, super love.... In God we trust, and everything goes by God. And now we say, thank you, Lord Jesus. Our film *Super Love* finally has come to an end. (1:09:35–10:42)

With the credits already running, this comment is immediately followed by a hilarious self-advertisement and a caution about buying "original" cassettes. Ironically, Mukandala's words match the last line of the film's credits: "© O.J. Productions 2003":

As usual, this film was translated into Swahili by Cpt. Derek Mukandala—L-u-f-u-f-u! If you are looking for films already translated into Swahili, call Mukandala Lufufu Videotheque—number 0754821169. Lufufu can send to you all translated films wherever you are in Tanzania and wherever you are in East and Central Africa. Beware of buying films in the streets where you will get bad copies and bad prints. Come straight to our library and get good original copies with stereo sound and brilliant pictures. All of you are welcome. (1:10:43–11:50)

The model of Mukandala's art of remediation is obviously the performance of the traditional African storyteller. Like a storyteller, Mukandala adopts different roles—as narrator and as the *dramatis personae*—and he provides a moral message. Like the traditional storyteller who reinvents preexisting stories according to the time, place, and context in which he retells them, Mukandala also works with preexisting material. Unlike the storyteller's "scripts," however, which are immaterial, Mukandala's audiovisual "scripts" exist outside him. Mukandala compared his art with "the transformation of rice into *pilau*" (*pilau* is a delicious Swahili rice dish). According to this metaphor, Nigerian video films are like raw or unprocessed foodstuffs that have to be prepared according to certain principles of local cuisine to become a palatable dish. In this way, video narration may be conceptualized as domesticating foreign films through remediation (Krings 2009). This implies that in Tanzania, such films are made digestible—to apply Mukandala's metaphor once again—through the use of another medium, the spoken word, and that their exhibition in video parlors is reconfigured in terms of the classical live performance of traditional storytelling. This is based upon the observation that live video narration in fact transfers video films into oral narratives. Freeing narratives from their audiovisual containers and reshaping them according to the principles of "primary orality" may well be considered a way of accessing and reconstructing meaning through an inversion of the process Walter Ong (2010) has described as "technologizing of the word."

THE INFLUENCE OF NIGERIAN FILMS ON BONGO MOVIES

While the consumption of Nigerian video films was still at its peak in Tanzania—that is, between 2003 and 2006—a viable local video industry was developing in Dar es Salaam. Early on, variously labeled Tollywood, Swahiliwood, or Bongowood—the latter being a composite of *bongo* (Swahili for "brain" and a nickname for Dar es Salaam) and "Hollywood"—this fast-growing industry soon began to release several so-called Bongo movies per week. Similar to its big sister, Nollywood, the Dar es Salaam–based industry had its roots in local drama and television production (Lange 2002). Most productions were realized by independent drama groups and were marketed nationwide (and beyond) by a handful of distributors (Böhme 2011).

Early on, Nollywood served as a reference point for Tanzanian filmmakers, their critics, and spectators. Actor and director Vincent Kigosi referred to himself as Mr. Nollywood (like the Nigerian actor Ifeanyi Ikpoenyi, aka Mr. Hollywood). A series of newspaper articles written by a certain Mapunda Selles was titled "Nilichojifunza Nollywood!" (What I learned in Nollywood!). Selles went to study in Nigeria. However, he spent two years attempting to break into the Nigerian video industry rather than attending classes. On his return to Dar es Salaam in 2006, his trip to the African dream factory Nollywood saw him turn into a critic of local production values and video film style.[3] By 2007, for some, Nigeria—or rather Nollywood—was still the promised land of African video film production. For others, Bongo movies had long since caught up.

In 2003, Tamba Arts group released *Nsyuka*, the "first Tanzanian horror movie," as its cover so boldly announces. The film about a revenant with a predilection for human flesh was a huge success, second only to *Girlfriend*—a local hip-hop movie released earlier the same year (Böhme 2007). *Nsyuka* set the path for a number of ensuing productions. Since then, director Mussa Banzi has produced a sequel and several other horror movies. Considering the fact that he himself is a horror film fan with a predilection for American and European horror movies (Mussa Banzi, pers. comm., September 13, 2007), it comes as no surprise that *Nsyuka* and his other films are stylistically influenced, strongly so, by the Western version of the genre, in terms of camera work; preferred settings, such as graveyards; character types, and the soundtrack—sometimes even copied directly from American horror movies (like *Nsyuka*, which derives part of its soundtrack from the American horror classic, *Friday the 13th*). However, far from simply localizing American horror movies, Banzi worked the other way around and adapted local folk beliefs to horror videos by applying some of the typical stylistic features of the Western horror genre.[4] At this point, Nigerian films come in as sources of inspiration as well, for Banzi is also a great fan of Nollywood movies. His second horror movie, *Shumileta* (2005), for example, a film about a seductive evil female creature—half "mermaid" (*mami wata*), half vampire—that wreaks havoc on men, is partially inspired by the Nollywood classic *Karishika* (1998; Krings 2007; Böhme 2013).

Like many Nollywood movies, Banzi's horror films always feature some kind of battle between spiritual forces and ordinary men, and these battles almost always involve *waganga*—local "medicine men" or "witch doctors." Unlike his Nigerian colleagues, however, Banzi, who is a Muslim, steers clear of any references to Pentecostal belief. But the way he and other Tanzanian directors following in his footsteps depict these battles—in particular the makeup, costumes, props, and settings—demonstrates a strong Nollywood influence. Similar to Nigerian films, witch doctors and witches alike know how to use *TV asilia* (original television), as Banzi calls it, for example, using a calabash full of water to see distant things or presenting a simple piece of cloth on a wall that turns into a screen at the press of a button on a magical remote control (Böhme 2015). Similar to Nigerian films, digital special effects render visible the magical power of witch doctors as well as those of mermaids, vampires, angels, spirits, and other strange creatures. Thus, colorful electric flashes shoot from their eyes and hands or out of magical tools. Again, similar to many Nollywood films, the typical witch doctor of Bongo movies is almost always depicted half naked, dressed only in blankets (often red, white, or black in color), with strange white patterns painted on his face and body. Most often he is adorned in paraphernalia signifying "tradition," such as cowrie necklaces and various amulets, and equipped with rattles or gongs to communicate with spiritual helpers.

However, the horror genre is only a small segment of Tanzanian video film production. The majority of Bongo movies explore gender relations, and many of the early productions of this genre tried to convey the "aura" of Nollywood films as well. This was achieved by adopting the constituents of Nigerian video film style, such as mundane settings, costumes, and props, as well as a certain way of acting (probably also some aspects of camerawork, montage, and sound typical of Nigerian video). Above all,

Mtitu Game's production company Game 1st Quality, which has become a major player in Dar es Salaam since 2005, is associated with a Nigerian video film style. Most of his films are set in huge mansions peopled by characters dressed in fancy clothes and driving luxury cars while sorting out the melodramatic twists of their lives.[5] Knives or guns are their weapons and cause bloodshed among lovers and characters, who tend to shout at the tops of their voices while quarreling heatedly with one another. Although a number of these details of film style may also be associated with the Latin American telenovelas, which are broadcast daily on Tanzanian television (cf. Ratering 2014), Mtitu Game's films were perceived as "copying" Nigerian movies. This critique has been launched by cultural elites who began casting a critical eye toward the local video industry, complaining that Game's films did not reflect the Tanzanian social and cultural reality. Whatever the case may be, the effect of this mimetic appropriation is that quite a number of Tanzanian dramas look just like Nigerian dramas set in urban Tanzania. Perhaps this is one of the main reasons (despite language) Bongo movies were able to supersede Nollywood videos in Tanzanian shops, rental outlets, and video parlors in just one year. Despite the nagging critique by cultural elites, however, Mtitu Game's films were and still are best sellers, a fact that reflects their popularity. Even a cursory glance at the trailers and VCD covers of numerous other Bongo movies produced between 2006 and 2009 shows that Mtitu Game was certainly not the only producer who shaped his movies after an acclaimed foreign model (see figure 5.2).

DAR 2 LAGOS: 4 RE-UNION

In 2006, Mtitu Game took the relationship between Nollywood and the Bongo movie industry a step further and produced *Dar 2 Lagos,* a film partially shot in Nigeria and starring both Tanzanian and Nigerian actors. The story is a twenty-first-century version of the biblical parable of the prodigal son: Mr. Maganga (David E. Manento) sends Kanumba (Steven Kanumba), a young man he raised as his foster son, to Nigeria to trace and bring back his biological son, Raymond (Emmanuel Myamba), who fled to Nigeria after a serious quarrel with his father. Since Mr. Maganga

FIGURE 5.2

Tanzanian film producer Mtitu Game in Lagos, June 2006. Courtesy of
Mtitu Game.

was once married to a Nigerian woman with whom he had two daughters, he suspects his son Raymond is staying with his half-sisters, in Surulere, Lagos. Kanumba arrives in Lagos just in time to prevent Raymond and his half-sister Misoji (Mercy Johnson) from committing incest. They had been unaware of their blood relationship, as the sisters had changed their names on their arrival in Nigeria (from Tanzania, where they were born). Kanumba then becomes the object of the other (elder) sister's desire (Bimbo Akintola). She happens to be the managing director of the hotel he is staying in, but he must rebuff her advances because of his commitment to another Nigerian girl (Nancy Okeke). Finally, Kanumba is able to accomplish his task and takes Raymond back to his waiting father in Tanzania.

Unlike productions that merely mimic Nigerian video film style and participate indirectly in the fame of Nollywood, Mtitu Game's video directly conveys the "aura" of Nollywood. This was the first Tanzanian film actually shot in Nigeria, with real Nollywood actors and a Nigerian director (Femi Ogedegbe). For Mtitu Game, who strived hard to realize the film, this exemplary coming together of the two national video industries had a deeper symbolic meaning—it demonstrated that the much younger Tanzanian industry was now on more equal footing with established Nigerian filmmaking. This equalization is addressed on the DVD/VCD cover in a number of ways: the title and subtitle, *Dar 2 Lagos: 4 Re-union,* not only refer to the story of the film but also allude to its symbolic nature. Behind the letters in the title, two shaking hands are visible, each with a wristlet in the national colors of one of the two nations involved. Behind the images of the leading actors (each of which have captions indicating the actor's name and country of origin), parts of a Nigerian and a Tanzanian map can be seen, merging together as if to overcome the real distance between the two countries and industries (see figure 5.3).

A mixture of self-referentiality and self-advertisement is apparent in the film itself. It starts with a scene in a video shop in Dar es Salaam, which serves to establish the noble personality of Kanumba (who is selling video films on the street before Mr. Maganga picks him up) but also to promote other films by Game 1st Quality, and to demonstrate that Tanzanian and Nigerian video films have equal production values. Kanumba asks the shopkeeper for Nigerian and Tanzanian videos. Among the Tanzanian

FIGURE 5.3

DVD cover of *Dar 2 Lagos* (2006). Courtesy of Mtitu Game.

videos is *Johari*—a film produced by Mtitu Game—and although none of
the Nigerian videos handed over to Kanumba is introduced by the title, he
comments on at least one of them (Chinedu Nwoko's *Private Affair*) with
a smile and admits that it is "a very good one." He is handed a package of
VCDs, which he starts counting and calculates a total of sixty-three Nigerian and twenty-four Tanzanian films—a ratio of roughly two and a half
to one, which in mid-2006 (when the film was shot) was quite common
in the video shops of Dar es Salaam but which had already been reversed
about a year later.

As Mtitu Game told me, beyond its entertainment value, he had hoped
to inform Tanzanians about life in Nigeria with *Dar 2 Lagos*. Nigerians do
not have the best reputation in Tanzania, where they are typically seen
as argumentative and corrupt or as fraudsters with an inclination toward
witchcraft.[6] The film addresses these stereotypes directly in a scene in
which Kanumba talks to three of his friends about his pending trip to
Nigeria. One of them believes that Kanumba will surely meet his death
in Nigeria because the country is torn apart by religious war and witchcraft, whereas the other two contradict him, saying that Tanzania is just
as "witchcrafty" as Nigeria (the video has English subtitles): "We have
many old witches here. How many people are turning into cats here?" The
film contains several other blueprints of Nigerian life and culture, which
the Tanzanian team encountered firsthand while shooting in Lagos in
June 2006: Steven Kanumba told me, for example, that Nigerian food was
much too spicy for his taste and that Nigerians "are only after the money"
(personal interview, August 31, 2007).

After experiencing a number of difficulties in Lagos, such as harassment by the police and a three-week wait, in vain, for an actress who ab-
sconded with an advance of 3,500 U.S. dollars, the video film was eventually shot—in just one week. *Dar 2 Lagos* was released in Dar es Salaam
on November 30, 2006, with a big launch party in Diamond Jubilee Hall.
Four Nigerians, two of whom had participated in the film, actress Mercy
Johnson and director Femi Ogedegbe, were special guests. Together with
the two other Nigerians—actress Nkiru Sylvanus and actor-scriptwriter
Emmanuel France—they stayed on for several months, enjoying Mtitu
Game's hospitality and working under his tutelage on four more films.

Mtitu Game became an official member of the Producers Guild of Nigeria and registered a branch of his company as Game 1st Quality Nigeria Ltd. in Nigeria. He hoped to distribute *Dar 2 Lagos,* whose Swahili dialogue were subtitled in English, on the Nigerian market. For patriotic reasons, he also hoped to spread some knowledge about Tanzania and its national language, Swahili, to Nigerian audiences and—since Nigeria exports video films far beyond its borders—to audiences in almost every corner of the continent.

AN AMBIVALENT RELATIONSHIP

When Nollywood movies arrived in Tanzania around the turn of the twenty-first century, popular audiences enjoyed them for their mise-en-scène of an African modernity, which somehow paralleled their own life-world and were yet different enough to allow for both an identification and a fascination prompted by alterity. They praised the welcome change Nigerian films brought to the cinematographic menu offered in Tanzanian video parlors of the era, which at the time consisted mainly of American, Indian, and Chinese genre films. First and foremost, Nollywood movies were valued as African films. Cultural elites, however, were more critical of them. As elsewhere across the continent, Nollywood videos were criticized for their preoccupation with the occult and their manifold explorations into the realm of the "powers of darkness" (Krings and Okome 2013b: 9–14). In Tanzania, cases of ritual murder that occurred around the year 2000 nourished the interest of popular audiences in Nollywood films, which seemed to offer explanations for such incidents. In neighboring Kenya, the films have even been held accountable for a perceived increase in witchcraft beliefs (Ondego 2005).

Cultural production in Tanzania, notably the Bongo movie industry, mirrors these ambivalent feelings toward Nollywood videos. Claudia Böhme (2013: 328–329), who did extensive research on the Bongo movie industry during its formative years (2006–2010), explains that when Nollywood films arrived in Tanzania, they functioned as an "initial spark," encouraging young cultural entrepreneurs to try making movies of their own. As the Bongo movie industry grew, however, the relationship of Swahili video films to their Nigerian templates became more controversial. Critical voices accused local video filmmakers of a lack of creativity and cultural authenticity, and that they were producing poor-quality copies of foreign originals. The filmmakers answered by calling for a "revolution" in Tanzanian filmmaking. Part of this revolution consisted of the gradual emancipation from the Nigerian template. While some producers, notably Mtitu Game, stayed close to the foreign model for a long time, others were keen to exorcize Nollywood from their films. Böhme quotes a director who, when he discovered props on the set he considered typical of Nollywood movies, shouted at the film crew: "We don't copy the Nigerians" (327)!

The Tanzanian appropriation of Nollywood began by remediating a singular film as a serialized photo novel and by subjecting several films to the process of video narration, which is a peculiar combination of translation and commentary modeled on oral storytelling. The printed photo novel transformed the listening spectator into a reader who had to fill in the "gutter" between the panels, opening up space for the imagination. Video narration, the local variety of dubbing, did not change the basic medium of video, but added another layer of meaning to the foreign audiovisual original and in a way produced a parallel appearance of original and copy. While the remediation as a photo novel did not meet with a favorable audience and therefore was limited to only one film, dubbed Nollywood films were selling relatively well on VHS cassette (and later on VCD). However, even these could not really compete with films produced in Swahili by the emerging Bongo movie industry. Unlike in other countries, where pirated Nigerian video films constituted a serious threat to local culture industries (Fuita and Lumisa 2005; Meyer 2010), the present Tanzanian video industry has completely taken over the market niche once filled by Nigerian films. Local filmmakers were able to achieve this by first imitating Nigerian videos and later emancipating their own films from the model of Nollywood movies.

6

Branding bin Laden

THE GLOBAL "WAR ON TERROR" ON A LOCAL STAGE

"OSAMA BIN LADEN is my hero.... My wife gave birth to our third child on 15 September and I named him Osama in honour of Osama bin Laden who has proved to the world that only Allah is invincible, by exposing America to shame despite its claim of being the strongest nation on earth." This statement by a Muslim from northern Nigeria, which was recorded by a BBC correspondent in Kano in late 2001, epitomizes the cult status Osama bin Laden attained in many parts of the Islamic world in the wake of 9/11 (*BBC News* 2002). In Nigeria, posters, stickers, and T-shirts with portraits of bin Laden were already selling extraordinarily well just a few days after September 11, 2001. Later on, the wars in Afghanistan and Iraq inspired screenplays for video movies, and Hausa bards composed songs in bin Laden's praise, pledging allegiance to the new "leader of Islam" (*jagoran musulunci*) and urging their fans to wage jihad.

The emergence of this type of merchandise can be explained by the logic of the economic utilization of political events by African cottage culture industries, a phenomenon for which Walter Armbrust (2007: 8), speaking of Egyptian culture industries in particular, coined the term "politicsploitation." This, however, does not address why these products were being bought. In this chapter, I explore the communicative functions bin Laden merchandise fulfilled in Nigeria's political context between 2001 and 2003 and ferret out why they aroused so much interest in the

Muslim north, in particular. I argue that the local signification of bin Laden as a Muslim hero needs to be understood in the context of the religious revival in northern Nigeria—epitomized by the reintroduction of sharia law from 2000 onward. This has sparked conflict on the wider national level, where the predominantly Christian south met, with considerable anxiety, the quest for religious and cultural self-determination of the predominantly Muslim north. Large numbers of southerners who were working and living in the north were particularly anxious about the consequences of sharia legislation.

As elsewhere, Nigerian producers and consumers of bin Laden merchandise appropriated the al-Qaeda leader as an icon of political Islam, which could be used for purposes of boundary making (Noor 2004). I argue that this appropriation process was substantially facilitated by a transformation in Nigeria's visual public in the early 2000s, which saw a marked increase in the promotion of commercial products and religious or political ideas based on the faces of prominent figures. Due to the ubiquitous presence of this strategy of visual communication in Nigerian urban spaces, consumers of bin Laden merchandise were perfectly prepared to turn Osama bin Laden's face into an icon for a new brand of radical Islam. I read this as an attempt to evoke a powerful external identification figure for use in domestic power struggles. On the national level, references to bin Laden could be used to increase Muslim agency and bargaining power at a time when Nigeria was headed by a Christian president; on the regional level, within the Muslim north, bin Laden evoked the notion of unselfish leadership, and many of the urban poor made use of his image to remind local elites of their duty to share their wealth with the common people, just as bin Laden was believed to have done.

A word of caution in terms of the methodology and scope of this chapter seems indicated. When writing this essay, I had to overcome certain limitations of my data based on my somewhat belated entry to the field. In 2003, I carried out three months of fieldwork in Kano and Lagos (including March, when the war on Iraq was going on), but I did not have the opportunity to do research in 2001 and 2002, when the production and consumption of bin Laden merchandise reached its peak. As a consequence, I was unable to obtain a proper audience ethnography. At the time of my fieldwork in 2003, circulation and consumption of bin Laden merchandise had already dwindled. To overcome my limited data on consumers, I resorted to reading cultural products—that is, bin Laden merchandise—against the historical context of their production and consumption, relying both on academic and journalistic sources and my own acquaintance with Nigeria built over the course of several research stays between 1991 and 2003. Since I did not observe actual consumers of bin Laden merchandise in their "natural" consumption settings, I am unable to differentiate the consumers in terms of their identification with any of the numerous denominations of Islamic belief in Nigeria. In other words, though I am fully aware that Muslims in northern Nigeria are heterogeneous internally (with Sufi brotherhoods on the one hand and on the other various factions of more or less radical orthodox groups, ranging from Abubakar Gumi's Izala, to more recent currents of radical Islam), I possess a rather incomplete vocabulary with which to speak about those who bought bin Laden posters and stickers in 2001 and 2002. All I know is that they were Muslims from the north. Hence, I set myself the humble task of trying to understand why bin Laden merchandise was bought and suggesting some plausible meanings bin Laden took on in post-9/11 Nigeria.

RELIGIOUS REVERSION AND THE UTOPIA OF JUST RULE

At the time of the terrorist attacks on the United States, the campaign for a reintroduction of sharia criminal law in northern Nigeria had just reached its climax. This campaign, which had originally been initiated by Ahmed Sani, a local politician in Zamfara state, as an electoral promise in the run-up to the gubernatorial elections of 1999, developed into a veritable grass-roots movement in the following years. As a result, by 2001, twelve states in the federal republic had reformed, or were in the process of reforming, their legislatures. Already in mid-2000, Murray Last (2000) observed a millenarian atmosphere in northern Nigerian towns preparing for sharia. The common people hoped that the divine law would put an end to all evil and bring about social justice and a fundamental improvement in their living conditions, which had dramatically changed for the worse at the close of the twentieth century. General mismanagement, corruption, and criminality, which had existed previously, increased enormously during military rule.

The millenarian hopes were based on the idea that because of its divine authorship, the religious law would compel even the highest authorities to act upon the rules of divine justice. The ideal of the unselfish and just ruler—epitomized by the Prophet Muhammad and his immediate successors, the four rightly-guided caliphs—became the benchmark for the political leaders of the new millennium. About 200 years earlier, Hausaland had witnessed the emergence of such an exemplary ruler: Usman dan Fodio, the founder of the Sokoto caliphate. Today, people still remember this religious reformer as showing genuine sympathy for the worries of the common people and living a very modest life himself (Harnischfeger 2006). The discrepancy between this ideal of a just ruler and the lifestyles of many among the political elites could not have been greater at the dawn of the new millennium. The elites were known to indulge in a lavish lifestyle—distributing the religious alms tax among their clients only as they deemed fit and paying little, if any, attention to the worries and needs of the common people. Hence, most governors of the northern states met the popular call for sharia implementation with considerable reservation. Gov. Rabi'u Musa Kwankwaso, of Kano state, for example, could not show himself in public without running the risk of being verbally harassed, cursed, or even pelted with stones (Last 2000). Only when several thousand people demonstrated outside his office, the so-called governor's palace, did he eventually yield to the people's will, introducing the sharia in January 2001. Two years later, in the summer of 2003, even the emir of Kano was battered with stones in his Rolls-Royce; the incident saw protesters vent their frustration and anger because the sharia still had not produced the desired effects (Harnischfeger 2006).[1]

Meanwhile, the so-called 'yan hisba had taken up the cause of cleansing northern Nigeria of cultural practices deemed un-Islamic and immoral. The 'yan hisba are a religious police of sorts, initially composed of independently acting neighborhood groups. Subsequently, however, they were integrated into the official bureaucratic machinery of the sharia states (Last 2008). The alleged agents of moral decay included Christians from southern Nigeria who, among others, ran bars and hotels in the so-called *sabon garis,* the foreigners' quarters of northern Nigerian towns, which go back to colonial urban planning. These quarters in particular saw scenes of bloody conflict following the implementation of sharia law, as Christian migrants were made the scapegoats of decades-long mismanagement by Muslim elites. One possible explanation for the increased propensity to violence against Christian migrants during the first years of the Fourth Republic is that for many northern Nigerians, the victory of Olusegun Obasanjo, a southern Nigerian "born-again" Christian, in the presidential elections of May 1999 was tantamount to a loss of political control. Up to that point, most politicians and military rulers governing Nigeria since independence had been from the north, and they had made sure that at least the political elites of the north had a grasp on the national finances.

On the eve of 9/11, an ambivalent mood prevailed in the northern Nigerian cities; on the one hand, people were weighed down with the sheer struggle for survival; they felt marginalized in terms of national politics and anxious about the loss of cultural integrity (see also chapter 4). On the other, there was the millenarian hope that reshaping cultural practices and public life in a manner agreeable to God would help overcome these threats. The "catch images" (Diers 1997) of the attack on the World Trade Center—produced by the terrorists, who claimed to be fighting for Islam, and then disseminated by global media—came just in time to be transferred to the local interreligious and interregional lines of conflict; after all, they seemed to bear witness to the power of a potentially violent Islam. As a result, as early as the evening of September 11, 2001, there were spontaneous, exuberant demonstrations about the "victory of Islam" in the streets of Gusau, the capital of Zamfara state. In Jos, a conflict between Muslims and Christians claimed several hundred lives. The dispute was about the filling of a local political office that had been smoldering since September 9 and that was rekindled by the satellite pictures from New York and Washington (Dan Fulani and Fwatshak 2002).

In complete accordance with the American dictate, which held Osama bin Laden and the al-Qaeda network directly responsible for the attacks, the popular imagination in Nigeria, too, began to focus on Osama bin Laden. Even before the outbreak of the war in Afghanistan, representatives of the Nigerian Council of Islamic Scholars proclaimed their unreserved support for bin Laden. During Friday prayers, imams called upon the faithful to pray for their brothers in faith who were fighting the American invaders in Afghanistan (Kazaure 2001). These and similar actions can be interpreted as expressions of a strengthened sense of belonging to the *umma*, the global community of Muslims. In this context, Last (2008: 59–60) refers to a "dual citizenship" that has emerged in the Islamic world in the past decades. Religious allegiance may thus eventually transcend sentiments of national belonging. This happened by October 2001 at the latest, when Nigeria, governed by a Christian president, joined the international antiterror alliance headed by the United States. Following the outbreak of the Afghanistan war, anti-American demonstrations in Kano turned into virtual proxy wars in which Muslim protesters vented their anger over the actions of the United States by committing extreme acts of violence against members of southern Christian migrant communities living in Kano and other northern cities.

POLITICSPLOITATION AND THE VISUAL PUBLIC

The fact that the catch images of the terrorist attack were efficacious in Nigeria was a function of both the globalized news channels—such as CNN, BBC, Al Jazeera, and the internet—and the local cottage culture industries that processed the global news material at the local level and turned it into videos, posters, and stickers. While it is true that cottage culture industries are based on "small media" (Sreberny-Mohammadi and Mohammadi 1994: 20–40), their commercial logic is by no means different from that of more formalized cultural production disseminated by "big media." Cottage culture industries, too, need a steady stream of "hot" new items to sell their products on a limited market.

Within the commercial logic of popular cultural production, a topic such as 9/11, which kept the world in suspense, and a character such as bin Laden, who was perfectly suited as both an identification foil for radical Muslims and a bogeyman for Christians, were ripe for commercial exploitation. Nigeria was no exception in this respect; similar phenomena have been observed in other parts of the Islamic world as well (in Malaysia, for example; cf. Noor 2004). With reference to the commercial exploitation of anti-American and anti-Israeli sentiments by the culture industry in Egypt, in particular, comes Walter Armbrust's term "politicsploitation." The logic of politicsploitation is comparable to that of so-called exploitation movies, which exploit their viewers' "base instincts" by celebrating sex and violence. Accordingly, Muslim politicsploitation in Egypt exploited the preexisting resentment for the United States and Israel. Armbrust (2007) draws a parallel to American blaxploitation movies of the 1970s (Koven 2001). The blaxploitation genre, which targeted black audiences, featured a reversal of common stereotypes found in mainstream movies: black gangsters and pimps were thus portrayed as heroes, white policemen as villains. A very similar change of perspective is found not only in the Egyptian video clips and TV comedies analyzed by Armbrust but also in Hausa video films in which the dominant Western portrayal of world affairs is reversed: Osama bin Laden is depicted as a hero, George W. Bush as a criminal. Armbrust points out that politicsploitation must not be mistaken for propaganda because those who employ it do not use their cultural products for purposes of political persuasion; rather, they mirror sentiments shared by their audience. According to Armbrust, the products do not generate anti-Americanism. On the contrary, anti-Americanism is the precondition for their existence. Before discussing Nigerian examples of politicsploitation in greater detail, I briefly talk about the "visual public" in northern Nigeria, which was a crucial prerequisite for the emergence of bin Laden merchandise and the way it was used for communicative purposes.

The "visual public" is a concept introduced by Peter Probst (2008: 7) in an attempt to question "the Western notion of the public—or 'audience,' for that matter—[which] is primarily a verbal and acoustic one," and to focus on the visual fabric of the public instead. All forms of image-based communication constitute visual publics. Apart from television and cinema, northern Nigerian cities did not have much of a visual public before the turn of the century. Billboard advertising was moderate. Painted signboards and murals were to be found mostly in the *sabon garis,* where southern Nigerian migrants, whose visual culture differed widely, had settled. There was one notable exception, however—communication by means of stickers. Already widespread by the 1990s, these were cultivated mainly by taxi and minibus drivers. Even though there was only a limited assortment of pictorial stickers, the overall choice of motifs was broad enough to enable diverse groups of people to communicate their religious or political associations. Supporters of the Muslim orthodox Izala decorated their vehicles with the portrait of Abubakar Gumi, the founder of that movement, while the cars of Sufi brotherhood followers boasted the faces of their respective sheikhs. Youth who wanted to express their antiestablishment attitude, emblazoned their motorbikes with stickers of Muhammadu Buhari, the military ruler whose brief term in office (January 1984 to August 1985) stood for radical measures against corrupt elites. Others used stickers of their favorite Bollywood stars to express their sense of modernity. The fact that the stickers were preferentially placed on means of transport increased their circulation and visibility. The stickers became iconic representations of the attitudes of those displaying them.

In this context, facial communication is in line with a strategy of visual communication widely used particularly in propaganda and advertising. Even though there were still no "torrents of facial images" comparable to those some observers have noted for the cities of the Global North (Macho 1996: 26), I noticed a remarkable increase in the use of faces for promotional purposes in northern Nigerian towns between 2000 and 2003. Due to the spread of digital technology, the reproduction and distribution of cultural material became much cheaper at the time, which was one of the reasons the global iconic turn in cultural production became palpable in northern Nigeria as well. In addition, local cultural production, notably the video film industry, witnessed a boom around 2000 (Haynes 2000). With the emergence of "stars" in the Hausa video film industry, for example, the faces of film stars were featured prominently on promotional movie posters in an attempt to attract audiences. The booming telecommunications business significantly expanded the spaces hitherto available for billboard advertising and also capitalized on the faces of film stars, using them for the purpose of product endorsement. Political parties stopped using simple symbols as icons of their parties, as they had done in the past, but complemented their canvasing during election campaigns with the prominent display of candidates' faces on T-shirts, stickers, posters, and banners. It is safe to say that around 2001 the visual publics of

FIGURE 6.1

Portraits of Osama bin Laden on small media, Kano 2002–2003. Author's
collection.

northern Nigerian towns manifested a certain degree of "facialization"
(Macho 1996: 26). Hence, when bin Laden merchandise began to appear
shortly after September 11, its buyers and consumers were already expert
users of images for communicative purposes, and bin Laden's face was
used just as easily as portraits of sheikhs, politicians, and video movie
stars (see figure 6.1).

BIN LADEN AS POSTER BOY

Soon after 9/11, posters showing pictures of the attack and its suspected
mastermind were offered by mobile vendors all over Nigeria. Such prints,
called "calendars" or "almanacs" in Nigeria, can best be characterized
as single-sheet tabloids targeting the common people.[2] Delivering sensational and curious news from all over the world, they were published
mainly by Christian Igbo in the southern Nigerian city of Lagos (Krings
2004b). When compiling the posters, the publishers appropriated images
and text fragments from international magazines and internet sources.

Their reassemblages follow the local tradition of sign painting. Tobias Wendl (2002: 18) characterizes the aesthetics of this tradition as an "aesthetics of economy and simplicity," in which "illustrations and advertisements from newspapers, magazines and books . . . are picked up, modified in a virtuous manner, quoted, commented, and reassembled." While these appropriative practices seemed to be subversive at first glance, they did not necessarily undermine the hegemony of the global mass media or the operational logic of the news coverage. As we see, the African appropriations did indeed have the potential to reverse the inherent value judgments of the hegemonic news media they copied from. However, the calendars' logic of "pictorial journalism," which was based on catch images and symbolic representation through faces, was no different from that of the dominant mass media.[3]

Appealing to people's curiosity about and desire for the sensational, the first bin Laden posters, which appeared in print as early as September 2001, did not yet address any specific target group in terms of ethnicity or religion. Calendar publishers in Lagos told me that this nonspecific targeting aimed to reach as broad a market as possible. However, as soon as the publishers realized that there was a huge market for posters in the northern part of the country that focused exclusively on Osama bin Laden, they began to develop new motifs. Text elements that had initially been presented only in English were now supplemented by captions in Hausa. After the Afghanistan war broke out, more and more posters became exclusively dedicated to the mystery-shrouded character of Osama bin Laden. As noted, poster publishers I talked to in Lagos in 2003 referred to their work as "pictorial journalism." A close look at the manner in which the source material taken from global mass media has been rearranged and supplemented by locally produced texts and pictures reveals that some of the "selectors" (or attractors) are at work, which Niklas Luhmann (1996: 53–74) identifies as typical for the construction of reality in a newscast. Most notably, this is the predilection for conflicts and transgression of norms, and the attribution of such occurrences to individual actors. The posters reduce complex world affairs to the agonistic moment of "America versus Islam," which is boiled down further to the confrontation between Osama bin Laden and George W. Bush. Hence, the two antagonists became emblematic figures, or icons, of two opposing ideologies.

Following Luhmann's line of thinking, posters exclusively devoted to the figure of bin Laden could be interpreted as "reports" that aim at elucidating his motives and background. This becomes particularly evident at the text level. The text block "Bin Laden's brief history in English," for example, which appears on several posters, gives not only biographical data but also lists reasons for bin Laden's struggle against the United States. The pictorial representation, which takes up more space than the text, is likewise intended to illuminate the motives behind bin Laden's actions. Religious symbols, such as the Koran, prayer beads, and the Kaaba (the "holy cube" also known as "house of Allah" inside Islam's most famous mosque in Mecca), set the stage for bin Laden in the role of a God-fearing Muslim (see figure 6.2). This is complemented perfectly by photographs showing him raising his right index finger—a gesture symbolizing the Islamic credo of monotheism. However, the focus is more often on bin Laden's ability to fight and his readiness for such fighting. On calendar sheets with titles such as "Facts about Osama bin Laden," he appears variously as a pilot flying a fighter jet, a soldier leveling an assault rifle, and a fighter wearing a bandolier across his chest (see figure 6.3). As authentic images of this type were not available, the publishers resorted to photomontages, mounting images of bin Laden's head onto pictures of any fighters whose bodies happened to be in a suitable position. Poster publisher Chijioke Obi told me that he wanted to visualize bin Laden's actual power, and these montages were the only way to do it. He said everyone knew that bin Laden had an arsenal of weapons at his command, but because there were no pictures of it, they had no other recourse than photomontages.

When the war in Afghanistan sparked anti-American demonstrations in northern Nigeria that escalated into miniature proxy wars, the government ordered a ban on the sale of the posters. Police in Lagos raided publishing companies and print shops, confiscated entire editions, and arrested individual Christian publishers, leveling the ludicrous accusation that the publishers were members of al-Qaeda and had disseminated Islamist propaganda.[4] Hence, the only poster with a clear Christian message, titled "The Global Christian Problem," remained unpublished (see figure 6.4). Emeka Frank, who designed the poster, told me that he did not have it printed for fear that he, too, might be arrested. The hand-painted artwork master shows bin Laden wearing Muslim clothes and holding the

FIGURE 6.2

Poster, Lagos, 2001. Author's collection.

FIGURE 6.3

Poster, Lagos, 2001. Author's collection.

FIGURE 6.4

Unpublished bin Laden poster, Lagos, 2003. Photo by the author.

Koran and prayer beads in his hands. Next to him is a caption reading "The global terrorist and his belief." In the pitch-dark of night and illuminated by an Islamic half-moon, he is hovering above the globe from which he expels a number of Christians with karate kicks and chops. Compared to their pursuer, the Christians depicted are the size of children. Some of them are lying on the ground, surrounded by a scattering of Bibles that have dropped from their hands; others seem to be begging for mercy: "Please let there be peace since we worship one God" is another caption apparently directed at the terrorists and like-minded beholders. The lower margin of the poster instructs the reader to look up the Gospel according to Matthew, chapter 24 (verses 8–28), for an explanation of the events of 9/11. At this place in the gospel, Jesus announces his return at the end of time, warning his disciples against false prophets who will then appear in his name. The poster thus interprets 9/11 as a foreboding of the biblical apocalypse and bin Laden as a false redeemer, deceiving his followers.

BIN LADEN AND SADDAM IN VIDEO MOVIES

The Nigerian video film industry—equally prolific as the calendar business and also matching it in terms of politicsploitation—reworked the events of 9/11 in two of its movies. Both films treat the serious matter in comedies. However, they differ profoundly in terms of religious targeting: while the southern Nigerian version features a Christian worldview and anti-Muslim sentiments, its northern counterpart promotes just the reverse. In 2002, Jesus Team Productions released the video *Osama Bin La*, by southern Nigerian director Mac-Collins Chidebe. Just like many other Igbo comedies, whose simple style is reminiscent of village theater plays, the movie was made in the Igbo language, re-staging, in a sense, the global theater on a local stage. The movie's key protagonists are stock characters: an old good-for-nothing, Joshua, who spends his corpulent wife's money on palm wine and a mistress; Joshua's sidekick, Anadi, who has obscene verbal fights with his spouse; a resolute female innkeeper; a lecherous cripple; and a self-confident village chief and his councilmen. "Osama bin La" and his accomplice, Clifford, fit in perfectly with the cast of characters: they are pilferers who return to "Ozallanistan," bin La's home village, following a successful thieving spree. Bin La, who turns out to be Joshua's son, has a long beard and wears turbanlike headgear in the style of the real al-Qaeda leader. His helper, Clifford, on the other hand, is introduced as a bogeyman by his very name, alluding to Clifford Orji, the "Cannibal of Lagos."[5] The two men continue their criminal escapades in Ozallanistan, eventually "terrorizing" the villagers by extorting protection money. Just as the Village Council is on the verge of hiring a militia to remedy the problem, American soldiers arrive, ordering the village chief to hand bin La over to them within one week, as he is wanted for the attacks on the United States. At this point, the movie ends and the audience is told not to miss the upcoming sequel, *Osama vs. America*. However, because the sequel was never produced, it is likely the video was not the blockbuster Jesus Team had hoped for.

Even though the movie was made in the Igbo language, it did not go completely unnoticed in the Hausa-speaking north. Abdullahi Aliyu, the editor of the magazine *Duniyar Fim* (Film World) published in Kano, wrote an ironic comment in which he seethed indignantly about the distorted image of Osama bin Laden promoted by the movie and cited the film as an example of why northern Muslims should not allow southern Nigerian Christians to meddle in Muslim culture and religion (Aliyu 2002). In the same commentary, however, Aliyu noted with some dismay that the movie's northern counterpart, *Ibro Usama*, which was released in May 2002, was not any better; admittedly, it did not portray bin Laden in a discrediting manner—but he deemed it simply a bad movie. *Ibro Usama* has some of the typical features of Hausa *camama* videos. This slapstick genre, produced cheaply and quickly, even by northern Nigerian standards, thrives on a limited number of comedians whose acting is characterized by clownish exaggeration and the obscene. The recurring, most essential motif of these movies is the constant violation of social norms. Rabilu Musa Danlasan (aka Ibro) is the undisputed star of the genre. The face of this comedian, shown on the cover of any videocassette or disc, is sufficient to increase sales, and it is safe to assume that this inspired the producers of *Ibro Usama* to cast the cream of northern Nigerian comedians in their debut feature (the vHS cassette cover for which can be seen in figure 6.5).[6] However, when Mato na Mato, the scriptwriter of the movie, was asked by a journalist about his motives for writing the screenplay, he

FIGURE 6.5

Videocassette cover of *Ibro Usama* (2002). Author's collection.

did not mention any commercial reasons but exclusively religious ones: "[Bin Laden] is a man who loves Islam and has taught a lesson to the other nations of the world. For that reason, I thought that we should make a movie about him so that every Muslim learns what Osama is doing, in order to advance the cause of Islam" (in Barkiya 2002: 22; my translation). This statement, however, was only made after the movie had already been released.

In the run-up to making *Ibro Usama,* the very casting of comedian Ibro as bin Laden sparked religious criticism, which most likely had an impact on the final script and its realization. Besides his many fans, actor Danlasan has always had many critics. A movie made in 2000, in which he satirized the syncretistic practices of local religious scholars, incurred the wrath of that powerful profession (Adamu 2004). The movies he stars in that feature suggestive dance scenes earned him the reputation of breaching Islamic values. Even before the shooting of *Ibro Usama* began, conservative religious scholars accused Danlasan of betraying Islam, as they feared the actor might ridicule bin Laden. The religious police in Kano intervened and tried to have the movie banned by the Censorship Board before it could be released. However, the censors objected to only a few song-and-dance numbers and released the movie as soon as these had been cut out. The clerics resorted to a religious antidote and had both the movie and its lead actor publicly cursed in several mosques. When the movie came to the video shops on May 10, 2002, it initially sold exceedingly well. However, viewers were disappointed because "Ibro" appears in but a very few sequences. Moreover, Ibro as Osama bin Laden comes off as strangely monosyllabic and lacks any of the humor commonly associated with the actor. In contrast, the comedians playing George W. Bush, Kolin Fols (Colin Powell), and Tony Nakunduba (Tony Blair) are given many more opportunities to display their talent. The movie's plot unfolds mainly in interiors, where Ibro Usama's enemies are forging the alliance against terror and preparing the landing of their troops in Afghanistan. Like Ibro as bin Laden, comedian Ciroki, who plays the Taliban ambassador in Pakistan (a Muslim), does not come across as very funny. Scenes shot in outdoor locations show troops of the Northern Alliance combating the Taliban and Ibro Usama. When the Taliban appear to emerge victorious in the battles, George W. Bush wants to go into hiding. The movie ends with this cliffhanger and the audience is referred to the upcoming sequel. However, this sequel was never realized, either.

Even though Danlasan and all other comedians playing Muslim characters in the movie kept their comical talent in check, the film inevitably provoked angry reactions from some viewers. In a letter to the Hausa film magazine *Fim,* a reader vented his anger as follows:

> Why on earth does Rabilu Musa (Dan Ibro) now feel impelled to even touch on religion in this shameless manner? Does he really think God will let him go unpunished if he strikes out at one of God's servants? There are people who have amassed riches without allowing themselves to get corrupted by these, who have dedicated themselves completely to God, His Prophet, and His religion; are we supposed to let such people be made into stuff for Hausa comedies? Just in case you don't know what I am talking about: I am referring to *Ibro Usama.* By God, if he continues to meddle with religion, we will beseech God to repudiate him immediately! (Aminu 2002; my translation)

Eventually, the controversy died down. As one of numerous past and future episodes of Danlasan's transgression of public morals, however, it added fuel to the negative image he had among conservative clerics, which would eventually land him in jail in 2009 (see chapter 4). In 2003, however, during the height of the war on Iraq, another director made a very similar film with Danlasan. This time the comedian played Saddam Hussein (the poster for the movie can be seen in figure 6.6). New director Kabeer Umar intended to present a role model to his audience—he envisioned Saddam Hussein as a brave fighter in a seemingly hopeless situation (personal interview, March 2003). In *Ibro Saddam*, the late comedian Lawal Alhassan Kaura (aka Kulu), who is featured as Ibro's sidekick in many *camama* movies, plays George W. Bush, or rather "George Kulu Bush." *Ibro Saddam* intentionally reverses the attributions of friend and foe in the dominant discourse of the West. It is not Saddam Hussein who is presented as the antithesis incarnate of the civilized world but his rival George W. Bush. The director told me that he took George W. Bush's last name literally, translating it according to West African cosmology, in which the "bush"—the wilderness inhabited by wild animals, spirits, and "pagan" people—is the antithesis of the human moral universe. Correspondingly, the film opens with a sequence in which Ibro Saddam comes across George Kulu Bush as a lost and uncivilized pagan child in the "bush." Any bid to civilize the ungrateful "bush man," however, is doomed to failure. Despite all attempts by Saddam at educating George Kulu Bush, the latter cannot shake off his origins—a Nigerian variant of "the name says it all." Saddam, on the other hand, is portrayed as a just ruler and upright Muslim. George Kulu Bush eventually travels to the United States, where he even succeeds in assuming the presidency. As president, he turns two prison inmates into his closest members of staff: Donald Rumsfeld, who is said to serve a sentence for multiple murder, and Colin Powell, imprisoned for rape. When the trio set about concocting war plans jointly with the United Nations (UN), it becomes apparent that access to oil is the real reason for the offensive; arms inspections to be enforced by the UN serve espionage and war preparation purposes.[7] There is a great scene in the movie, set in a Nigerian factory, where Hans Blix, the head of the UN Inspection Commission, played by comedian Ciroki, is using a measuring tape and a stethoscope in his search for weapons of mass destruction; he does not find any. George Kulu Bush therefore travels to Iraq in person and tells his rival: "Your sharp incisor alone is enough of a weapon to justify war," which wryly highlights the determination of the United States to wage war. This movie, too, is still awaiting a sequel.

FIGURE 6.6

Poster for *Ibro Saddam* (2003). Author's collection.

There are various reasons the logic of politicsploitation was successful with poster and sticker production but not in the marketing of video
movies. In Nigeria, video movies sell through cassette/CD covers, poster
promotion, and word-of-mouth advertising. Neither the southern bin
Laden video nor its northern counterpart lived up to the promise of its
cover, because in both movies the bin Laden character appears only in a
few sequences. Moreover, both movies have very low production values,
even by local standards. In northern Nigeria, matters were made worse
by the fact that the comedic treatment of the subject, and in particular
the portrayal of bin Laden as a buffoon, was considered sacrilegious. The
whole fuss preceding the movie's release had doubtlessly aroused a great
deal of interest, and when it eventually came out, it sold well in the first
week; however, sales soon nosedived when word got around that Ibro in
the role of bin Laden was by no means at his best.

The reversal of the dominant Western perspective on international
political events is most aptly realized in *Ibro Saddam*. Even though the
movie built on a consensus apparently existing among some factions of
the northern Nigerian populace, it was a box-office failure, and no sequel
was made, and this was the case with the two other comedies as well.
On the one hand, the movie was released too late; when it came out in
September 2003, it had already been overtaken by reality—Iraq had been
defeated, and Saddam Hussein, who went into hiding, was no longer suitable as a hero. On the other, Nigerian Muslims were reluctant to accept
Hussein as an icon of Islamic religiosity because his public image—unlike
that of bin Laden—was missing most of the typical markers of a devout
Muslim.

ENCODING/DECODING BIN LADEN

The Nigerian signification of bin Laden between 2001 and 2003 involved four different "actors": bin Laden himself, or rather al-Qaeda's
media production house, As-Sahab; CNN & Co., who disseminated bin
Laden's iconic self-stagings; Nigerian media producers, who reassembled
these images and spiced them up to cater to certain audiences; and last
but not least, the local consumer, who decoded the images encoded by the

first three actors according to personal conviction. Al-Qaeda's media machinery staged bin Laden as a belligerent, holy warrior, unselfishly committed to fighting the cause of the Muslim plight. In bin Laden's iconic self-stagings, an AK-47 automatic rifle and a camouflage uniform served as visual synecdoches for bellicosity. The Nigerian poster publishers added numerous types of other weapons—all the way to airplanes featuring bin Laden as a pilot or commander-in-chief. For Nigerian audiences, bin Laden in uniform referenced a number of "strong men" whose portraits on stickers and posters had circulated before; among them domestic military rulers, such as Murtala Mohammed, Muhammadu Buhari, Ibrahim Babangida, and Sani Abacha, as well as foreign dictators, such as Muammar al-Qaddafi and Saddam Hussein. The latter had already been quite popular at the time of America's first Gulf war in 1991. I remember the merchandise for sale at Kano's central market at the time: Qaddafi posters and locally produced calabashes, which were decorated with carved and painted portraits of Hussein. Some of the young people I spoke with back then viewed Qaddafi and Saddam as anti-capitalist, anti-imperialist social rebels who fought against the economic and cultural hegemony of the West on behalf of the poor and marginalized of the world. This would somehow relate the two dictators to bin Laden, who was viewed in the same light about a decade later. On the smaller national level, domestic military dictators became identification figures for similar reasons. All of them were, or still are, Muslims hailing from the north, who—while ruling the country with an iron hand—ensured the north's political dominance over the predominantly Christian south, which many northern Nigerians feel is better kept in check.

Al-Qaeda's media machinery was equally careful in crafting bin Laden's public image as a righteous Muslim. This was also accomplished metonymically by way of visual synecdoches. Both the terrorist's iconic self-stagings and the Nigerian merchandise frequently show him wearing a turban and caftan; Koran, prayer beads, long beard, and the raised index finger of his right hand (as a gestural profession of faith) signify deep religiosity. The iconography of these pictures has parallels to visual representations of prominent, late spiritual leaders venerated in northern Nigeria for decades. These include Sheikh Ibrahim Niasse, the Senegalese *muqaddam* (teacher) of the Tijaniyya brotherhood; Sheikh Nasiru Kabara, the

Nigerian governor of the Qadiriyya brotherhood; and Sheikh Abubakar Gumi, the founder of the fundamentalist Iszala reform movement. Stickers featured the late Ahmadu Bello, who was a great-grandson of Caliph Usman Dan Fodio and officiated as prime minister of the Northern Region from 1954 to 1966; because of his qualities as a politician and his unselfish commitment to Islam, he is still revered as a political and religious icon. The degree to which the signification of bin Laden overlapped with that of these local religious icons is nicely illustrated by a printed sheet combining several bin Laden stickers, with a sticker showing Ahmadu Bello (see figure 6.7).

Another element of bin Laden's iconic (and acoustic) self-staging—the image of the ascetic religious reformer—did not go unnoticed in northern Nigeria. In his analysis of bin Laden's rhetoric, Navid Kermani (2001: 1) refers to a staged humility: "[It is] precisely this eager humbleness of expression that aims at touching the hearts of the fellow believers. Whenever [his] garb and the location chosen for a video are supposed to create a *prophetic aura*, the asceticism of [his] language picks up the thread of the military and political inferiority of the early Muslims for which they made up manifoldly, however, thanks to the purity of their faith" (italics mine). Bin Laden's retreat into the mountains of Afghanistan, which evokes associations with the Prophet Muhammad's historical "exile" (*hijra*), combined with a seemingly unselfish relinquishment of the wealth accumulated

FIGURE 6.7

Detail of stickers showing Osama bin Laden flanking Ahmadu Bello, Kano, 2003. Author's collection.

before—all this was in stark contrast to the conduct of the Nigerian elites, who cultivated a luxurious lifestyle behind walls reinforced with barbed wire. Bin Laden's contempt for the Saudi Arabian establishment echoed the rebellious attitudes of young hotheads toward the domestic elites, whose privileges were believed to have been abolished when the sharia was reintroduced. In that respect, bin Laden served as the ideal example of a righteous Islamic leader who commits himself to the Muslim community and uses his fortune for its benefit. Students from an Islamic school in Kano told a journalist that they thought bin Laden was a "good leader" because he was "uncorrupted" and did "not want anything for himself" (Wiedemann 2006: 7). I got a similar comment on bin Laden's relevance from Abubakar Aminu, the critic of the *Ibro Usama* movie I quoted previously above. He explained: "As you well know, Osama is rich; and yet he has abandoned money and his pleasant life in order to aid religion and to support people in the whole world in their struggle against oppression by the Americans and the Jews—for example, in Palestine, Iraq, Afghanistan, and elsewhere" (email, August 16, 2003; my translation).

According to Murray Last (2008: 41), Muslim ideas about the Last Days still have some currency in northern Nigeria. Such beliefs include the appearance of the *Mahdi*, a messiah who is to herald the beginning of the apocalypse and help the faithful triumph over the enemies of Islam. At the end of the nineteenth century, this notion of the apocalypse had a powerful impact on the Sokoto caliphate. At that time, thousands of people who interpreted colonial conquest as an augury of the imminent end of the world set out east toward Sudan, where the Mahdi was believed to have made his appearance in the person of the political and religious leader Muhammad Ahmad. In conversations I had with friends in Kano in 2003, some were pondering whether the attacks of September 11 should be interpreted as premonitions of an imminent apocalypse. While bin Laden was not explicitly referred to as the *Mahdi* of the Last Days, I think that for some, he at least served as a "surrogate prophet" of sorts (cf. Furnish 2002).

In 1999, when Olusegun Obasanjo, a "born-again" Christian from southern Nigeria, became the country's president, many northerners felt politically marginalized. At the same time, there was a dearth of political icons that could adequately represent the northern quest for self-determination (which was associated with the reintroduction of sharia) vis-à-vis the south. For lack of local faces, bin Laden was appropriated as a symbol of political and religious aplomb—if not by all, at least by those who bought bin Laden merchandise. Admittedly, there were stickers showing the face of Ahmed Sani, the governor of Zamfara state, who had sparked the sharia debate in 1999 and was later proclaimed *mujadidi* (religious reformer; Last 2008: 41). But Sani was a civilian and therefore did not possess any militaristic qualities. On the other hand, bin Laden's public image combined war and religion. That is, he exhibited qualities which, to this point, had been allotted to two different categories of northern Nigerian identification figures—domestic dictators, with the power and violence they once wielded, and religious leaders, with their spiritual rallying of the flocks.

IMAGES OF BIN LADEN AS MESSAGES

From 2001 to 2002, images of bin Laden were used in northern Nigeria for communicating religious and political messages on a number of levels. First of all, those who affixed such stickers and posters to their motorcycles, cars, shop walls, and homes expressed an awareness of belonging to the global community of believers as well as their approval of political Islam and its radicalization—which meant an association with bin Laden in particular. This key message was the basis for two additional messages directed at two different categories of audiences inside and outside the Muslim community of northern Nigeria. Addressees *inside* the community were the local elites who were expected to make a far greater personal commitment and give their wealth to the community. Until then, none of them had endeavored to do so. This referenced bin Laden as an exemplary model of a pious and unselfish leader, qualities most Nigerians missed in their own leaders. Identifying with bin Laden meant expressing a critique of the elite lifestyle in the name of religious orthodoxy, which implicitly referred to bin Laden's fight against Saudi Arabia's ruling dynasty. Young men used images of bin Laden to communicate their radicalism and their dissatisfaction with the general conditions they found themselves in, just as a generation earlier had done with stickers of General Buhari and Sheikh Abubakar Gumi. Addressees *outside* the Muslim community were

Nigerian Christians hailing from the south. Users of bin Laden merchandise thus communicated their determination to continue with the social and cultural transformation of the northern states implied by the reintroduction of sharia law. In other words, bin Laden images became symbolic tools of boundary making within Nigerian ethno-religious politics. In this context, it makes sense to remember that at the turn of the century, Nigerian visual publics transformed and expanded considerably. With the spread of video, satellite TV, the internet, and advertising billboards, the logic of visual communication gained more and more ground in Nigerian urban spaces (Ukah 2004, 2008). Wherever this is the case, Muslims must face a problem when competing against Christians in communicating their religious identification. As I have argued herein, one of the central features of promotional visual communication involves associating consumer goods or ideational products (such as religions) with faces, which is an important tool of branding. In contrast to Islam, Christianity has a rich tradition of iconizing religious figures, which enables not only the believers to see their religious credo reflected by portrayals such as Jesus Christ, the Virgin Mary, St. Paul, and numerous other figures, but also to outwardly communicate their religious identification. Since this is impossible for Muslims due to the prohibition of images in Islam, "surrogate prophets" need to be found. Within the Nigerian visual public from 2001 to 2002, bin Laden served this communicative function perfectly.

Of course, no faithful Muslim would have called bin Laden explicitly a "surrogate prophet," as this would immediately conjure up connotations of blasphemy. By the same token, it is unlikely that Nigerian users of bin Laden images, if asked directly, would have subscribed to the communicative functions I mention. Most likely, such questions would have elicited no more than quite general responses, such as, "I like Osama because he tells the truth," which was a motorbike owner's reply to a journalist asking why he had put a bin Laden sticker on his vehicle (Doyle 2001: 2). One of the differences between visual and verbal communication is visual communication can be much more opaque and ambiguous than its verbal or written equivalent. Whoever puts a sticker displaying bin Laden's portrait on a motorbike is communicating a nonverbal message; moreover, since images are polyvalent, the motorcyclist cannot be held responsible for what gets communicated. This holds true for the symbolic

communication of politico-religious radicalism—be it directed at the local Muslim elites or Christian migrant laborers—and also for the potentially idolatrous stylization of bin Laden into a "surrogate prophet."
Both significations are easily veiled by the less controversial expression
of belonging to a global community of faith, which can be communicated
by bin Laden stickers as well.

As a trademark of radical Islam, Osama bin Laden has joined the
ranks of global politico-religious icons. Global mass media reproduced
bin Laden's face millions of times and because only a limited number of
photos were available, time and again showing the same attributes (beard,
turban, caftan, or camouflage jacket), he also has a high degree of brand
recognition. As an icon of politico-religious radicalism, bin Laden may be
located halfway between Jesus Christ and Che Guevara, whose antithetic
meanings he seems to combine. Both Nigerian popular culture and the
global art scene have discovered bin Laden's resemblance to conventional
portrayals of Christ already.[8] His affinity with the antiestablishment icon
Che Guevara, however, seems to have been realized so far only by clothes
vendors in Thailand. Islamic studies scholar Farish Noor (2004: 198) reports visiting a Thai market where bin Laden T-shirts were on sale beside
Che Guevara T-shirts. When Noor asked the Muslim clothes vendor who
that guy was with the beret and beard, pointing to Guevara, the man replied: "Osama's brother, of course!"

7

Master and Mugu

ORIENTALIST MIMICRY AND CYBERCRIME

ON FEBRUARY 14, 2009, I received an unsolicited email message offering me a once-in-a-lifetime chance to get rich. It read, in part: "I am
Barrister Gerry Meyer, the attorney at law to Late Michael Krings, a national of your country, and a gold merchant here in Republic of Benin
West Africa. Herein after shall be referred to as my client. On the 27th of
May 2004, my client, his wife and their only child were involved in a car
accident along Sagbama express-road. All occupants of the vehicle unfortunately lost their lives." I was further informed that the late Michael
Krings left a huge deposit with the "Banque Atlantique Benin," which
needed to be cleared soon lest it fall into government hands. The barrister
continued:

> Since I have been unsuccessful in locating the relatives for over two years
> now I seek your consent to present you as the next of kin of the deceased
> since you have the same last name so that the proceeds of this account
> valued at $18.5 million dollars can be paid to you and then you and me can
> share the money. 50% to me and 50% to you. I will procure all necessary
> legal documents that can be used to back up any claim we may make. All I
> require is your honest cooperation to enable us seeing this deal through. I
> guarantee that this will be executed under a legitimate arrangement that
> will protect you from any breach of the law.

I never replied to barrister Gerry Meyer. I had had email exchanges, however, with a number of cyber scammers who were working with comparable "formats" even before I received his proposal.

In this chapter, I focus on Nigeria-related advance-fee fraud. Unsolicited email messages suggesting "Urgent business proposals" or "100 percent risk-free" transfers of several millions of hard currency are familiar to most users of electronic mail around the world who may find such proposals in their in-boxes almost every day. Their authors operate in the guise of the sons or widows of African ex-dictators, high government officials, managers of national banks or ministers responsible for natural resources, lawyers, and even Nigeria Police Force. Invariably, such emails refer to vast sums of money available for transfer into the addressee's bank account. He or she is offered a fair share of the money as recompense for his or her assistance. Enticed by the prospect of a once-in-a-lifetime chance to get rich quick, the victim is then lured into paying advance fees that invariably arise in the guise of fictitious taxes and transfer costs or bribes to fabricated officials. Getting their hands on this money, which flows from Europe or America to Africa, and not in the opposite direction, as suggested in the seductive emails, is the fraudsters' ultimate aim. My main interest in this chapter is to gain an understanding as to how the "Yahoo Boys," as the scammers are referred to in Nigerian popular discourse, operate.

I argue that scammers deliberately mimic orientalist notions of Africa when crafting their emails. This argument is inspired by Jan Beek (2007), who suggests that the scam letters are built on stereotypical Western images of Africans, and also draws on Andrew Smith's (2009) textual analysis of 550 such emails. On closer scrutiny, many scam letters turn out to tie in with Western representations of Africa as perpetuated by news broadcasters and other genres of dominant global mass media. The mimicry of such representations is one of the strategies scammers use to induce credibility in their Western marks. What is involved here is a special case of contact and copy, in which the copy is not only used to evoke its original (the common Western imagination of Africa) but actually turns against those who are associated with the "sphere" of the original. Other copies, such as forged bureaucratic paperwork and documents relating to international business procedures, also play an important role in the subsequent course of such scams. For the scammers to succeed, the copies must be as faithful to their originals as possible. By providing visual evidence in support of false claims, such bogus copies are important tools in the context of the fraudsters' strategies of persuasion. This conscious manipulation of the deceptive effects of visual evidence links advance-fee fraud, targeted at Westerners, not only to local forms of confidence tricks directed at Nigerians themselves but also to the sphere of magic and ritual. Hence in this chapter, I outline a tentative genealogy of Nigerian fraud, which is based on the same psychology and operational logic as magical performances.

Driven by a desire to look behind the letters and to find out more about the mysterious Yahoo Boys, I conducted email and chat room interviews with four cyber scammers and exchanged emails with a few more. This approach was inspired by email interviews conducted by a self-proclaimed anti-scamming activist who posed as a reporter with the pseudonym Rick Hunter (2011) and offered 5,000 U.S. dollars per interview. Like Rick Hunter, I sent out an interview request to approximately 200 email addresses of scammers collected in February 2008. Unlike Hunter, however, I did not assume a false identity and offered payment of only one hundred euros per completed questionnaire or online interview. Moreover, I actually paid my four respondents for answering my questions. Although admittedly problematic, in both ethical and methodological terms, my interviews allowed me not only to draw a tentative picture of the social organization of a veritable industry based on cybercrime but also to recount the scammers' own perspectives on their illicit craft. Additional information gathered by Hunter, Daniel Jordan Smith (2007), and two journalists (Buse 2005; Dixon 2005), who succeeded in conducting face-to-face interviews with scammers, enrich my own data.[1]

NIGERIAN FRAUD AND ITS ORIGINS

The fortunes offered in Nigerian scam emails are invariably explained as originating from illegal sources. Thus, Mariam Abacha, widow of Nigeria's late military head of state, Gen. Sani Abacha, offers 25 percent of "the sum of 36.2. million USD (Thirty six million, two hundred thousand)," which she intends "to use for investment purposes outside Nigeria and hopefully in your country," and further explains that she received this huge sum of money "from one of the various payback contract deals I arranged during my late husband's regime, this one in particular, from the Russian firm that handled our country's multibillion dollar Ajaokuta steel plant construction." Such emails are of course intended to entice their recipients and represent initial attempts at establishing a hook for confidence tricks, which are also known as 419 (four-one-nine) scams and are named after the relevant section of the Nigerian criminal code. A recipient who shows interest in such a "business proposal" will sooner or later be confronted with demands for fictitious fees that need to be paid before the money can be released. After the payment of a first fee (usually through a money transfer service, such as Western Union or Money Gram), additional fictitious fees arise repeatedly until the victims finally realize that advance-fee fraudsters have duped them. Their losses may well amount to several hundred, often thousands, and sometimes even hundreds of thousands of dollars. "It's like being a gambler who throws good money after bad—the deeper you get in the more reluctance you have to back out" (James Caldwell, U.S. Secret Service, in Glickman 2005: 468). Average losses per victim amount to 50,000 U.S. dollars (Peel 2006: 5), but the biggest single loss ever reported was 242 million U.S. dollars, paid by a senior official of Brazilian Banco Noroeste, who was led to believe that his bank would finance the building of the new national airport at Abuja (Basel Institute on Governance 2007). In 2009 alone, the total losses incurred by the victims of such scams were estimated to have reached a new peak of more than 9 billion U.S. dollars (Ultrascan 2010).

Despite its strong ties with Nigeria and expatriate Nigerians, advance-fee fraud is not a Nigerian invention. Its origins are, in fact, European. The so-called Spanish prisoner scam, which is said to have originated in the sixteenth century, could well be described as a primary script of letter-initiated advance-fee fraud. This early version of the format involved a fictitious captive of Philip II of Spain, an English nobleman, who pleaded for bail in his letters to the English gentry and promised in exchange a generous reward for his release. The French Revolution and World War I provided other backdrops for updated versions of this fraud scheme (Edelson 2006; Seltzer n.d.).

Although Nigerians may not have invented fraud, they have certainly contributed to its honing and perfection. Most observers of 419 scams locate the roots of the current phenomenon in Nigeria to the late 1970s and early 1980s. Ironically, foreign, and by and large Western, companies played an important part in laying the foundation on which 419 scammers would later build their enticing legends. During the Shehu Shagari administration (1979–1984), corruption became deeply embedded in the Nigerian economy. The oil boom years had brought petrodollars into the national purse, money that was used, in part at least, for large-scale infrastructure projects. This facilitated "kill-and-divide" practices—the awarding of contracts by corrupt government officials to companies or individuals under secret agreements that included "certain percentages of the contractual amount as commission" (Tive 2006: 14). Nigerian and foreign contractors conspired with corrupt government officials to loot the country's economy through such shady deals. Many of these contracts were awarded but never executed, others were executed but "over-invoiced," a practice that involved sharing the difference between the actual costs and the costs listed in the invoice between the contractor and his contract-awarding partner in a so-called "payback deal." Money transfer–style 419 emails typically refer to such practices to explain the origins of the huge sums of money referred to.

When the economic crisis of the 1980s set in, the petrodollars of the earlier decades had produced not only a generation of well-educated young Nigerians who lacked adequate job opportunities but also a number of dismissed civil servants. The latter were former employees of government institutions, such as the Central Bank of Nigeria and Nigerian National Petroleum Corporation, and they were well versed in the practices their former bosses had used in the past to siphon off Nigeria's wealth with the assistance of foreigners. According to Simon (2009: 7), these former office workers were the first Nigerians to send out advance-fee fraud letters to foreigners. They used the same schemes as previously used by their bosses, "albeit with the intention of defrauding their 'business partners.'" When they received these offers and became aware of Nigeria's shadow economy, foreign businesspeople sensed the opportunity to make easy money—even without the detour of building infrastructure in Nigeria—

and purportedly responded enthusiastically. Simon quotes a popular anecdote among Nigerian scammers. In the early days of advance-fee fraud, when scammers would "send out ten letters 'requesting assistance' for transferring money abroad, they would receive 12 responses signifying interest" (8). Therefore, without ignoring the agency of Nigerians, I find it useful to keep in mind that from the outset, European and American businesspeople played some part in laying the groundwork for Nigeria-related cybercrime.

A CYBERCRIME INDUSTRY

Over the past thirty years, the magnitude of 419 activity picked up the pace, not only in keeping with the decline of the Nigerian economy caused mainly by looting military dictators and the hardships of World Bank–imposed structural adjustment programs that left thousands of aspiring young men without jobs but also thanks to the spread of new information and communication technologies. The history of 419—its transformation from a confidence trick based on a few type-written letters posted around 1980 to "a globe-girdling blizzard of instantaneous importunings" (Glickman 2005: 473) in the wake of the digital revolution around 2000—provides a powerful example of how new media technologies are appropriated within specific social environments and adapted by their users to meet their very specific needs. Internet, email, and mobile telephone technology made scamming a lot cheaper, faster, and, through the anonymity offered by these technologies, even safer for individual scammers. Hence, technology broadened the scope of 419 exponentially (Simon 2009). Experienced scammers were able to transfer and adapt their knowledge to the new communicative environment, which was made up of computer-savvy newcomers whose numbers grew by the day. Thus, the internet and email literally "democratized" scamming.

Men dominate the practice of advance-fee fraud. It is carried out both by scammers working alone and by hierarchically organized groups. At the top of such groups is a "chairman"; at the bottom are so-called "boys," the majority of whom appear to be in their twenties. The boys are responsible for the large-scale dispatch of the emails, a process referred to as "bombing." This is carried out mostly in ordinary internet cafés but sometimes in offices set up especially for this purpose (John Kuti, personal interview, February 24, 2008).[2] Daniel Jordan Smith (2007) estimates that in 2004, around one-fifth of all the computer terminals in average-sized Nigerian internet cafés were occupied at any given time by young people involved in 419. For Smith's, Hunter's, and my own informants, 419 was a full-time occupation, at which they worked up to twelve hours a day. The recipients' email addresses are sought either manually on the internet, collected using special software or purchased from internet providers for a small fee. If the scammers work in groups, the chairman pays the boys' internet costs (Fred Walker, personal interview, March 4, 2008). The emails are often sent at night because the internet cafés offer reduced nighttime rates. The rate of response from "clients," who are also referred to by the Yoruba term *mugu* (fool), is around 2 percent. "When you get a reply, it's 70% sure that you'll get the money," one scammer claims (Dixon 2005: 3). The boys, however, do not necessarily themselves reply to the positive responses received from potential victims; instead, they hand them over to more experienced group members higher up in the hierarchy. If a scamming attempt is successful, the profit is supposed to be divided in a ratio of seventy to thirty between the chairman and the boy. However, the boys are often left empty-handed, as they in turn are cheated by their bosses and never find out whether a "client" they landed was successfully defrauded. For this reason, sooner or later the boys try to defraud "clients" themselves and go into business on their own.

The different types of scamming genres are known as formats. Most of the scammers work with formats that they did not invent themselves. The scammers I contacted, who claimed to have composed their email letters themselves, provided terse and vague replies to my question about how they came up with ideas for new formats: "through normal conversation," or "ideas are gotten from all walks of life" (Fred Walker, email, February 25, 2008). In fact, the formats circulate among the scammers and are updated, adapted to new circumstances, and constantly modified as to their details. This also explains the significant qualitative discrepancies observed in the emails. Some betray major formal weaknesses and substantive inconsistencies (Blommaert and Omoniyi 2006). The style and usage in others would suggest that their authors have considerable practice in bureaucratic correspondence. "Like the one I once worked with. He is a top government man in this present regime and he belongs to the Federal House of Representatives; he is good in making such fabricated write-ups and when I left him I was able to know how it is done and I started writing mine" ("Vanity," quoted in Hunter 2011: 12). The few famous cases of convicted high-level 419 scammers, such as Fred Ajudua, a Lagos-based lawyer (Buse 2005), and Emmanuel Nwude, the former director of the Nigerian Union Bank (Peel 2006), bear witness to the fact that 419-related activities are also practiced in supposedly respectable social circles. However, even the so-called Yahoo Boys are anything but school dropouts. "Contrary to popular belief," wrote a certain Davis Pui, who declined to participate in my interviews, "people that do these things are mostly graduates with knowledge of social engineering and networking, I am a BSC holder in one of the famous universities in Nigeria" (email, February 15, 2008). His assessment of correspondents' level of education corroborates both those of my informants and Hunter and Daniel Jordan Smith. The scammers include qualified lawyers, holders of bachelor's degrees (in information technology and geography, for example), and secondary school graduates.

Expatriate Nigerians have long helped high-level scammers internationalize their business. "The fraudsters here have contacts in America who wrap up the job over there," said Samuel, a former scammer from Lagos interviewed by *Los Angeles Times* reporter Robyn Dixon (2005: 3). "For example, the offshore people will go to pose as the Nigerian ambassador to the U.S. or as government officials. They will show some documents: This has presidential backing, this has government backing. And you will be convinced because they will tell you in such a way that you won't be able to say no." According to Samuel, his former boss, a scammer called Shepherd, had seven Nigerians working for him in the United States, including four graduates in psychology (4). Back home in Nigeria, not only do the chairmen and their boys profit from scamming but so do an equally large number of people who supply the scammers with counterfeit documents, bogus websites, and the like. The cybercrime industry feeds thousands or, more likely, tens of thousands in Nigeria alone.

Despite the growing attention attracted by and knowledge of Nigeria-related advance-fee fraud in the Global North, the scammers are not running out of business. The simplest but nonetheless most efficient strategy is to maximize output through "mass-bombing": sending neutrally addressed formats to as many people as possible. Another strategy is to customize such formats to individual addressees, like the email I received from barrister Gerry Meyer of Cotonou. This method involved gathering individual email addresses through search engines, yellow pages on the web, and company websites, and then feeding them manually into email programs by copying and pasting. This was a time-consuming process and necessitated the modification of the format each time a new addressee was inserted (Igwe 2007). To speed up this process, scammers used a combination of different media and software, including the chat program ICQ and its search tool "people search":

> During the day, they would watch foreign TV shows and documentaries and read foreign magazines and newspapers, scouting for names of victims. At night, they would invade all the cyber cafés with lists of names. They would open their ICQ, type in a name, choose an age range, and all e-mail addresses bearing that name would appear. . . . A respondent told me that ICQ was a place where one could find "real *mugus*." (Igwe 2007: 34)

With the help of email extractors—programs that extract email addresses from portions of text copied from the internet, such as the lists obtained from ICQ—lists of plain email addresses of people bearing the same names could be produced and then copied and pasted into an email program. This enabled the scammers to combine "mass-bombing" with customized formats using individual names.

Another reaction to the increased attention to 419 scams is the creation of new formats, such as lottery scams, charity scams, and romance scams, which no longer refer to Nigeria, or even Africa, but to many other places around the globe (Igwe 2007: 76–85). Despite this textual shift away from Nigeria on the surface of the scam letters, and although advance-fee fraud is spreading around the world at a considerable rate with the result that dubious unsolicited business proposals are also sent from computers located in Europe, the United States, and elsewhere, at the time of my research in 2008, two-thirds of the emails still originated in West Africa, most notably Nigeria (D. J. Smith 2007: 39–40).

MIMICRY AND OTHER SCAMMING STRATEGIES

According to Nigerian popular belief, it is the lure of easy money that makes recipients of 419 letters fall for the scam. While there may be some truth to this argument, it downplays the agency of the authors who craft the scam letters with the help of rhetorical strategies. Based on a close reading of about 550 scam emails, Andrew Smith (2009) suggests that their effectiveness in inducing credibility lies in the fact that they rely on cunning mimicry of the common forms of the Western representation of Africa. Referring to a phrase extracted from a 419 email, Smith (2009: 32–33) contends: "These scams rely upon their ability . . . to speak in the context of the stories 'you might have heard' about Africa." This holds true not only for the news content and documentaries broadcast by CNN and the BBC via satellite television, insists Smith, but also for Western feature films and novels set in Africa. Moreover, such material not only shapes and represents the common Western perspective on Africa but also the seemingly "natural" relationship between Africans and Westerners. Feature films like *King Solomon's Mines, Out of Africa, Hotel Rwanda,* and *Blood Diamond,* all of which circulate in Africa as well, continue to present stereotypes about Africans and the roles they are supposed to play vis-à-vis Europeans. Glickman (2005: 364) notes that "scammers are playing on a racist stereotype: that Africans are childlike, intellectually unsophisticated, innocent in business ways, and probably corrupt." Within this logic, an apparently naive and backward African who stumbles on a huge sum of money and does not know what to do with it, comes as no surprise and it may appear only "natural" that he should seek the assistance of a European or American to invest this money abroad (Peel 2006; A. Smith 2009). One may even question with Glickman whether emails containing an above-average number of misspellings are composed with the deliberate intention of instilling a sense of superiority in their recipients. In other words, what those who write the scam letters do—either consciously or intuitively—is mimic Western orientalist notions about Africa and apply these within their rhetorical strategies. This orientalist mimicry serves to instill credibility and lull the victims into a false sense of security. If the story presented to a mark remains within the framework of what he or she already knows about Africa and Africans, why should he or she be suspicious?

Hence, a number of emails depict Africa as a place where strange customs abound; for example, this is an email I received from Saratu Ouattara in Burkina Faso:

> Dearest one
>
> I am writing to seek your partnership in the investment of my inherited fund (USD$17.5M) from my late father who died mysteriously last year. It was very evident that he was poisoned to death. In my culture, when a man dies without a mail [*sic*] child, the brothers share his property leaving both the wife and the daughters empty, they took [everything] including the house we lived in. This is the exact case with me as I am the only daughter of my father. I lost my mother when I was barely a year old and my father refused to re-marry another wife because he felt solely responsible for my mother's death. (February 2, 2010)

The writer, who pretends to be a woman, obviously mimics the Western discourse of gender equality while tugging at the heartstrings of potential victims by relating a touching story about misery and orphanhood. As Andrew Smith (2009: 35) notes, scammers sometimes deliberately "speak with the voice of the figure who mediates between an unfamiliar local reality and a Western reader, and who gives their reader knowledge that is tacitly empowering." This observation helps to link Smith's initial interpretation of 419 emails as mimicry of Western representations of Africa to that of his namesake Daniel Jordan Smith (2007), who reads such emails as popular cultural texts containing local interpretations of corruption in Nigeria and beyond. I suggest both readings are valid. Scam letters contain local interpretations of African social reality *and* the mimicry of Western representations of African reality precisely because they need to connect two systems of knowledge—that of those penning the letters and that of the recipients. Scammers are mediators between two different lifeworlds and their dominant imaginaries. Letters that consciously mediate between the two must surely have the greatest chance of success; hence, they carry imprints of both.

A tradition that both the West and Africa have come to share is the exploitation of this resource-rich continent to the advantage of the Global North and disadvantage of ordinary Africans down through the history of Euro-African bilateral relations. It is no coincidence that so many of the dead expatriates referred to in the next-of-kin format worked in the gold trade or oil business, a fact that appears sufficient to explain why they would leave millions of dollars in personal bank accounts. As Daniel Jordan Smith (2007: 47) points out, this is an illustration of "the widely held Nigerian assumption that expatriates in Nigeria who work in the oil industry are getting fabulously rich." At the same time, the high salaries paid to European engineers who work on construction jobs in Africa are well known to the average European. To a certain extent, such workers may indeed be seen as modern-day descendants of colonial adventurers. The exploitation of Africa has a long tradition and by signposting that the money referred to in the money-transfer scams derives either from work in a resource industry or from shady deals, which come very close to overt theft, scammers allude to the global order of things, in which Africa remains a source of enrichment for others.

Scammers are obviously acquainted with the important function accorded the mass media in Western systems of knowledge production. In an attempt to invest their own stories with the level of truth their Western marks associate with serious media coverage, many scam emails refer directly to such coverage. "You must have heard over the media reports and the internet on the recovery of various huge sums of money deposited by my husband in different security firms abroad," states the widow Mariam Abacha in her email quoted earlier. It was posted in 2003, following international media reports that detailed attempts by the Nigerian government to recover the money deposited by the late military dictator Sani Abacha in British and Swiss bank accounts. In an attempt to link their own texts even more closely to "official" media texts, some scam emails contain hyperlinks to the web pages of the *New York Times, BBC News,* and similar organizations. Serving as backdrops for new 419 email legends are events such as the airplane crash in "Mahale National Park, in Tanzania on 13 December, 2005," which left "Mr. Allan Williams" dead together "with his wife who happened to be his only family" (September 22, 2009), or the arrest of Charles Taylor, "who was the former president of Liberia, now facing trial at the Hague in Europe" (March 18, 2010).[3] Given the efficiency of this strategy, which plays on the intertextual properties of the internet's hypertext medium, it comes as no surprise that in recent years, scammers have broadened considerably the geographical scope of their scam legends. Thus, Sgt. James Herron, who is "an American military soldier, serving in the military with the army's 3rd infantry division" in Iraq, is in "very desperate need for assistance and [has] summed courage to contact" the recipient of his email about the transfer of "the sum of twelve million United States dollars (US $ 12,000,000)." The email goes on to explain the source of the money and lends credence to its existence with a link to a *BBC News* story:

> Source of money: some money in various currencies were discovered in barrels at a farmhouse near one of saddam's old palaces in tikrit-iraq during a rescue operation, and it was agreed by staff Sgt Kenneth buff and i that some part of this money be shared Between both of us before informing anybody about it since both of us saw the money first. Find the story of this total money found on the web address below: http://news.bbc.co.uk /2/hi/middle_east/2988455.stm. (October 2, 2010)

Similarly, the Asian tsunami of 2004, Hurricane Katrina of 2005, and the Haitian earthquake of 2010 were used as backdrops for charity scams, in which scammers posed as penniless victims, as well as for a variation on the next-of-kin format to explain a bank client's death. Even if no hyperlink is inserted, scammers play on the intertextual properties of the internet with the full knowledge that a reference to a "tragic plane crash on the Lenana Peak, Mount Kenya, Saturday, the 19th day of July, 2003" (April 22, 2010) may be verified easily through a quick internet search.

This general awareness of the epistemological function of the media in the West and strategic employment of certain media's capacities are not only evident in the scam letters I have discussed so far but also in the subsequent stages of the scam process, when contact between a scammer and his mark has been firmly established. The production of visual evidence is the most important tool for dispelling any doubts the mark may still have. This takes the form of a simulacrum of official documents (Wizard 2000), such as letters printed on either bona fide or counterfeit government, bank, or law-firm letterhead, which are stamped and signed and ultimately resemble official documents as closely as possible. Similarly, the victim is issued an official-looking receipt for every fictitious fee paid. Whereas the initial scam letters rely on the mimicry of Western notions about Africa, "follow-ups"—as the role-play that develops from such letters is called in scammer parlance—hinge on the mimesis of official business proceedings. One author observes that "419 is a business where the powerful influence of official documents on millions of people all over the world is made manifest" (Igwe 2007: 65).

According to Chidi Nnamdi Igwe (2007: 57), who presents remarkable insights into scammers' strategies gained through interviews with fraudsters in Nigeria, scammers differentiate between "obedient *mugus*" and "stubborn *mugus*." "The stubborn ones are those who ask a lot of questions. They are likened to the doubting Thomas, who was always curious and doubtful, and who acted only when he saw enough convincing evidence." Although "stubborn *mugus*" are difficult to handle, scammers prefer these kinds of victims because once all their questions are answered and all their doubts dispelled, such victims rarely turn back. Among the sophisticated tools used to convince reluctant marks are fake websites—scammers create websites for bogus institutions (banks, security firms, lottery companies) or bogus websites for real institutions (Glickman 2005). A victim may even be asked to open an account at a sham internet bank operated by the scammer, eventually seeing a large sum of money transferred to the account, only to learn that another fee is required to move the money to the victim's own bank account abroad (Edelson 2006). A similar tactic—also based on the notion that seeing is believing—is what scammers call "flashing the mugu's account" (Igwe 2007: 75). This involves depositing an electronic check in the victim's bank account. The mark can then see the money has arrived.[4] The victim may be told the deal will fall through unless a final fee is paid by a certain deadline; he or she pays the fee for fear of losing out. As it takes several days for an e-check to clear, the fraudster then cancels it before payment is delivered, and he disappears into the ether.

Under certain circumstances, when scammers finally meet their victims face-to-face, 419 scams may develop into elaborate scenarios. In such cases, scammers continue the rouse, upping the stakes by perpetuating the fraud in person, at staged meetings, held either on the premises of institutions at which they pretend to work or nearby—for example, in offices rented in the same building as a bank branch. Barrister Usman Bello provided the following description of a successful but costly case:

> The best scam I have done is from Russia, crude oil investment supply. I only used Yahoo mail and the search machine of Google. After searching

the correct fax number of my client, I faxed the format to the Russian
client that the Nigerian National Petroleum Corporation is seeking a sup-
plier of crude oil servicing parts to enable the refinery [to] service
their Kaduna refinery and Warri refinery. The Russian client replied
through my fax line that he has what it takes to service the refinery.
(email, February 21 2008)

Bello then asked his "client" to present a detailed estimate for a three-year
project, which the client duly provided. The proposed sum was in excess
of 20 million U.S. dollars. The victim then had to register as a foreign contractor with the Nigerian National Petroleum Corporation. He paid the
associated sum of 25,000 U.S. dollars into a foreign account, which he had
been led to believe was the Nigerian government's account. Finally, the
victim traveled to Nigeria to sign the contract and pay the required fees:

After registration, he had to come down to Nigeria to sign the contract
agreement document and he paid the sum of USD 7,500.00 and on his arrival to Nigeria he brought 4 ROLEX wrist watches (his & hers), neck ties,
and 4 pairs of suits for the top Government officials (all of which belonged
to me and my partners in the deal). We took him to Kaduna refinery to
examine the state of decay in the company (all these with the help of NNPC
staffs). The Mugu was so glad when he was going home, believing that the
contract had been signed. On his arrival to Russia, a letter was sent to him
from the Office of the Accountant General of the Federation that he has
to effect the payment of 3 years tax clearance to enable the Ministry [to]
approve his contract. He effected the above payment of USD 258,000.00
with a foreign account as [a] Government agency account. Thereafter he
complained of having no money again. That was the end of the best business I have ever done since 1998. (Usman Bello, February 21, 2008)[5]

A staged encounter, such as a tour of a run-down refinery, provides visual
evidence. Whatever critical intuition the mark may have retained, if such
an encounter is performed well, the effect is devastating. Based on this
strategy, a German industrialist was swindled out of 1 million pounds by
a scammer who held meetings with him in the open lobby of a Lloyds TSB
branch on London's Oxford Street (Peel 2006), and a Saudi victim lost
100,000 U.S. dollars to scammers who created a fake South African embassy in Amsterdam (Glickman 2005). This conscious use of the deceptive
power of visual evidence connects international 419 scams to local forms

of confidence tricks based on face-to-face communication and persuasive strategies that, though less mediatized, are rooted in similar techniques of make-believe.

THE MAGIC OF FRAUD

The Master (2005), a Nigerian video film about the rise and fall of a scammer, illustrates this continuum of confidence tricks. At the beginning, Denis, the would-be scammer, is fleeced by a compatriot. He is lured into a shared taxi where he overhears, supposedly by chance, a conversation between a seller and an agent—the fraudster and an accomplice—concerning the sale of used clothing. The scammer pretends to be a vendor from Ivory Coast who speaks very little English and appears to have no clear idea how much the goods are worth in Nigeria. With this masquerade, which builds on the traditional prejudices of Nigerians vis-à-vis the inhabitants of this smaller West African country, he lulls the victim into a false sense of security and bolsters his feelings of superiority. Back home, and after parting with his money, Denis discovers he has been fooled. The sacks he bought are actually full of sand that has been hidden with a covering of rags (for earlier versions of this trick, see also Adogame 2009). The strategy is the same as the one used by the authors of the 419 emails when they assume the role of the naive African.

Another traditional confidence trick is the so-called "wash-wash," which is a special form of "money laundering." Famous in Nigeria and Cameroon, this trick involves a trunkful of "black money" (black paper cut into the size of dollar notes), which is said to have been defaced for security reasons but may be "washed" using a certain liquid the scammer offers his mark. As proof of his claim, the fraudster washes a number of these notes in the victim's presence (Igwe 2007: 41–43). The scammer offers to help the victim purchase the alleged chemical that is so expensive the scammer, who pretends to be low on funds, cannot afford to buy himself. The main point of the trick is the conscious use of the deceptive power of visual evidence—the transformation of a few pieces of black paper into real dollar notes right before the mark's eyes.[6] Under certain circumstances, even transnational 419 scams initiated by email may develop into such local forms of trick-based fraud. This is the case, in particular, when scammers who operate transnationally finally meet their victims face-to-face (Wizard 2000).

The Hausa say, "Seeing is better than hearing" (*gani ya kori ji*), that is, visual evidence—seeing something with one's own eyes—is always superior to hearsay. A certain alhaji (a Muslim who has been to Mecca), who approached two of my friends from Kano in 1996, in the hope that they would help him "wash" a boxful of black notes he had bought, must, in fact, have been blinded by this maxim. When they showed me samples of this "black money" (*ba'kin kud'i*), I initially thought that this was a case of an overliteral interpretation of "money laundering." At the time, I was not yet familiar with the "wash-wash" trick. I only realized what was going on a few years later when I read about a confidence trick in a local German newspaper. Accordingly, a Turk living in Mainz had fallen victim to two Africans who had sold him a suitcase full of dyed "money." In the meantime, a Nigerian friend named Tahir had told me how he had once become the accomplice of such confidence tricksters. His story, however, involves a variation on the black money scam, as it concerns white notes which were supposed to be transformed into real money with the help of a mysterious machine. Again, the presentation of visual evidence is the main scamming mechanism used here.

Tahir is a radio mechanic. I met him while doing research in the Nigerian Lake Chad area at the end of the 1990s. When he told me how he had built a money-making machine according to the fraudsters' instructions, I asked him to build a replica for me (see figure 7.1). The machine works on the principle of a box with a false bottom. An apparently empty drawer is opened, a white note is placed inside, and the drawer is closed. A button is pushed and the machine starts working: lights flash; the noise of an electric motor and beeping can be heard. Finally, the drawer is opened again and a bank note appears. If the victim is taken in, he or she is shown part of the machine's interior, which contains small bottles of different-colored liquids—the "printing dyes." As the level of the liquids is low, there obviously is not enough dye to produce more notes. Therefore, new dye must be purchased before any further processing can take place. What emerges from a visit to a rich dealer, an accomplice, to whom the fraudsters take their victims, is the fact that the dyes are very difficult to obtain and hence

FIGURE 7.1

Replica of a money-making machine, 2003. Author's collection.

very expensive. The first payment must be made immediately. Meanwhile, the fraudsters deliver huge volumes of white notes packed in boxes to the victim's house. When the dyes arrive, it turns out that the machine does not work properly with the new dyes and has to be sent to Europe to be repaired. The victim must now also cover the courier's travel costs. Eventually, the victim receives a message to the effect that a suspicious machine has been confiscated at the airport and the police are seeking the owners. The victim is thus forced to acknowledge that his or her investment in money production has failed.

Apparently, this trick also exploits local conceptions about the technical prowess of Europeans and the supposed ease with which they earn money in Europe. The fact that the money machine comes from Europe is an integral part of the scam. Therefore, in this case, the tricksters exploit local conceptions of the difference between Africa and Europe in exactly the same way as the authors of 419 emails do—but in the opposite direction, so to speak. Things that are impossible at home appear entirely feasible in exotic, far-off places.[7]

Tahir's money machine is a secular version of an old story involving the magical generation of riches. Sacks full of money and false-bottomed boxes were also featured in stories told by my two friends from Kano, whom the alhaji had approached, not entirely by coincidence, with the request for help with "money laundering." As spirit mediums, Lawan and Husseini were in contact with spiritual beings, which, according to local beliefs, could grant not only health and protection to their supplicants but also power and wealth. A basic precondition for seeking the intervention of the spirits is the presentation of sacrificial offerings (see chapter 1). The spirit mediums conduct these sacrifices on behalf of their clients, who either have to provide a sacrificial animal themselves or pay for it in advance. In most cases, they are not even present when the sacrifice is made. In any case, only the blood of the sacrificial animal is intended for the spirits; the meat may be claimed by the mediums. Therefore supplicants, spirits, and mediums all benefit from the transaction.

Given that an advance in the form of the sacrifice is built in to the local belief system, it is easy to see how the spirit medium format provides an ideal platform for fraudsters. Lawan and Husseini have occasionally also been asked for assistance by persons who had been taken in by fraudsters masquerading as spirit mediums. The payments made for the supposed sacrificial animals in these cases were horrific—after all, the expected return was nothing less than sacks full of money with the help of the spirits—and can, therefore, be understood as the equivalent of the fictitious customs-processing charges, bribes, taxes, and levies that arise in all forms of fraud. And as in the case of the "secular" variants—in which receipts, faxes with official or seemingly official letterheads, and eventually tours of run-down oil refineries act as proof and, hence, bait, in these "sacred" forms of fraud—the tempting evidence takes the form of sacks full of money. These are shown to the victims but cannot be touched by them (and like sacks of secondhand clothing that function as bait in *The Master,* only the surface layer contains the material claimed by the fraudsters).

It would appear, however, that the alhaji did not fall for false mediums. Instead he fell victim to the secular "wash-wash" scam. He probably turned to my friends for their assistance because the production of money by magic is actually an element staged in the genuine rituals of the bori cult. In his desperation, he hoped that his worthless black money could be transformed into real money, in the same way that dirt is literally magicked into money in actual bori rituals. During these theatrical performances, the mediums embody their spirits and demonstrate the spirits' power to the audience by performing numerous tricks for them. One of these tricks consists of transforming dirt into money with the help of a palm-sized leather purse, which has identical openings on the top and bottom. With a theatrical gesture, the medium pours sand gathered from the ground into one of these openings and begins to dance and swirl around. Coins fall to the ground as soon as the purse is reopened.

Tricks like this make up part of the repertoire of magicians and shamans throughout the world. They feed the ritual rhetoric that aims to convince the participants of the ritual's efficacy. In northern Nigeria, the purpose of the tricks is to present both evidence of the spirits' authenticity and to demonstrate the ability of the mediums to act genuinely. If Michael Taussig (2003) is to be believed, even local observers do not take such tricks at face value, and it is an open secret that such performances are, indeed, tricks. In the case of the shamanic healing performances discussed by Taussig, the shaman provides a model that he hopes is copied by effective spirits who are capable of healing. Hence, the trick serves to inspire the spirits to imitate the shaman's action and not to dazzle the participants in the ritual. Magic tricks are of interest in the genealogical analysis of 419 fraud because the sacred roots of all forms of confidence tricks can be identified here. Magicians are not fraudsters—the exceptions prove the rule here, as skepticism and magic also go hand in hand, says Taussig—but act in the context of a complex belief system they themselves subscribe to. Unlike confidence tricksters, who aim to fleece their victims without providing the promised goods or services, magicians and shamans act in good faith. Some may use their tricks for advertising purposes, that is, to assert their position vis-à-vis their competitors, but the promised service—for example, mediation between supplicants and spirits—is usually carried out when a client consults the medium.

The magic purse in the bori ritual, the money machine from Europe, the suitcase full of black bank notes, and the fake official documents in transnational 419 scams are all skillful means of visual persuasion. Their purpose is to persuade by presenting visual evidence. If there is something in Taussig's theory that magic tricks are generally understood as tricks and the clients of shamans and spirit mediums are, so to speak, their best critics, it could be speculated that Nigerians and other Africans are such good advance-fee fraudsters because they are familiar with similar techniques of persuasion from ritual contexts. According to this view, 419 scammers would have developed a particular knack for such activities through their familiarity with the practice of magic.[8]

VINDICATIONS OF SCAMMING

Despite the real damage scamming does to the Nigerian economy and the efforts to fight it by the Nigerian Economic and Financial Crimes Commission, it is considered a more or less petty crime in popular discourse. It is referred to as a "game" that favors the witty and cunning to the disadvantage of the gullible. In his song, "I Go Chop Your Dollar," Nkem Owoh sings:

419 is not a crime, it's just a game that everybody plays / I done suffer no be small / Upon say I get sense / Poverty no good at all, no / Na im make I join this business / 419 no be thief, it's just a game / Everybody dey play em / if anybody fall mugu / ha! my brother I go chop em.

CHORUS: National Airport na me get em / National Stadium na me build em / President na my sister's brother / You be the mugu, I be the master / Oyinbo man I go chop your dollar / I go take your money and disappear / 419 is just a game, you are the loser I am the winner.

The refinery na me get em / The contract, na you I go give em / But you go pay me small money make I bring em / you be the mugu, I be the master / na me be the master ooo!!!!

When Oyinbo play wayo / dey go say na new style / When country man
do him own / them go dey shout: bring em, kill em, die!

That Oyinbo people greedy, I say them greedy / I don't see them tire /
That's why when they fall into my trap o! / I dey show them fire.

This song, which is featured in the soundtrack of *The Master,* mirrors the
popular attitude to fraud: poverty and unemployment explain why young
people enter into the "business," the double moral of the *Oyinbo* (white
man) who exploits Africa but "shouts" if Africans invent a means to turn
the tables, and finally the tireless greed of the *Oyinbo* to explain why so
many Europeans and Americans fall for the scam. In *The Master,* Denis, the 419 fraudster played by Owoh, tricks the European businessman,
Mr. Littlewood, into believing that he, Denis, is the "King of Nigeria"—
hence the song's allusions to the national airport, the president as his
"sister's brother," and so on—who can help him get a contract awarded to
rebuild a refinery. When Mr. Littlewood finally discovers that he has been
duped, he complains to a public prosecutor and calls Nigeria "a country
full of rogues." On hearing this, the prosecutor becomes furious: "You
wanted to cheat my country and now you have been cheated. Who is the
rogue? Your greed has gotten the better out of you!" The agency of the
scammers is thus downplayed and the responsibility for being victimized
is shifted onto the European victim.

How does one become a 419 scammer? All of the scammers I interviewed specified the general lack of job prospects in Nigeria as the main
reason for taking up this illegal activity. The ostentatious behavior of successful scammers who publicly proclaim their expensive lifestyle with the
slogan "What do you do? I yahoo!" may play a role in attracting others to
the activity (Peel 2006: 23). As fraudster John Kuti told me, the call to join
the game can be hard to resist:

> In Benin City there where so many boys who later engaged in this,
> someone you see today trekking in the street the next day you see the
> person driving a big car. Boys living from grass to grace, they were being
> admired by everyone. During this time I was doing nothing and [couldn't]
> continue to remain like this. I had to look for another means of going
> back to Lagos to start it fully. I told a friend about it and he told me he had
> bigger boys in Lagos who are into this big time and we both arranged a

date of going to Lagos to hook me up with these guys. (personal interview, February 24, 2008)

Some scammers are ashamed of their behavior and take care to ensure that nobody outside the scammer networks finds out how the money is earned. "I don't really enjoy the game of scam," wrote "Vanity" in an email interview with Rick Hunter (2011: 6), and went on to explain: "Don't think that scammers don't have a sense of good morals. When you see a cheat, there is always something that drove him/her to the crime." Davis Pui sent me the following email:

> Please tell the world that con artists are not devils or heartless or whatever bad name that they call us. We are human like each and every one of them, but life has treated us the way we do not have a choice. It is painful to let you know that most of us are university graduates without job or any form or means to survive without doing this. Ask me, will it not be better if we scam people without using any gun on them? (February 15, 2008)

At least one scammer, with whom I exchanged emails, had sympathy for his victims; however, most do not share this feeling. Scammers "have the belief that white men are stupid and greedy. They say the American guy has a good life. There's this belief that for every dollar they lose, the American government will pay them back in some way" (Samuel, quoted in Dixon 2005: 1). Scammers also try to justify their criminal activities in light of colonial and postcolonial power relations. Scamming is thus labeled "retribution" for the atrocities Africans suffered at the hands of white slavers and colonizers or through the current postcolonial terms of trade. "White people used our old fathers as . . . slaves and took away all our money and resources, thinking we will not revenge," a scammer wrote me, calling himself Angelina Davis (!). He went on to say, "There we are today. I have made a lot of money, and will make more" (February 15, 2008). Another scammer elaborates on this argument:

> Tell your fellow white that the reparation due to Africa for 300 years of rape and violation will be paid in full either by hook or by crook, from this generation or the next. And unless the white man confesses and takes a positive proactive action for restitution, he can never be free. This is the ideology of the scammers. Would you want to know how Europe and America underdeveloped Africa? Would you want to know more about the perennial debt burden of the third world countries and the refUSl of

the so called Industrialised Nations to accept debt repayments instead of insisting on debt servicing? What do you call this? A scam of international scale or is it international politricks? (quoted in Edelson 2006: 51)

"Now it's payback time" is the general shorthand for this argument. This justification for scamming also appears in *The Master,* when Denis, the arrested 419 scammer, in his closing monologue, takes his leave of the journalists in the film and, hence the audience, with the following statement:

What do you call 419, you journalists? They came here, the white man came here long-long time ago. Our great grandfathers. . . . They parceled them, they put them into a chamber, they sent them across as slaves, they sent them to go there at a two million level; what do you call that? Is that not 419 on a superlative order? And you don't write about it, and you don't ask questions about it!

The monologue is cut with images of journalists nodding in agreement with Denis's argument, thereby suggesting the public's consensus. Indeed, the so-called Yahoo Boys, who take pride in their dubious success and boast publicly about their ill-gotten wealth, have become a role model of sorts. Nigerian musicians indicate their admiration in public. In his hit song "Yahoozee" (2003), singer Olu Maintain celebrates the good life with references to luxury cars, champagne, and easy women:

If I hammer	If I strike a fortune
First thing na Hummer	I will buy a Hummer
One million dollars	One million dollars
Elo lo ma je ti n ba se si daira	I have made enough naira
Monday, Tuesday, Wednesday, boys dey hustle	Monday, Tuesday, Wednesday, boys are hustling
Friday, Saturday, Sunday, gbogbo aye	Friday, Saturday, Sunday, everybody
Champagne, Hennessy, Moet for everybody	Champagne, Hennessy, Moët for everybody
Ewo awon omoge, dem dey shake their body	Look at the girls, they are shaking their bodies[9]

Although the singer takes care not to directly reference cybercrime as the source of the "One million Dollars" he sings about, his lyrics—and more so the accompanying video clip—have been interpreted as rather direct allusions to the lifestyle of the Yahoo Boys. "The song is fast becoming a national anthem of sorts among youths who now believe that some day, in the not too distant future, they will 'strike gold' or 'hammer' the elusive dollars from Monday to Friday (working days!) of intense 'hustling' doing night browsing and sending scam mails in a cybercafé," writes Bayo Olupo-hunda, an antifraud activist in Lagos (quoted in Kilpatrick 2009: 1). Kelly Hansome, another Nigerian singer, is not as cautious as Olu Maintain. His song "Maga don pay" (The fool has paid, 2008) glorifies cybercrime directly as an easy way of getting rich. The song's video clip shows him in a fancy suit, dancing in front of a Rolls-Royce, surrounded by sexy female background dancers, both African and European, who appear to enjoy his wealth. "Too much money / problems how to spend it / plenty dollars . . . maga done pay / shout hallelujah!" The song's success triggered a critical debate about its promotion of an inappropriate role model for Nigerian youth. In February 2010, eight Nigerian artists responded with a collaborative work called *Maga No Need Pay* that seeks to dissuade young people from engaging in cybercrime by promoting an almost Calvinist work ethic as the route to success. This project was financed by the "Microsoft Internet Safety, Security, and Privacy Initiative for Nigeria" (MISSPIN). The enormous number of comments posted on the song's YouTube page reveals its mixed reception. While many, Nigerians and non-Nigerians alike, approve of the song's message, other contributors, who admit to being Nigerian Yahoo Boys, condemn the artists for their alleged hypocrisy (ameer4dad, August 2010). A more moderate commentator writes: "Let the magas pay, after all our fathers were enslaved and whipped and caused to work more than [they] could, without pay. . . . Pls let the magas keep paying, but i advise people to change course as soon as they hammer, to reduce the nemesis, because what goes around comes around" (DeChakaZulu, July 2010). It would appear that this familiar trope will continue to haunt the Nigerian discourse on scamming for quite some time.

EPILOGUE

Scamming reverses the general distribution of agency in Africa's relationship to the Global North. Jean-François Bayart (1999: 116) predicted this momentum more than a decade ago when he stated that "informal and illicit trade, financial fraud, the systematic evasion of rules and international agreements could turn out to be means, among others, by which certain Africans manage to survive and to stake their place in the maelstrom of globalization." In fact, the scammers' vindication of their illicit craft as "retribution" carries yet another punch line. For as Andrew Smith (2009) points out, the ongoing history of Western capitalist and imperialist expansion is part of the condition for the success of Nigerian scams, a dialectical irony already identified by Karl Marx. "There is in human history something like retribution," wrote Marx, in reference to the 1857 rebellion in India, "and it is a rule of historical retribution that its instrument be forged not by the offended, but by the offender himself" (quoted in A. Smith 2009: 29). This not only holds true for the media technology the scammers employ (a material instrument forged by the offender), but also for the orientalist representations of Africa (an ideological instrument forged by the offender) which the scammers mimic in their scam letters to induce credibility. In this case, the copy not only "draws on the character and power of the original, to the point whereby it assumes that character and that power" (Taussig 1993: xiii) but turns against the "producers" of the original or their proxies—that is, the beneficiaries of the ongoing history of Western capitalist and imperialist expansion. It is significant, perhaps, that the successful scammer is called "master." This term can refer not only to the mastery of something but also to ownership and power over people. In a postcolonial setting such as Nigeria, the connotations that inevitably come to mind here are the "colonial master," the "slave master," and the "master of servants." To a certain extent then, scamming turns former masters, or at least the proxies of former masters, into mugus—into a category of people foolish enough to be "owned" and exploited, just as slaves and colonial subjects were, and postcolonial subjects continue to be. The attribution of exploiting and being exploited, of agency and "patienthood" (Gell 1998) is thus reversed: masters turn into mugus and mugus into masters.

In the course of my online interviews, I experienced something of this reversal of power relations myself. In the spirit of foolhardy honesty, I revealed my true identity in the interview requests I dispatched by email and provided a link to my website by way of authentication. I also believed that radical honesty offered the only currency with which I could prosper in a context ridden with fraud and lies. This approach worked well with at least four interview partners. However, I reached my limit during my exchange with the fifth, a certain Mike Cahill. He initially responded by email to my questionnaire. His answer to the question about how he found ideas for new personas, which he assumed in his scam formats, should have sounded alarm bells for me. He provided the following sample scam email:

> Dear madam or sir,
>
> my name is Matthias Krings, I am a professor of Anthropology teaching at the University of Mainz, Germany. Check this link to know more about me: http://www.ifeas.uni-mainz.de/ethno/PopKultur/Matthias_Krings .html.
>
> Until recently when I was crippled by stroke, which left half part of my body paralysed. I also had extensive eye surgery, which has resulted into poor vision. For the past two years, I have been looking for a miracle all to no avail. Recently, my doctor told me a dishearten news about my health that, the probability of my surviving until the next three months is 1/2. I contacted you therefore bla bla bla . . ." (email, February 19, 2008)

Nonetheless, I arranged an in-depth ICQ instant messaging interview with him that lasted two hours and twenty minutes. He was very evasive and ended up finding out more about me than I did about him. The interview ended as follows:

> M. CAHILL: 'Bye for now and thank you for the waste of our time. May I ask you a question?
>
> M. KRINGS: Yes.
>
> M. CAHILL: Are you truly who you say you are?
>
> M. KRINGS: Yes.
>
> M. CAHILL: Good. As from tomorrow, you will owe your friends some explanation. You waste my time and you seem happy with that. I will waste yours.
>
> M. KRINGS: I don't think I wasted your time.
>
> M. CAHILL: Good.
>
> M. KRINGS: Since I reciprocated with much more information about me than you offered me about yourself. Isn't that so?

M. CAHILL: You are smart, aren't you?

M. KRINGS: If I have offended you, I beg your pardon.

M. CAHILL: No, no offense.

M. KRINGS: Let's part on good terms.

M. CAHILL: Maybe I will ask you that tomorrow.

M. KRINGS: OK, I am off.

M. CAHILL: You have just started the game. We will play it together.

(ICQ, February 19, 2008)

A minute after our conversation, my email inbox filled up with responses to an email that had been dispatched in my name and using my address. In this email, I offered anyone who would help me with a transfer of several million dollars a considerable proportion of this sum. I received more than 1,000 emails during the night. These were automatic responses issued by the spam filters of some of the recipient addresses distributed throughout the world. The actual number of emails sent in my name would have been considerably higher. Mike Cahill even had his fun targeting the addresses of members of Johannes Gutenberg University Mainz. Hence, I found myself owing explanations to a few newfound "friends" the next morning: the first query came from the press office, followed by another from the Institute of Physics, and so it continued for a few more days. Mike Cahill succeeded in making a mugu out of me and asserting himself as master, thereby maintaining the reversal of the roles of agent and patient implied by the coinage "master and mugu."

It is perhaps just consequential that in their search for new formats and scamming strategies, 419 fraudsters also infiltrate the sphere of academic communication—even without being given a perfect draft like the one I sent to Mike Cahill. On two occasions in the past few years, I have received emails from trustworthy African colleagues who claimed to have been robbed of their money and mobile phones by thieves while on trips to Accra and London, and therefore to be in desperate need of a quick infusion of a few hundred euros, preferably to be sent via Western Union money transfer. Scammers who stole their identities and used their email contacts had clearly hijacked these two colleagues' email accounts.

In recent years, a format involving conference scams has been gaining prominence. Such scams invite people to register for international conferences on topics invariably associated with development discourse—HIV/AIDS awareness, racism and child abuse, youth health, and so on—and aim to collect registration fees from would-be participants. The themes of such bogus conferences would suggest that development workers and academics are the primary target group. In April 2010, I received the following email for conference participation through the Listserv of the Africa-Europe Group for Interdisciplinary Studies (AEGIS):

> Following my role as the Chair of the UN-AU Panel on Peacekeeping Operations in Africa, the Foundation for World Wide Cooperation, which I chair, in cooperation with The Johns Hopkins University SAIS Bologna Center, will present the conference "Africa: 53 Countries, One Union" to be held in Bologna on 21 May 2010. The conference will address the strong need for continental integration of Africa as a prerequisite for political, social and economic development.
>
> The Draft of the Conference Program is attached for your information. I do hope that you will be interested to attend it. Should you wish to be present, please fill out the Registration Form and return it to the e-mail address indicated therein, not later than 10 May 2010.
>
> Best regards,
>
> Romano Prodi
> President
> Foundation for World Wide Cooperation

One of the list members, historian Jan-Bart Gewald, immediately replied: "Why is it that I have a strong 419 feeling with this call?" It eventually transpired, however, that the conference and the call for participation were genuine. Although Gewald's question was intended to be rhetorical, its possible answer is disquieting. Romano Prodi's letter had a number of signifiers that sounded alarm bells: a prominent and internationally renowned sender, internationally established institutions, and a conference title and theme that are—I regret to note—as full of development jargon as any of the bogus conferences announced in 419 scam letters. As fraudulent copies of genuine correspondence, scam emails have become so close to their originals that they have not only acquired the character and rhetorical power of their originals, they even call bona fide emails into question—in the eyes of readers acquainted with 419 scams, at least. The copies have negative repercussions for their originals, and it may well become increasingly difficult in the future to differentiate between genuine correspondence and fraudulent 419 copies.

8

"Crazy White Men"

(UN)DOING DIFFERENCE IN AFRICAN POPULAR MUSIC

IN NOVEMBER 2013, I went to Hamburg for a concert by Mzungu
Kichaa, a cosmopolitan Dane who plays Tanzanian pop music and sings
in Swahili. That night, Mzungu Kichaa, which literally translates as "crazy
white man," performed together with three members of his backing band,
Bongo Beat, all of them black Tanzanians who had been flown in from
Dar es Salaam to Copenhagen a few days earlier. Their performance was
part of "Danish Vibes," a promotional showcase financed by a Danish
government agency, which was meant to v Danish musical talent to representatives of the German music industry. Of the four bands performing
that night at the Mojo Club, Mzungu Kichaa and his band were surely
the most exotic. I met two young Tanzanians in the audience who were
living in Hamburg temporarily. One of them was Peter Maziku (aka Peen
Lawyer), a rapper and graphic designer from Dar es Salaam. He had come
to Germany for half a year of vocational training via the Hamburg–Dar es
Salaam city partnership. The other was a young soccer talent who played
for the junior team of the Hamburg St. Pauli Club. While the framing of
the event suggests the majority of the audience was German and Danish
and perceived Mzungu Kichaa above all as a Danish musician, the two
Tanzanian spectators recognized him and his band as part of the Tanzanian pop-music scene and had come to celebrate a bit of home away from
home. As I watched them dancing among the crowd and singing along to

his songs, which they knew by heart, I had the feeling they were also a bit proud of how far Bongo flava, the genre of Tanzanian pop music Mzungu Kichaa subscribes to, had traveled that night. In an interview I conducted earlier that day, Mzungu Kichaa told me that "in terms of identity," he felt pretty much like a "mixed-race person." Elsewhere he describes himself as "the personification of indifference towards racism, stereotypes and the belief of 'otherness.'"[1] The enthusiastic response of his mixed audience that night indicates that his cosmopolitan attitude and the resulting musical output are met with approval.

Mzungu Kichaa is not the only "crazy white man" currently performing African popular music in and out of the continent. Equally prolific are White Nigerian, a Nigerian national with Levantine roots whose tagline reads "arrogantly Nigerian," and the German-Namibian EES, who performs Nam flava, Namibian pop music with a Kwaito influence from South Africa. In this chapter, I propose to view the artistic output of the three musicians within the framework of cosmopolitanism. According to Ulf Hannerz (1996: 103), cosmopolitanism "is first of all an orientation, a willingness to engage with the other" that "entails an intellectual and aesthetic openness toward divergent cultural experiences." The concept is rooted in Greek political philosophy; cosmopolitanism was thought of as paradoxical and reflected "skepticism toward custom and tradition," as Kwame Anthony Appiah (2007: xiv) explains. Unlike the ordinary citizen in Greek civilization, who owed loyalty to the *polis,* or "city-state," he belonged to, the "cosmopolite" was conceptualized as a "citizen of the world." Theories of cosmopolitanism are manifold and have developed along different lines of thinking. Among the six perspectives Steven Vertovec and Robin Cohen outline in their introduction to *Conceiving Cosmopolitanism* (2002), four are more or less relevant for the purposes of this chapter. In reference to the "crazy white men" whose works and lives I intend to discuss, it makes sense to conceive of cosmopolitanism as (1) "a kind of philosophy or world-view," (2) "a political project for recognizing multiple identities," (3) "an attitudinal or dispositional orientation," and (4) "a mode of practice or competence." Subscribing to the last perspective, Ian Woodward and Zlatko Skrbis (2012) suggest the need for empirical studies that look out for "the performative, situational and accomplished dimensions of being cosmopolitan." However, despite advocating a performative approach, they still subscribe to the rather ontological formulation of "being cosmopolitan." If we are taking their argument seriously, I suggest we must go a step further and ask how cosmopolitanism is actually being *done*. If cosmopolitanism entails the openness to difference, then how is this openness actually performed? The three musicians' artistic and banal performances—such as their music, songs, video clips, as well as their written and visual postings on social media platforms—constitute ideal empirical objects for the study of cosmopolitanism as a form of practice. It is through their practices, their musical and social performances, that they actually constitute their cosmopolitan subjectivities, their "being cosmopolitan." Borrowing a coinage from Harvey Sacks (1984), I suggest we actually need to observe their *doing "being"* cosmopolitan.

Taking into account that the musicians under consideration are not only artists but also entrepreneurs who struggle to make a living from their music, I propose reading their musical performances as deliberate plays, with both difference and sameness. As I discuss, their cosmopolitan ventures are characterized by the paradox of transcending and marking difference at the same time. While their "epidermal difference" (Nava 2007: 9) makes them stick out from the masses of fellow musicians in Africa—something which can be turned into an advantage in a competitive professional environment—their performances and linguistic competences signify just the opposite: sameness. Thus, they thrive on the (un)doing of difference, and I argue that it is exactly this feature that accounts for their popularity with African audiences, as it embodies the cosmopolitan potential of African popular music. As they break the boundaries of conventional categories, the three musicians demonstrate an attitude of openness, in Hannerz's words, "a willingness to engage with the other." And since at least two of them also work hard to internationalize their music, they also provide viable links to the world outside Africa.

DIFFERENT SHADES OF WHITE

Mzungu Kichaa, whose real name is Espen Sørensen, was born in Denmark in 1980.[2] Coming to Zambia with his parents at the age of six, he spent three years of his early childhood in rural Africa. In 1989, the family relocated to London, and only six years later, when he was fifteen, his parents took him to Ngorongoro, Tanzania, where they had found jobs. During his schooling in Dar es Salaam and Moshi, he established two bands that played various styles of music—rock, reggae, and Congolese rumba (Sanga 2011). Mzungu Kichaa is a multi-instrumentalist who plays violin, flute, guitar, and percussion. Through one of his former school-mates, P-Funk Majani, owner of the Bongo Records label, he became involved in the Bongo flava music scene as early as 1999. However, it was to take him ten years before he eventually released his first solo album, *Tuko Pamoja* (We are together, 2009). Meanwhile, he had been studying in London at the School of Oriental and African Studies, where he obtained a bachelor's degree in music and social anthropology and a master's in African studies with a special focus on music. During his time in Britain, Mzungu Kichaa jammed with African musicians who were playing Congolese rumba. Then in 2006 he founded yet another band, Effigong, in Copenhagen. Back in Tanzania, where he relocated in 2008, his song "Jitolee!" (Volunteer!), featuring Tanzanian rapper Professor Jay, proved a big hit and was third on the East African TV video charts. His EP, *Hustle*, which contains a duet with Kenyan singer Dela, came out in 2012. Mzungu Kichaa has been nominated twice for a Danish World Music Award—in 2009 in the category of Best World Album for *Tuko Pamoja* and in 2012 in the category of Best World Track for "Twende Kazi" (Come and work).

EES (aka "Easy" Eric Sell) is a Namibian of German ancestry.[3] Born in 1983, he is from the Namibian capital city of Windhoek. He started his career in Namibia in 2001 as a musician and music producer. Beginning as a hip-hopper, whose German raps addressed primarily the German-Namibian minority, he later switched to Kwaito, singing mainly in English and therefore expanding his fan base considerably. After receiving vocational training as a professional sound engineer in Cape Town, South Africa, he left for Germany. EES has been living in Cologne since 2004 and spends several months each year in Windhoek, where he runs the music label EES records and the fashion label EES wear. By 2013, he had released twelve albums, most of which fall under the Kwaito category. In southern Africa, his musical career gained momentum in about 2008. Since then, he has won several awards in Namibia, including the Namibian Annual Music Awards (2009) accolade Artist of the Year. For the video clip of his hit song "Ayoba," featuring the South African Kwaito legend, Mandoza, he won his most prestigious award thus far, the Channel O Music Video award in the category Best Kwaito (2012). Referring to his music also in terms of a political project, EES believes he has a "responsibility to 'do something good' to help his country become 'a rainbow nation, living together in one country, no matter what the skin colour.'"[4]

White Nigerian, whose real name is Mohammed Jammal, is a Nigerian with Levantine roots. Born in Jos, Nigeria, in 1988, he grew up in a Hausa-speaking environment—a language he has mastered like a native speaker. He is equally fluent in pidgin English, Nigeria's everyday lingua franca. In 2010, while still studying in London to obtain a master's degree in global management, he was discovered on YouTube by Nigerian stand-up comedian AY, who invited him to perform on his live London show. On his return to Nigeria in 2011, White Nigerian gradually made a name for himself as a comedian and also joined the Nigerian house and hip-hop music scene. His song "Taka Rawa" (Let's dance) gained some recognition as supposedly "one of Nigeria's best club songs of 2011" (Alhassan 2012). Since then, he has collaborated with other Nigerian artists and produced several more songs. From 2012 to 2013, he joined the National Youth Service Corps (NYSC)—a one-year civil service program that is compulsory for every Nigerian citizen after graduation from college. Serving as a teacher in a local government area near Abuja, he explained: "I'm white. I'm Nigerian. I'm corper NS/12C/09XX and I'm proud to be serving my country."[5]

(UN)DOING DIFFERENCE

Footage from White Nigerian's first public guest appearance on stage—during "AY Live in London" 2010, in front of an audience of 5,000—shows an African crowd cheering and applauding in face of the conflation of categories brought about by his performance. A YouTube viewer calling himself Edy M, whose background is most likely Nigerian, comments on White Nigerian's second clip, *London or Naija,* in which White Nigerian talks in Nigerian pidgin English about his strange experiences in London. The viewer expresses his feelings as follows: "I have watched this more than 10 times today already. The funniest part is that I don't see any white in him anymore and I am not even talking about his color. It is the way [he] reasons, the way he sighs and talks with his hands like a correct naija boy that I so much enjoy." Despite the fact that this commentator reports "not seeing any white in him anymore," which is an interesting and valuable observation in itself, I contend the very fact that a white man is displaying the habitus and the language proficiency of a typical Nigerian are what fascinate the viewer and make him watch the clip "more than 10 times a day." And I am almost certain he would not be as interested if the same stories had been related by a fellow black Nigerian (a "correct naija boy," as he puts it).

African music economies have changed considerably in the past decade. With the coming of music television and digital media, recorded music is no longer simply heard but rather heard and watched. In Tanzania, Nigeria, and southern Africa, music videos have become important promotional tools, and artists who want to be successful need to produce them (cf. Hacke 2014). This trend works in favor of the three musicians I discuss in this chapter. In a media environment that privileges audio*visual* media more than ever before, looking different proves an asset. White performers of African music thus become the exotic eye candy of local TV programming dominated by the unmarked norm of "blackness."[6] This is not to say that white performers were previously absent from the African music landscape. Johnny Clegg in South Africa and John Collins in Ghana are two famous examples, and I am almost sure there must have been other less well-known performers here and there, too. But unlike (at least two of) the three musicians I am considering here, Clegg and Collins did not capitalize on their skin color in their stage names.[7]

Being white is a double-edged sword for popular African music artists, however. On the one hand, their white skin allows them to stand out from their many African counterparts and gives them an exotic quality. On the other, it has the disadvantage of coming with a host of ambivalent or even negative signifiers that could kill a music career before it got started. "White" is the color of colonialism, apartheid, and tourism, and thus associated with people who were, and still are, detached from the day-to-day struggles of ordinary people, to say the least. For African audiences to accept their work, the musicians need to engage in complex negotiations about the significance of their skin color and the associations that come along with it. Paradoxically, they need to highlight and downplay their difference at the same time.

Mzungu Kichaa and White Nigerian reference their skin color in their stage names. At first, Mzungu Kichaa had a tough time accepting his *nom de scène*. In an interview with Imani Sanga (2011: 199), he reports how Juma Nature, one of Tanzania's Bongo flava "superstars," began calling him "crazy white man" in a playful manner: "At the beginning, I didn't want the name because in my life I did not want to be called *Mzungu*. I didn't want to be segregated. You know how it is when they call you *Mzungu* while you don't feel to be one!" Nevertheless, Mzungu Kichaa chose to use the nickname, initially given him in 1999, as his proper stage name when he released his first solo album in 2009. In this sense, his situation is comparable to White Nigerian's. Even though the racial reference in their stage names is articulated somewhat tongue in cheek, their *noms de scène* still allow the musicians to capitalize on their epidermal difference and thus to establish their appearance as a constitutive part of their public image.

It is perhaps significant that the German-Namibian EES does not exhibit his difference like the two others do. Neither does his stage name contain any reference whatsoever to the color of his skin, nor does he play with the discrepancy of being white and acting black. Of the three artists, he makes the least use of an African language in his songs. Instead, quite a number of his songs are written in German or its Namibian variant, formerly called Südwesterdeutsch and now popularized by Eric Sell (n.d.) as "Nam-släng." It seems that EES is about the normalization of German-Namibians as a kind of Namibian ethnicity, which can be read as a reverberation of a larger discourse among white settler communities in southern Africa, where being white and African is not necessarily seen as a contradiction.

The three musicians perform sameness—the flipside of difference—in several registers. The most obvious is language. By singing in local languages, such as Swahili and Hausa, or in local variants of English, like Nigerian pidgin, difference is undone. EES, as already mentioned, is more limited in his use of African languages. Quite frequently, though, he uses phrases or words from African languages as hook lines. Examples are his songs "Mahambeko," which is "blessing" in the Oshiwambo language, and "Ayoba," a slang expression of amazed approval originating in South African township culture. In terms of lyrical content, it is safe to say that EES's and White Nigerian's song lyrics are very simple. They boil down to celebrating the moment ("Boys and girls, if you wanna have a good time, let me see you wind it, wind it . . . ," White Nigerian—"Taka Rawa") or life in general ("Life is what you make it, so let's make it beautiful, because that's what it is . . . ," EES—"Mahambeko"). In this sense, their lyrics are similar to those of many other singers the world over—not just African. Mzungu Kichaa departs from this observation, as several of his songs contain prosocial messages. His song "Jitolee!" (Volunteer!), for example, is a reflection on the deplorable condition of present-day social relationships and a plea for compassion and to help others selflessly. He displays an attempt to educate his audience through music. This kind of edutainment is typical of many Bongo flava musicians who are keen to deliver social messages and therefore follow in the tradition so well developed in Tanzania (Reuster-Jahn and Hacke 2014). On the one hand, this is hardly astonishing, as Mzungu Kichaa wrote his master's thesis on music in development and also has worked in some development contexts himself.[8] On the other hand, it demonstrates that Mzungu Kichaa cast his artistic work with a strong orientation toward local popular culture, and it may also be read as an appeal for sameness. In terms of sound, all three artists tune in to the localized African variants of global pop music. With EES, it is Kwaito; with White Nigerian, electronic music, such as house and hip-hop of a particular Nigerian type; and with Mzungu Kichaa, Bongo flava—Tanzania's specific blend of hip-hop, R & B, reggae, and local music traditions. In short, the sound of their music is comparable to the sound of the latest urban trends within the particular music environments they subscribe to.

EES, White Nigerian, and Mzungu Kichaa frequently collaborate with other artists. These collaborations take the form of "featuring," which is a well-established practice in the global pop music business and quite common in the music economies of Namibia, Nigeria, and also Tanzania. Featuring may be used for symbolic reasons and marketing purposes, and it usually implies a certain hierarchy between the two musicians involved. Mostly, the featured artist is a well-established musician and his guest appearance in a newcomer's song and video can be read as a solid stamp of approval. The newcomer may also pay homage to a star by featuring him. It is noteworthy that the three musicians in question make frequent use of this practice. It is surely no coincidence that all their award-winning songs and videos feature big stars. In his award-wining music video *Ayoba*, EES features South African Kwaito legend Mandoza (see figure 8.1), and in the video *Mahambeko,* Lady May, Namibia's most famous female rapper, has a guest appearance. White Nigerian's video *Taka Rawa* features Nigerian rapper and record producer JJC (Abdulrashid Bello); and for his hit song and video, *Jitolee!* Mzungu Kichaa got helping hands (or rather voices) from Professor Jay, a well-established artist, and the female singer Mwasiti, by then a rising star on the Tanzanian Bongo flava scene.

On a symbolic level, this communicates equality and serves to undo difference. Well-established black artists welcome white newcomers in their midst. In terms of acceptance and popularity, they also serve as stepping-stones for the white newcomers' careers. EES explained to me

FIGURE 8.1

EES and South African musician Mandoza, 2012. Photo by Manni Photography.
Courtesy of Eric Sell.

that his collaboration with the Namibian rapper Gazza, for the song "International" (2006), paved the way for his acceptance among black Namibian audiences.[9] And as if to attest to this, a certain Remigius Kalimba comments on the YouTube video clip of this song by ironically writing: "Thank you Germany for leaving this boy behind after [you] gave us independence. . . ." Various paratexts to the songs and music videos serve the same purpose of demonstrating equality. White Nigerian, for example, who also seeks to establish himself as a comedian, has uploaded a short clip[10] on his YouTube channel that shows him talking to Nollywood stars Osita Iheme and Chinedu Ikedieze, who tell the public: "He's our brother. He speaks Pidgin fluently. He's a white Naija boy!" EES has produced a documentary about his career so far (*Yes-Ja: Following the Journey of a Unique Leader*, 2010) which is remarkable for the number of Namibian musicians letting him (and his audience) know they accept him as one of their own. In the film, the musician Big Ben explains: "The first moment when he came out, it almost looked ridiculous in a sense that here is a guy from a totally different background trying to do something totally black. But then he proved to them that music has no boundaries. . . . His contribution is significant." The Dogg, another prominent Namibian rapper, adds: "I checked him out on TV: I did not know who he was, I was like 'Now, who is this white boy trying to be a nigger?' He is very talented and he knows how to promote himself. He will go far."

Another register for the production of sameness is habitus and clothing. Like their black African counterparts, the three white musicians reference American hip-hop videos in their physical performances. They also dress in a global urban fashion—T-shirts, baseball caps, sneakers, sunglasses, and a style of dress they share equally with many black African musicians. Here and there, some reference to ethnic dress or "African" attire is made (Mzungu Kichaa wears a Maasai necklace in the *Jitolee!* video and a Maasai hairdo in the *Oya Oya* clip; White Nigerian dons a typical Hausa hat in the *Taka Rawa* video), but altogether this seems to be less important than the general display of urban dress codes. By creating his own fashion line of street wear, and promoting it in his video clips, Namibian rapper EES is perhaps the most consequential in this regard. Unlike the others, White Nigerian—at least in two of his music videos (*Dirty Wine* and *Party Time*)—also models his image on the nouveau riche type of character frequently displayed in hip-hop videos, in which male rappers are surrounded by such quintessential icons of wealth and male fantasy as fast cars, luxury mansions, and loose women. (The promotional poster for White Nigerian's *Dirty Wine* can be seen in figure 8.2.)

There are also many symbolic references in terms of national belonging—in the case of White Nigerian and EES, who are citizens of Nigeria and Namibia, respectively—and of Pan-Africanism—in the case of Mzungu Kichaa, in whose music videos red, gold, and green, the quintessential colors of Africa and its diaspora, appear quite frequently. In his earlier videos, White Nigerian can be seen wearing a black jacket that resembles a Nigerian police officer's uniform with a national flag stitched on the lapel. The national colors, green and white, are also often referenced in the visual material that makes up his public image. His Facebook page contains several pictures that show him serving his country as a youth "corper," the coinage of which comes from Nigeria's mandatory National Youth Service Corps program. In an essay written for a society magazine, he describes his national belonging as follows: "They say 'never judge a book by its cover' and that's exactly right. A lot of people see me and assume I am an 'Oyibo' ['European']. I'm not and let my color not deceive you. It's what's inside that counts and for me apart from the color, I am Nigerian to the core. Born and bred in Jos, I grew up speaking Hausa and of course Pidgin English. I have one passport and it's green" (White Nigerian 2013). EES, also known as "Nam-boy," is no less outspoken in claiming his national identity. Namibia's flag appears quite often in his music videos and stage performances; likewise, a certain type of hand sign—made by bending fingers in such a way as to represent the contours of Namibia on the map. When asked by Channel O (2013) about the reason for these patriotic references, EES replied:

> So when you're outside Africa that's when one realizes what he or she is truly missing and then I'm like, "Damn, Namibia that's my home. Okay let me put a Nam flag here" just to represent [Namibia] and then [the] next video, "Oh let me put a Nam flag here as well," and it just developed into a habit. . . . I couldn't just represent any one tribe since we are one Namibia; we are very diverse, like 13 to 15 different cultures so let me represent them all. Then my hand sign, because it looks like Namibia on the map. Also the other reason is that I looked at the other countries music-wise and I analyzed why they are successful, especially on the hip-hop scene,

Poster promoting *Dirty Wine*, by White Nigerian, and featuring Tekno, 2013.
Courtesy of Mohammed Jammal.

because that was the big genre back then. So I realized that they enforced their own culture, their own way of dancing, of graffiti and of emceeing and I wondered how they [did] it. Looking into that I saw that they put the American flag up everywhere and I thought maybe we can learn from them so I started putting the Nam flag up everywhere; I must tell you it works. I mean in 2010 [2010 FIFA World Cup] South Africans know, you put the flag up everybody—black, white, Asian, Indian, everybody: we are one. So Namibia needed that after independence and so did South Africa and that's the second reason why I did that.

Of the three artists, Mzungu Kichaa stresses his "being African" the most. Maybe this is due to the fact that unlike the two others, he cannot claim to be a born African. Perhaps it is safe to say that he is African by affection. "I am African," reads the T-shirt he sports on the cover of his 2012 single, *African Hustle* (see figure 8.3).

In a different song, "Ujumbe" (The message, 2009), he explains his emotional attachment to Tanzania and his desire to become a citizen:

Nimetunga nyimbo ya Watanzania wenzangu!	I have composed a song for my fellow Tanzanians!
Ebu sikiliza ninachotaka kuwaambia	Please listen to what I want to tell you
Nimepapenda sana hapa nchini	I am very much in love with this country
Watu ni wazuri kweli kweli	The people are really very nice
Wamenikaribisha vizuri sana	They have welcomed me so well
Mpaka nimesahau nilikotoka	until I have forgotten where I came from
Nikiulizwa leo ni Tanzania	Today, when I am asked, it is Tanzania
Kwa mila niliyopata nikilelewa	For the culture I was socialized into as I grew up
. . .	. . .
Nimekuja Tanzania kuwaomba uraia	I have come to Tanzania to request citizenship
Niwaeleze nini, ili mweze kuniamini	What shall I explain to you, so that you can believe me?
Nyama, ndizi, ugali, mchicha, yote natumia	Meat and plantain, ugali and spinach, I eat it all
Kwa nini isitoshe kunipatia uraia	Why shouldn't this suffice for me to be granted citizenship?

Nitakwama hapa hapa, niliyotaka sitapata	I will get stuck right here; I will not get what I want
Ujuzi na uwezo wa kupita miamba	The skill and capacity to skirt the rocks
Nisingeyajua, si tayari ningekwama	If I didn't know them, wouldn't I have got stuck already?

FIGURE 8.3

Mzungu Kichaa and Kenyan singer Dela, 2012. Photo by Kreks Carter. Courtesy of Espen Sørensen.

In a 2010 interview on Kenyan TV's *Patricia Show*, the host introduces Mzungu Kichaa as an "internationally acclaimed musician who seems to be immersed in everything African," and they chat about how he grew up in Zambia, how he danced with the Maasai when his parents moved to Tanzania, and so on.[11] He even proves right there in the studio his ability to dance and jump like a Maasai ("I was a very good dancer"). At a certain point, he relates how he came back to Denmark as an "African kid" after spending three years in rural Zambia: "I didn't like to wear shoes, I didn't know how to eat with knife and fork. . . ." The Kenyan show master replies: "Oh, was it that bad?" And Mzungu Kichaa answers: "No, it was that great." In some of his songs and also in the liner notes of his debut album, *Tuko Pamoja* (the title of which translates as "we are together," which is also significant in the context discussed here), he refers equally to his many experiences in Africa. In a bid to construct an African origin for himself, he even goes as far as insinuating that he might be an albino born of African parents. *Oya Oya*, an early music video, which consists of still images and has a self-made touch, begins with a picture of an elderly African couple with an albino child. This image fades into a portrait of Mzungu Kichaa, as if to suggest the child in the first picture represents the musician's younger self.[12]

VOICES OF FANS AND CRITICS

In the absence of street-corner interviews, user comments on YouTube clips are a rich source of getting an idea of people's opinions about the three performers. Needless to say, this source has certain limitations in terms of representativeness and reliability. Only rarely do commentators introduce themselves and explain where they come from and where they are while writing the commentary. Often, however, clues can be found between the lines. The majority of commentators seem to be diasporic Africans writing from abroad, where the streaming of YouTube videos, because of broadband internet access, is much easier and cheaper than in most African countries. Also, unlike the numerous but rather short fan postings on the three musicians' Facebook pages, which are always positive, comments on YouTube videos appear to be more critical. And this is despite the fact that they can be edited and deleted by the channel owners—that is, the musicians.

Most of the almost four hundred comments on White Nigerian's two earliest YouTube clips, in which he talks in pidgin English and Hausa about his life in London, are positive and encourage him to continue posting similar clips. Some even suggest he should try starting a career in the Nigerian video film industry. A number of comments are almost anthropological (and reminiscent of the nature-versus-nurture debate), as they point out that White Nigerian questions the whole notion of "race." A certain MrDejoo1 thus suggests: "Now, this is an evidence that the only difference between a black man and white man is culture. Not necessarily the color. If you raise a white man in a black man's household, he would act like a black man, vice versa. Let the white supremacy fools see this video, perhaps, they would think twice."[13] User dlfunky1 adds: "Colour is not the only thing that defines people, it's culture and upbringing too," and pickerpiker draws on a computer metaphor to conceptualize the relationship between "race" and "culture":

> This guy just prove say human being na [= is] like computer without an operating system when they are born, they only become whoever depending on the kind of os installed on them, whether windows or linux or e.t.c. oh boy na naija os dey your head, no wahala i dey enjoy u [There is a Nigerian operating system in your head, no problem, I really enjoyed your clip].

For a certain Vivian, White Nigerian (Mohammed Jammal) also displays a rare, but ideal combination of form and content: "U ar[e] the kind of guy am lookin for all this time a white guy in 9ja [= Nigerian] body i will like 2 know u." Still others discuss the nature of his whiteness, raising the question of what kind of European he is or whether he is one at all. Some demand information about his parents' backgrounds. One commenter even asks whether he is an albino, proving that this explanation has also gained some currency beyond Tanzania. Lastly, a certain Dog Heart urges other users not to take White Nigerian's stage name at face value: "When will Nigerians stop calling Arabs and Indians whites? This guy is a proper Syrian or Palestinian who lives in Lagos or P[ort] H[arcourt] or Warri doing all kinda bad business. He prolly was born in Nigeria." Contrary to this rather negative judgment that draws on common Nigerian stereotypes of Levantine traders, another user, calling himself inanna, even develops high political hopes for White Nigerian as he considers his skin color a sign of righteousness: "We need people like you in Nigeria, especially in our politics. Nigeria needs someone who can be considered neutral to help heal our politics. I am so proud of you as a fellow Nigerian. Keep up with the good work." As if to respond to comments like this, White Nigerian released the song "President" in 2013. The Hausa lyrics are quite explicit: "Ni ne shugaban k'asa, White Nigerian shugaban k'asa" (I am the president, White Nigerian is the president), and the song's animated video clip grants him a significant promotion, from ordinary member of the National Youth Service Corps to head of state. Needless to say, this song is not meant to be taken too seriously. However, it can be considered reminiscent of an era in Nigerian popular culture during which the late Fela Anikulapo Kuti, the country's most popular musician, made a serious run for the presidency. It was 1978. Though the Federal Electoral Commission disqualified the Movement of the People, his affiliated party, Kuti is still widely remembered as the "Black President," which is also the title of one of his records (Veal 2000: 169).

In terms of high hopes, Mzungu Kichaa's music video *Wajanja* (2009) prompts a comment in a similar direction. This song praises Tanzania's young generation. Its hook line is a statement about the intelligence and cunningness of Tanzania's youth ("vijana wa bongo ni wajanja"). The video depicts the artist as a man of the people—in fact, as one of the young people he sings about.[14] A commenter, who calls himself afrocentricmilitant7, is impressed by the humility Mzungu Kichaa shows and contrasts this with the comportment of African American musicians:

> ive got so much love for this guy, cos it just shows me how fake everything else is. this white guy goes to the hood and sings in swahili. fuck any u.s. rapper talking about africa. them man are black and whenever they come africa they sleep in 5 star hotels. this guy analala [sleeps] under roof ya mabati [corrugated iron]. huu msee kichaa [This is a respected "Mister kichaa"]. he gives me hope for the world.

This particular comment got thirty-five "likes" by other YouTube users. Due to the nature of his songs, many of which address social issues and show a general concern for the problems of the common people, and for his comportment in his video clips, in which he presents himself as a man close to the people, Mzungu Kichaa seems to earn a lot of respect among Tanzanian fans of Bongo flava music. Serious critiques or so-called hater comments are absent from the commentary lists of his video clips on YouTube.

This differs from EES (Eric Sell), whose many music videos on YouTube inspire controversial commentaries also. In her friendly comment on *Ya Rocka* (EES feat. Fresh Family, 2012), Brown Timoteus, who most likely is a young female black Namibian well acquainted with Kwaito and its latest top acts, has this to say: "EES!!!! Yes jaaaa.... he's probably the only white Namibian that can dance kwaito. lol ... I love it!!!"[15] And a certain nauta51, who is a "Namibia[n] student in Greece," calls EES "my bro" and also lets him know: "i really love your music cos you promote nam-music very well with nam-flavor, just keep it up, and say hi to all nam-people there if you are still in namibia, sharp!"[16] Others have more qualms with EES's claim to represent Kwaito, Namibia, or even the whole of Africa. Thus, the music video *T.I.A.* (This is Africa), which is a collaboration between EES and the Namibian rapper Gazza, has prompted an interesting debate among commenters. The song title refers to the initialism tiA (for "this is Africa"), which in southern Africa is frequently used—especially in tourist contexts—as an ironic or even sarcastic comment on any kind of shortcoming or difficulty believed to be typically African (cf. Mboti 2011).

EES and Gazza's song is first of all a dance tune with a moving beat. On a somewhat deeper level, however, it turns the pessimistic notion of tiA into something quite positive: it invites the assumingly foreign listener to come and experience Africa and adjust to the life there: "Yes, Ja, I would like to invite you to the beautiful continent of Africa / Where we say 'Ja' / This is t.i.A. 'Ja' / So what's up? / What ever you do / You have to do it, like we do / Don't freeze / You gotta move to the beat [...] Africa—We are the future." Commenting on this clip, a certain monaomar1 begins by saying, "Good song ... but not as good as K'naan's T.I.A."[17] This is a reference to the Canadian Somali rapper Kaynaan Cabdi Warsame, more widely known for his music video *Wavin' Flag* (chosen as Coca-Cola's promotional anthem for the 2010 FIFA World Cup in South Africa). In his own *T.I.A.* song, K'naan ridicules the gangster attitude of African American rappers and invites them "on a field trip" to Africa to see real hardship ("You don't know how hard it is here / The streets is tricky in these parts here"). This is part of hip-hop's "keeping it real" discourse, which also echoes the comment quoted above that contrasts Mzungu Kichaa's presumably humble self-portrayal with the rather grand attitude of U.S. rappers. The debate over EES and Gazza's video versus K'naan's *T.I.A.* is continued by someone criticizing K'naan for having "lost his African roots," before returning to the Namibian song, which a certain Mattman Key believes "is better than K'naan's" because it "has a Kwaito sound." The reply by MissDarkAngel777, who seems to be a black Namibian woman, is harsh:

> Knaan is awesome. . . . He is true and good and I am proud to be a[n] African when he is singing, which is a lot more than I can say for EES. . . . Nothing about him is real. . . . And he is probably some afrikaans kid, and has to change his accent just to sound slightly kwaito. . . . He is such a wannabe WIGGER. . . . I am ashamed to call myself a namibian when I hear this shit, and I can't believe he is spreading it to the rest of the world. . . . EES is like a disease!!!

Calling EES not only a "wigger," which is a conflation of *white* and *nigger*, usually considered derogatory, but even more so a "wannabe" wigger, is to deny the Namibian's musical project of any legitimacy. Moreover, it expresses a sense of perplexity in view of EES's claim to represent Namibia, and between the lines is also an allegation of cultural appropriation. I return to this point later. Mattman Key replies by pointing out: "He's not really the first White person to do Kwaito," and referring to *Lekgoa*, a "White dude from South Africa."[18] And Sam Miwe, a user who claims to be from Zambia, suggests, "We have to [be] open-minded that Africa is white and black."

IN SEARCH OF EUROPEAN AUDIENCES

Whether black or white, making a living from music is not easy in African countries where the buying power of the majority is low and ordinary people are less likely to spend money on music. EES and Mzungu Kichaa run their own labels, EES Records and Caravan Records, respectively, using their own websites and iTunes and amazon for distribution and sales. However, piracy and their own promotional activities of offering free downloads tend to minimize their revenues. White Nigerian doesn't even attempt to sell his songs. Gate fees from live acts are another source of income. However, they do not book enough concerts to make this a reliable source of income. To make ends meet, all of them display a considerable amount of creativity. In addition to his music, EES sells a whole Nam flava lifestyle, offering EES-wear apparel—sneakers in Namibian national colors, shirts, pants, and hats—and even an energy drink called Wuma. White Nigerian engages in promotional activities ("Car wash with White Nigerian") and runs a nightclub in Abuja. Mzungu Kichaa has been able to secure financial support from sponsors such as Swiss Air and World Music Denmark, and has also experimented with crowd funding.

Trying to access audiences with more buying power is yet another option for the three musicians, and at least two of them, Mzungu Kichaa and EES, are very active at internationalizing their careers and thus broadening their fan bases. Performing African music in Europe as a musician with a European complexion comes with its own challenges, though. While their skin color may work as an exotic signifier in African music markets, it is not necessarily an advantage in Europe. Where "whiteness" constitutes the norm, white performers of African music are considered "wannabe" Africans, as they do not conform to the image of the exotic other. Mzungu Kichaa discovered this early on when launching his career in Scandinavia and Germany: "Some organizers of festivals have dropped me from their list when they discovered that although I sing in Swahili, I am actually a mzungu" (quoted in Banda 2010). According to him, it was the credit given by diasporic Africans who came to his concerts that helped to authenticate his music for European audiences (Sanga 2011). He has since gained some recognition within the tiny margins of the world music scene. In 2009, his album *Tuko Pamoja* was nominated in the category of Best World Album on the Danish World Music Awards in Copenhagen, and since 2010 he has been featured regularly at music festivals in Scandinavia. The fact that he has been frequently performing together with Tanzanian musicians—Ashimba, Fid-Q, and his backing band, Bongo Beat—on European stages may have been equally important for raising his credentials among European lovers of world music. His switch to English lyrics on his latest releases may be read as an attempt to make his music more accessible to his European fans.

EES has been particularly industrious at accessing new audiences. After coming to Germany in 2004, his initial hopes of starting a quick career in the music business were shattered. At first, he attempted to popularize Kwaito music in Germany but could not get airplay for his songs. This is because the music industry still has a strong grip on music business in Germany and radio stations rarely feature independent artists on their programs. Also, unlike Mzungu Kichaa's music, EES's is less likely to be sold in the world music segment. Kwaito is electronic music—somewhat close to European house music—and perhaps EES's particular variety of it does not sound different or "African" enough for German audiences—despite its lyrics in accented English and interjections in African languages and Afrikaans. Next to continuing with the production of Kwaito tracks, he began producing songs in German, featuring upcoming stars of the German YouTube v-logger scene, such as LionT and T-ZON, the latter being a German-Namibian musician who is also living in Germany. To further promote his music and business ventures, EES also opened a YouTube channel called EES-TV and took part in several shows on German television.[19]

EES-TV is meant to mediate "Africa" for German YouTube users by introducing them to a particular form of Namibian lifestyle. It is produced in German, or rather "Nam-släng," the updated variant of Südwesterdeutsch EES seeks to establish as his linguistic signature. The channel consists of short documentary clips about the seemingly exotic and adventurous life of a German-Namibian Kwaito star. Shot during EES's trips to Namibia each year, and uploaded every week, these clips combine the conventions of an exoticized touristic gaze at Africa with the aesthetics of raw, behind-the-scenes video footage. In the channel trailer, *Introdakschen am Pool,*[20] EES introduces himself and his mission, talking into the camera while standing in a swimming pool. Most remarkable about this seven-minute clip is the way he explains his African roots and how he belongs to the community of the so-called "forgotten Germans" of Namibia. His reiteration of this group's history, though visually enhanced by a number of old still photographs, barely mentions the colonial period of 1895–1918. This is remarkable, as the commemoration of the German war on the Herero and Nama (1904–1907) was high on the agenda—in both Namibia and Germany—after EES came to Germany in 2004, leading to controversial public debates about Namibian reparation claims (Förster 2010). Historical consciousness of the uneasy history of black and white relations in southern Africa is thus lacking in "Easy" Eric Sell's attempts to sell his Africa and his products to German audiences. His account of the history of Kwaito in the same clip is no less idiosyncratic: while floundering about in the pool and talking about the foundation of the musical genre in Soweto, only images of his own performances are shown as inserts, somehow insinuating that he played a crucial role in Kwaito's origins. Though a certain amount of bragging and a lack of humility are common ingredients of show business, the unquestioned implicitness with which EES assumes the role of representing Namibia and Kwaito music is perplexing. Who speaks for whom about what and who is not problematized on EES-TV. Instead, EES seeks to normalize his presence and that of the "forgotten Germans" of Namibia. It fits into this program that the majority of the clips on EES-TV portray a Namibia which seems to be full of white people. EES is thus shown taking a sundowner with German-speaking friends, surfing dunes with a German-speaking crowd, and so on. If black Namibians appear at all on EES-TV, they do so only as colorful backdrops. EES-TV has to be understood as a paratext to Sell's music videos; a paratext designed especially to access German audiences. The puzzling thing about this particular paratext is that unlike the music videos, where collaborations with black Namibian artists are the norm, it displays a Namibia that is almost literally whitewashed.

SOCIAL MEDIA AND COSMOPOLITAN ENGAGEMENTS

The internet and social media are infrastructures that afford "cosmopolitan engagements at a distance" (Woodward and Skrbis 2012: 134). Being artists and cultural entrepreneurs at once, the three musicians know how to use these infrastructures virtuously. All three connect with their fans via Facebook and Twitter and navigate networks of followers that stretch across different continents. As of January 28, 2014, the number of followers each had on his Twitter page looked like this—White Nigerian: 6,122, Mzungu Kichaa: 5,655, and EES: 672. This ranking corresponds to the frequency of tweets sent by each musician each day. It reverses if we look at the number of "likes" on their Facebook pages, which reflect a combination of both how long each artist has been on this platform and the duration of his career: White Nigerian joined Facebook in 2010 and, as of January 28, 2014, had more than 5,000 "likes." Mzungu Kichaa also joined in 2010 and could count about 30,000, whereas EES got on Facebook in 2009 and had more than 80,000. Of course, these figures are nothing more than mere indicators of interest by Facebook users and should not be mistaken for expressions of real fandom—whatever that is. Moreover, since Facebook "likes" (and Twitter followers, too) have been turned into commodities that can easily be bought in bulk for small amounts of money and, in the case of Facebook, may also be gotten through its sponsored ad service, the analytical value of these figures must be treated with some reservation.

In terms of commitment, the total number of subscribers to a page is a better indicator. However, only the page owner knows this. A page's weekly interaction rate remains a somewhat weaker indicator of user commitment: As of January 28, 2014, White Nigerian had 167 people "talking about this" (3.3 percent of his total likes), Mzungu Kichaa had 3,211 (10.7 percent), and EES had 1,977 (2.5 percent).[21] Facebook offers its page owners statistical tools allowing them to learn some basic facts about the people who "like" their pages. Some of this data can also be extracted with the help of external tools.[22] As table 8.1 shows, with respect to the three musicians in particular, it is possible to learn from which countries the "likes" of a page originate. Regarding the pages of the three musicians, it comes as no surprise that the vast majority of "likes" are from those countries with which the musicians most identify: 72.8 percent of Mzungu Kichaa's "likes" were from Tanzania (also, 10.8 percent were from Kenya and 3.2 percent from other African countries), 59 percent of White Nigerian's "likes" were from Nigeria (and 3 percent from other African countries), and 38 percent of EES's were from Namibia (and 13 percent from other African countries).[23] While White Nigerian had a considerable number of likes from Britain (12.4 percent) and the United States (11.3 percent), which correlates with the high number of diasporic Nigerians living

TABLE 8.1

Percentage of Facebook "likes" by country for the three musicians
(as of January 28, 2014)

Country	White Nigerian	Mzungu Kichaa	EES	
Nigeria	59	0.1	0.1	(0.15)
Tanzania	0	72.8	0	(0)
Namibia	0.1	0	37.6	(52.5)
Africa (excluding Nigeria, Tanzania, and Namibia)	3	13	13	(18.8)
Great Britain	12.4	1.5	0.4	(0.5)
United States	11.3	2	1	(1.4)
Denmark	0	4	0	(0)
Germany	1.3	1	6.2	(8.6)
Continental Europe (excluding Denmark and Germany)	4.8	2.4	14.2	(5.4)
Other	10.1	3.2	27.5	(12.4)

Note: Figures in parentheses do not include "likes" from India or Serbia.

in these two countries, the other two musicians were considerably more popular in continental Europe. As one might expect, Mzungu Kichaa scored highest in Denmark (4 percent) and the rest of continental Europe (2.4 percent), whereas EES scored highest in Germany (6.2 percent) and in the rest of continental Europe (14.2 percent).[24] Given the considerable amount of energy Mzungu Kichaa and EES spend on internationalizing their careers, these figures seem to be rather low, correlating with the observation that the white cosmopolite who performs African popular music is a figure rather difficult to sell in European music economies.

Growing rates of Facebook "likes" are also interesting to compare. From June 2013 to January 2014, Mzungu Kichaa had a growing rate of 200 percent—by far the highest of the three musicians; White Nigerian had 25 percent and EES 11 percent. This correlates with public performances, of which Mzungu Kichaa, who toured Scandinavia and some African countries during the second half of 2013, clearly had the most.

How do the musicians employ social media? All of them use Twitter and Facebook as promotional tools, updating their fans about their daily lives, whereabouts, and latest projects. Twitter allows them to keep in touch with their followers with a level of regularity and intimacy which no other social media is able to provide. Several tweets per day create an "ambient awareness" (Reichelt 2007) of their activities among their followers, keeping the musicians present in their fans' lives—for example, "I will be live on ITV in 15mins! ITV Nigeria not UK lol" (White Nigerian on Twitter, January 27, 2014). Often, tweets are formulated as teasers meant to arouse their readers' curiosity. Links provided in such tweets redirect to the musician's pages on other internet platforms, such as Instagram, Facebook, or YouTube, where images, music, videos, and other information are disclosed: "Watch the history of Mzungu Kichaa through 34 videos on Youtube. Which is your favourite? and why" (on Twitter, January 16, 2014)? Encouraging the active participation of their followers, the musicians often ask for their fans' opinions on a particular project. This keeps their followers involved and the feedback they receive may help the musicians with their future projects.

Facebook and Twitter are also important tools for mobilizing "friends" and "followers" to perform certain tasks, such as donating money or casting a vote in favor of the musician. On January 9, 2014, Mzungu Kichaa asked his followers for help with the release of his EP *Relax*. His Twitter post read as follows: "We need your support! Please share our crowd-funding project to raise funds for new music with Mzungu Kichaa." The message provided a link to a project called Connecting Cultures through Music, which he had created on Boomerang, a Danish crowd-funding site, where he posted the projected release date of his EP. EES is particularly good at mobilizing his fans to cast votes for him in awards venues organized by TV channels, such as the MTV Africa Awards or the Channel O Music Video Awards. Following his nominations in 2009 and 2012, respectively, EES campaigned heavily on his diverse websites and social media pages. Since he asked both his European and his African followers for support, his African "Best Kwaito" award of 2012 was at least partially produced by European votes, a somewhat paradoxical effect of EES's cosmopolitan career. On the other hand, he sought to secure his Namibian fans' votes during his participation in the talent show *Millionärswahl* (Millionaire's poll) on the German television channel SAT1. Prior to and even during the final show, which was live-streamed on the internet on January 25, 2014, EES's Twitter account and Facebook page were literally overflowing with his pleas for votes. While he called upon his German Facebook fans to vote for him to "show how big the Nam flava family is" (January 25, 2014), he appealed to his Namibian Twitter followers by linking his personal project to national sentiments: "1 HOUR LEFT before the start of the big online TV show *Millionärswahl*—ARE YOU READY TO VOTE FOR NAMIBIA???" This was his appeal to followers on Facebook a few days before the show: "Watch the show live from anywhere in the world at www.connect.prosieben.de and VOTE FOR NAMIBIA—and EES to bring it home" (January 22, 2014)![25]

For their friends and followers, the musician's Facebook pages mediate cosmopolitan awareness and provide a space for realizing their own worldly engagements and tentative performances of cosmopolitanism. By reading the postings of their co-subscribers and looking at their faces that bespeak of different origins, they experience epidermal, cultural, and linguistic difference. Mzungu Kichaa's page contains messages in Swahili, Danish, and English. English, German, Nam-släng, and Afrikaans converge on EES's page, whereas English, Nigerian pidgin English, and Hausa converge on White Nigerian's page. Visitors and subscribers are able to witness the frequent travels of their "stars" by reading their updates and looking at the uploaded snapshots. For some of the subscribers, these pages are like windows onto a world of difference hitherto unknown to them. One of EES's German fans, Desiree Reiter, posted this message on his Facebook page: "i hope sometime my dream come true and then it's like your life . . . in afrika with a bus and learn the spirit of other people" (the "bus" refers to EES's Volkswagen bus, baptized "Shaggon Waggon"). Sometimes, fans perform their own tentative border crossings by posting messages in one of the languages or linguistic codes used on a particular page, which is not their own. On EES's page, some black Namibians leave short messages in German, and some of his German fans try Nam-släng. While this is done in a playful mood, there is also a remarkable number of Scandinavians posting well-formulated messages in Swahili on Mzungu Kichaa's page. On closer inspection, this turns out to be by people involved in East African–related development work. On all three pages, messages by subscribers and visitors almost always address the page owner and only very rarely other subscribers and their postings. Of course, individual subscribers may easily contact one another via their own Facebook pages, "friend" one another, and start a conversation, which would turn the musician's page into a hub for cosmopolitan connections. However, until further proof, this remains a possibility only.

DIFFERENT SHADES OF COSMOPOLITANISM

At the heart of the cosmopolitan ventures of the three musicians, we find what Mica Nava (2007) calls "domestic cosmopolitanism." Unlike other theorists of the cosmopolitan who have focused on travel and staying abroad, Nava proposes to take into account that "a good deal of inclusive thinking and feeling . . . takes place in the micro territories of the local: at school, in the gym and the café, *at home*" (135). While, today, the three musicians are also leading cosmopolitan lives in a conventional sense, epitomized by their frequent travels between the continents, the roots of their cosmopolitan thinking and feeling are situated in the domestic sphere of their African home countries, Namibia, Nigeria, and Tanzania. Significantly, all of them revert to the inclusive experiences of their childhood and schooling days when accounting for the origins of their cosmopolitan attitudes. In our interviews, Eric Sell and Espen Sørensen also mentioned their families and thus another of Nava's "micro territories of the local." Using her own family history as an example, Nava argues for acknowledging the importance of family to understand how individuals develop a disposition toward cultural difference. I wish to combine this idea with another, which I borrow from Peter van der Veer (2002), who argues for the necessity of taking the enabling conditions of engagement with the other into account when studying cosmopolitan orientations. In other words, we not only need to think of family histories but also of past and present power relations that, as enabling conditions, shape the form domestic cosmopolitanism and "conviviality" (Gilroy 2004) take in a given society. This helps us better understand the different shades of cosmopolitanism the three musicians have developed.

Eric Sell is fifth generation German-Namibian. During the late nineteenth century, his ancestors arrived in the German colony Deutsch-Südwestafrika, as Namibia was called back then. Sell entered school in 1990, the year Namibia achieved independence from South Africa, and the terms of black and white conviviality changed. During our interview, he explained how, despite the official end of apartheid, white and black pupils still gathered in separate corners of the schoolyard. He eventually came into contact with Kwaito music by socializing with children from both groups and swapping hip-hop CDs with black friends. His style of domestic cosmopolitanism therefore developed against the backdrop of a society in social transformation. The descendants of four generations of white settlers had lost their privileges and were now seeking to define a place for themselves within the new political situation. Sell's frequent use of the national flag, which is perhaps the most striking feature of his performances, has to be understood in this light. It is at once an emphatic claim of belonging and a dedicated confession to commitment—also a clever way of branding.

As we have seen, Mohammed Jammal, alias White Nigerian, shares this frequent use of national symbols. He, too, belongs to a category of people that arrived during the colonial past. As so-called middlemen between colonizers and the colonized, the Levantine traders of West Africa benefited from the colonial economic system. Prejudices against the K'wara, as they are called in northern Nigeria, originate in their past privileges. After 1960, their allegiance to the independent state has often been questioned, as they are known to maintain ties to their ancestral homelands and the Levantine diaspora elsewhere. It is against this backdrop that Jammal stresses that he carries only one passport, which is Nigerian, and that he "wrote history" by being the first "white man" ever to join the Nigerian Youth Corps Service. The domestic cosmopolitanism of the K'wara of northern Nigeria starts literally at home, through African nannies and housekeepers, and though Jammal discloses little about his past, we may assume that his family also enjoyed this privilege. Apart from Nigeria as a whole, Jammal also identifies with Jos, or "J-town," as it is called in Nigerian slang, where he grew up and went to school. Significantly, Jos has a long history of cosmopolitan encounters, attracting people from all over Nigeria and also missionaries and development workers from Europe and America. Committed to the well-being of his hometown, Jammal took part in a number of media campaigns dedicated to the restoration of peace in Jos, which since 2001, has witnessed a series of bloody conflicts along ethnic and religious lines.

While Jammal and Sell share a history of growing up in Africa, so-journing in Europe, and eventually returning to Africa, Espen Sørensen's biography is even less fixed according to geographical and cultural terms. Growing up in a family who cultivated a cosmopolitan lifestyle, his formative years were spread out across four countries—Denmark, Zambia, England, and Tanzania. Of the three musicians, he attests most to Nava's argument that a cosmopolitan orientation may also be tied to a family habitus. Sørensen's maternal family developed just such a habitus, across several generations: his mother was born in Bangkok and grew up in Borneo, where her father, a Dane who had served in the British Royal Air Force, worked in the timber business. His mother's mother, born in Bangkok, too, had a British father, who served as legal adviser to the King of Siam. His paternal family, though less cosmopolitan, has Danish and Polish roots, his father being half Polish. As he told me in our interview, his parents were very liberal in terms of his upbringing: "They always let me be whatever I wanted to be. If I wanted to be a Zambian kid, when I was in Zambia, I was allowed to." The political economy of development work is the enabling condition of Sørensen's early cosmopolitan experiences. This brought his parents to Africa and Sørensen himself later on when he worked as a coordinator for the Pilgrim Foundation, the socially responsible affiliate of a Danish jewelry company of the same name.

Cosmopolitanism has sometimes been criticized as a category mostly held by elites (Vertovec and Cohen 2002). While the three musicians surely do not belong to the lowest strata of the societies they live in, calling their performances and lifestyle elitist would surely misrepresent them. On the one hand, they thrive on certain privileges, which in one way or another are implicated by the history of European imperialism. On the other hand, they try as much as possible to emancipate themselves from this legacy. Ian Woodward and Zlatko Skrbis (2012: 130) differentiate between "reflexive and banal forms of cosmopolitanism." Whereas the reflexive type is "related to a deep capacity for inclusive ethical practice," the banal form comes closer "to sampling and superficial enjoyment of cosmopolitan opportunities in a variety of settings." As the musicians demonstrate, however, these two ideal types must not mutually exclude each other. If cosmopolitanism, at its most basic level, implies transcending boundaries—geographical, cultural, social, and political—the three musicians perform both reflexive and banal kinds of cosmopolitanism. They are frequent travelers and border crossers. They enjoy "cosmopolitan opportunities in a variety of settings," which is the rather banal face of their transnational lifestyle. Their Facebook pages carry many photos showing them in different locations across the globe. For Mzungu Kichaa, the iconography of travel seems to be of particular importance. Many photos capture him in transit: at airports, about to board a plane or having just arrived. These testimonies of banal forms of cosmopolitanism, however, should not prevent us from acknowledging the "inclusive ethical practices" that are at the heart of their individual ventures: their engagement with musical, linguistic and cultural registers conventionally considered different from their own ("a white boy trying to do something totally black," as one of EES's Namibian colleagues put it). In fact, Mzungu Kichaa's frequent travels and EES's sojourning in Europe are both a consequence and an indicator of their dedication to African music. For economic reasons, they need to leave the continent to continue with music making. Applying Woodward and Skrbis's nomenclature too strictly, though, and calling their performances a "reflexive form of cosmopolitanism," would fall short of accounting for the visceral and affective dimensions of their ventures. This is not to say that they do not reflect on what they are doing, but their performances touch upon and express something that lies beyond the cognitive. What I find in them is not just "a positive attitude towards difference" (Ribeiro 2001: 2842) but rather a desire to blend into the other that goes far beyond staged performances and strategic maneuvers, and pervades their whole lives. Their crossing of cultural boundaries is a special case of appropriation in which copying means becoming a kind of permanent mimesis—but actually, no longer mimesis, as the copy turns into an original, and the difference between original and copy may cease to exist.

Coda

MIMESIS AND MEDIA IN AFRICA

MIMESIS IS A BASIC human way of approaching the world. We understand by imitating, we appropriate through copying, and we connect to other people and things by shaping our artistic products or ourselves after them. According to Gunter Gebauer and Christoph Wulf (2003: 8), "Mimetic processes can be conceptualized as iterative creations of antecedent worlds through which humans make these their own, however, not by means of theoretical thinking but by means of the senses, that is, aesthetic" (my translation). Our mimetic faculty combines with and is extended by that of "mimetically capacious machines" (Taussig 1993: 243), which are able to produce likenesses and also form the basis of larger media apparatuses, replicating them en masse. Mimesis and media are inextricably linked: mimesis not only mediates but is always already mediated. Mimesis depends on media. Even at its most basic form, it needs the medium of the human body to produce likenesses of other humans, animals or things. However, as representational media, such as paintings, sculptures, books, and modern mass media, are also difficult to imagine without mimesis, the dependency is mutual.

Across the chapters of this book, I am interested in instances of mimesis and media in African encounters with cultural difference. By its very definition, mimesis is built upon a difference between the imitator and the imitated. Even if an actor plays himself or a painter draws a self-portrait, mimesis is used as a distancing device, allowing the imitator to view himself or herself as an "other." Seen in this light, the imitation of others who are experienced as embodying the essence of a different "culture" by cultural producers in Africa is only a gradual extension of the basic binary constellation of any mimetical operation—ego representing an alter. The mimesis of alter beings, such as spirits, animals, and human others, has a long tradition in many African societies, where it was and often still is enacted in a variety of performance genres, including rituals, masquerades, dances, storytelling, and theater, as well as plastic arts. Audiovisual media—cinema, television, video and the hyper-medium of the internet—have considerably multiplied encounters with representations of alter ways of living. At the same time, audiovisual media technologies provide new means of appropriating cultural difference through mimesis. As I recapitulate below, some of the meanings attached to the older forms of mimesis have been carried over into these new forms, which combine the human mimetic faculty with that of mimetically capacious machines. It is also important to note that I deal with two different but related notions of mimesis: (1) people imitating (the manners of) other people and (2) people imitating the (artistic) work of others. Sometimes, these two notions converge. A film that emulates another film is a good example of this. In this case people imitate other people's artistic work, which consists of imitating other people (or at least scripted templates of other people).

How mimesis and media are used, conceptualized, and evaluated in Africa depends on the contingency of different social contexts. It is therefore impossible to break down the range of meanings attached to mimesis and media to a single definition. Hence, in the following I recapitulate different notions of mimesis and media in Africa under five headings. I consider each of these notions relevant beyond the particular examples outlined in this book. Interestingly, I find a striking resonance between some of the recurring themes of the previous chapters and Platonic and Aristotelian thinking about mimesis. The two ancient philosophers offered me the right impulses to distance myself from the material at hand, take a fresh look at it, and eventually flesh out the following five notions of mimesis and media in Africa.

THE NOTION OF THE INTERMEDIARY

Across the chapters of this book, we see a wide range of mimesis in terms of the similarity between template and copy. We witness almost faithful replicas but also adaptations which are far less similar to their models. Within the perspective developed in this study, similarity is only a means to an end, not an end in itself. In *Mimetische Weltzugänge* (Mimetical approaches to the world), a follow-up study to *Mimesis,* their seminal history of the mimesis concept, Gebauer and Wulf (2003: 9) state: "Frequently, the results of mimetic acts can only be insufficiently explained by a reference to similarity. More important than the existence of similarity is the fact that contact is established; for example, by an artist to the works of other artists, . . . by one human being to other human beings, by ritually acting individuals to other ritual actions and performances" (my translation). It is this intermediary nature of mimesis which we see at work across the various examples I outline in the chapters of this book. Drawing on Michael Taussig's explorations of mimesis and alterity, I seek to capture this notion within the formula of "contact and copy," an operational logic which equally includes its reverse—"copy and contact." Mimesis invokes the other (understood in the widest sense of that to which a representation, as a copy, refers) to participate in some of its qualities. We see this logic at work in religious and ideational contexts, such as Babule mediums invoking the power of the European colonialists and radical Muslims conjuring that of Osama bin Laden. We also see mimesis at work in the more mundane contexts of emerging culture industries, where cultural producers tie their own products to already successful foreign templates (films from Hollywood, Bollywood, and Nollywood, for example). They thus seek to confer the global appeal and success of these templates on their own work. The secondary purposes attached to mimetic relationships may vary, as they depend on the contingencies of changing social contexts, but the primary function of invoking and participating in the qualities of that which is copied remains the same.

Mimesis' intermediary nature is highly ambiguous because along with the positive and valued qualities of a given model that are acquired through imitation come its undesired and negative aspects as well. Hence, mimesis is frequently considered dangerous for those who undertake it. The belief that imitators are affected by the imitated is already present in Plato's *Republic*. It can be traced throughout European theater history and is also present in African performance traditions involving possession-trance (chapter 1). Similar convictions also exist in Nigerian and Tanzanian video filmmaking where actors and actresses are often associated with the types they play. In northern Nigeria, for example, critics have equated actors with the immoral behavior of the characters depicted in Hausa videos. In her study of Pentecostal television drama production in Kinshasa, Katrien Pype (2012) explains how the producers take precautions through praying and other preemptive measures to prevent the devil from conquering the souls of the actors who are imitating wicked characters. The underlying logic is that of sympathetic magic in which like produces like and "imitating is copying and becoming" (140). Imitating immoral behavior is almost like inviting the devil to come and take a seat within the imitator's soul. Such ideas about the dangers of mimesis have been observed among southern Nigerian and Ghanaian video filmmakers as well (Meyer 2006).

However, mimesis may be considered potentially dangerous both for those who engage in it and for the audiences who are deemed likely to imitate what they read in books or see in plays, films, or video games. This conviction, again already mentioned by Plato, informs much of the critical debate about the imagined negative effects of media on youth—not only in African societies. We may wonder whether it is due to the physiology of sensing—"seeing something or hearing something is to be in contact with that something" (Taussig 1993: 21)—that mimesis is believed to also be contagious to its audiences. In the preceding chapters, we first come across a variant of this type of discourse in the contemporary Kenyan critique of the Lance Spearman photo novels, which were targeted for their "violence and gangster dialogue" and were believed to have caused an increase in crime in East African cities during the 1960s. Most prominently, however, we see it at work in the controversies surrounding vice and videos in northern Nigeria. Because of their imitations of "other possible lives" (via their taking models from Indian popular cinema), Hausa videos were considered harmful to their audiences. Parents and elders feared that the films would "destroy the moral upbringing" of their children whom they observed copying the forms of dress and behavior shown in the movies. Religious hardliners propagated symbolic acts, such as public immolations of videocassettes, and Kano state, home of the Kanywood video film industry, introduced censorship. The latter is a parallel to Plato's call for strict control of the arts in the *Republic*. Unlike Plato, however, whose utopian state remained on paper only, the Kano state legislators aspired to founding an ideal state for real. Though the foundations on which these two states are built differ—reason here, religion there—their treatment of the arts, of mimesis, is remarkably similar.

EXPLORING THE POSSIBLE, INVENTING "AFROMODERNITY"

Mimesis produces both similarity and difference. Throughout this book, all examples of mimesis—either of other possible lives or the artworks of others, and most often a combination of the two—are copies with a difference. The cultural producers, whose appropriations of foreign works I discuss herein, alter their source material significantly to suit their own purposes. The Hausa remake of Cameron's *Titanic,* for example, changes some of the characters and the imagery to adapt it to a new reception context, despite being faithful to its model in an overall sense. This is in keeping with the Aristotelian conception of mimesis as "copying and changing in one" (Gebauer and Wulf 1995: 54). And like Aristotle, for whom the mimesis of tragedy is no longer defined as mere imitation of the real (as in Plato) but comprehends "both the possible and the universal" (54), African cultural producers have used the photo novel, the comic, the video film, and the music video for their own explorations of the possible. Since the blueprints of other possible lives developed on these media platforms are in part inspired by foreign audiovisual media, they tend to take on the characteristics of both the strange and the familiar.[1] In Tanzanian video films, the Swahili-speaking characters are portrayed as living in luxurious mansions full of opulent furniture reminiscent of Nollywood settings, and the Hausa-speaking lovers of Kanywood videos act in ways which are more typical of Bollywood cinema than of Nigerian everyday life. I conceptualize such films as material results of the "symbolic distancing" process which scholars of transnational media consumption describe as one of the attractions global media has for local audiences. According to John Thompson (1995: 175), the appropriation of foreign media enables spectators "to take some distance from the conditions of their day-to-day lives—not literally but symbolically, imaginatively, vicariously," and to critically question their own lives and living conditions.

In Africa, this process has been observed, for example, with the consumption of Bollywood movies in northern Nigeria (Larkin 1997) and Kenya (Fugelsang 1994), and with Nigerian video films in Botswana (Kerr 2011) and South Africa (Becker 2013). Unlike the vast majority of such audiences, the cultural producers whose work I discuss do not content themselves with merely imagining how local life would look under different conditions, but they express their visions of other possible lives and hence their "symbolic distancing" from their day-to-day existence through their own cultural production. This kind of appropriation, which I define as "mimetical interpretation," never implies simple reproduction but always copying *and* changing. Thus, Kanywood films and Bongo movies, which usually entertain mimetical relationships to both alien and local forms of cultural production, offer their audiences particular visions of "Afromodernity." According to Jean and John Comaroff (2004: 202), who coined this term, Afromodernity is not "a response to European modernity, or a creation derived from it," but "a complex formation" that "is actively forged, in the ongoing present, from endogenous and exogenous elements of a variety of sorts." The African appropriators whose work I discuss herein are among those who are "actively forging" Afromodernity. This holds equally true for the "crazy white men" I discuss in chapter 8. They participate in Afromodernity and give their particular brand of it a certain cosmopolitan spin. Their success with African audiences proves that by and large their contributions meet with approval.

As we see in this book, explorations of the possible may occur not only on the representational level of the finished cultural products but also during their production processes. In chapter 4, I call Kanywood film sets quintessential heterotopian spaces because they were marked by a noticeable difference in terms of social conduct. During the film shoots, which usually lasted only a few days and took place in spatial seclusion, many of the constraints governing everyday male-female interaction in

northern Nigeria lost their validity. Instead, actors and actresses, directors, producers, and technical staff seized the chance to create their own
"live" versions of Afromodernity.

BINDING AND BANNING ALTERITY

African cultural producers mediate alterity for local audiences by appropriating foreign media content and domesticating it within their own
cultural work. Their mimetical interpretations are as much about the exploration of the possible as they are about the binding and banning of
alterity. Seen from this angle, media such as the photo novel, the comic,
the video film, and the music video have inherited some of the functions of
older forms of mediation, which have been employed previously to come
to terms with alterity. Like rituals of spirit possession, masquerades, and
wooden figurines, which were and still are used to fix and contain alterity
within the temporal and spatial confines of performances and material
objects, the media I discuss are the privileged instruments and sites for
engaging and containing cultural difference today. Media producers may
be called the heirs of ritual specialists. Like the priests of traditional cults,
media producers specialize in the mediation of alterity. They produce images of cultural difference by means of various media, including their own
bodies. And like the alter beings portrayed previously in rituals, masquerades, and wooden figurines, the other possible lives portrayed currently
in popular media are marked by a fundamental ambiguity, as they are at
once fascinating and repulsing.

As specialists of mediation, cultural producers act on behalf of the
common people. They perform and produce audiovisual representations
of alterity so that the viewers are spared undergoing mimesis themselves.
The audiences of such cultural forms are thus privileged to engage with
alterity from a safe distance—through TV screens, for example, which
function as windows and walls at the same time. This is reminiscent of
the Aristotelian notion of the distancing effect of mimetic arts, as seen
in painting and drama (particularly tragedy). According to Aristotle, mimesis allows its audience to take pleasure in viewing and gaining understanding about things that might otherwise appear disgusting, if seen

unmediated. If we substitute Aristotle's "basest animals and corpses" for "other ways of life" and likewise "tragedy" for "popular media," we grasp the (cathartic) effect the various imitations of other possible lives have on their spectators. Gebauer and Wulf (1995) describe Aristotle's view of mimetic identification as follows:

> The concern of tragedy is to offer the audience pleasure. This feeling arises from the spectators' re-experience of the tragic events, which broadens their range of experience, knowing all the while that they themselves are not entirely subject to what happens on stage. The pleasure taken in trag-edy is linked to the desire to survive. . . . mimetic identification with the horror expressed in tragedy suggests to Aristotle precisely the promise of fortifying oneself against the "horrifying" and "pitiful." (56)

In my reading, mediatized imitations of other possible lives offer their audiences pleasure and insights through a similar process. Though placed on screens in front of the spectators, alterity is fixed, bound, and kept at a safe distance within such representations. The final sentence in the extract from Gebauer and Wulf might be rendered as follows: mimetic identifica-tion with other possible lives as expressed in popular media suggests pre-cisely the promise of fortifying spectators against other ways of life and ul-timately also against altering their own ways of life. It is important to also remember that it is a double-mediated and therefore somewhat diluted alterity seen in the representations I discuss in this book. Representations such as the *Titanic* comic, Lance Spearman look-reads, Hausa videos, and Bongo movies are already translations of European, American, Indian, and Nigerian ways of life, respectively, as they are adapted from media originating in these alter social spaces. While my reading—in borrowing from Aristotle—suggests that these diluted forms serve to contain alterity even more so because of their substitutive nature (the audiences do not have to undergo mimesis themselves, as others—actors—do it on their behalf), the interpretation of local critics is just the opposite and thus reminiscent of Plato's critique of mimesis. The critics of Nigerian Hausa videos, for example, consider such adaptations even more dangerous than their foreign originals in terms of fostering imitation by their audiences. According to their interpretation, the foreign originals, though problem-atic in and of themselves, would be still far enough removed from local reality to be contagious. Unlike the foreign originals, however, the local copies are much closer to local social reality and thus would be more likely to serve as templates for imitations by audiences, as they provide images closer to home. However, except for the occasional nickname and clothing accessory, and the rare invention of new performance forms (e.g., Hausa youths imitating the famous song-and-dance sequences of Hausa videos live on stage by dancing and miming to playback tunes), not much has actually left the screen and become manifest in public life. This suggests that the critics' contentions should be understood as expressions of their fear of social change rather than observations of any real changes in social life induced by popular media. Instead of setting the ambivalent forces of alterity free, media such as Kanywood videos serve to fix and bind them.

SIMULATION, MIMICRY, AND DECEPTION

Gebauer and Wulf (1995: 36) mention "simulation" as one of the many meanings of mimesis to be found in Plato's Book III of *The Republic:* "Something is represented of which it is known that it does not correspond to the truth because it is in some sense advantageous to do so" (36). Imitators may thus use an imitation to deceive audiences, tricking them into believing that they are facing something genuine, when they actually are not. Today, this notion of mimesis is expressed through the term *mimicry.* As such it corresponds to the deceptive nature of the 419 letters, which simulate genuine business proposals and can lead to the many fake documents that mimic bureaucratic business procedures. Other instances of mimesis as simulation are to be found in *The Master,* the Nollywood film that looks behind the scenes of 419 scams. To trick his European victim into believing that he has the power to authorize a contract to refurbish the Kaduna oil refinery, Denis mimes the "King of Nigeria." This invention, which is perfectly in tune with the European conception of Africa, serves to assuage any fears the victim may have and Denis eventually succeeds in turning him into a *mugu*—a "fool" blinded by his own greed and the mimetic talent of the fraudster, willing to pay fictitious fees for fake documents.

Mimesis as deception is also a trope in African critical discourses about popular media, in which doubts about the genuineness of certain representations in terms of their cultural authenticity are quite common.

Debates about video filmmaking in Kano and Dar es Salaam are replete with talk about a so-called copycat syndrome. This is shorthand for criticizing the filmmakers for a perceived lack of originality and as copiers of foreign ideas. In critical Kanywood parlance, Hausa remakes of Indian films, which are not true remakes in a conventional sense, as my discussion in chapter 4 shows, are called *wankiya*. This is a colloquial expression for "deception." As a label for a type of film that hides its relationship to a foreign template, the term *wankiya* refers to the deception of the audience who is left in the dark about the film's true nature. What is interesting about this debate is that it is not so much concerned with the creativity and originality of the director-auteur (as European debates about imitating in the arts would have it) but with making viewers believe they are being presented with representations of local life as it is, or ought to be. Debates about *wankiya* are not so much concerned with the genius of filmmakers as with their social integrity and the cultural authenticity of their films. Kanywood debates are haunted by the Platonic doubt of mimesis as deception turned on its head. While Plato criticizes mimesis because like a mirror it produces only reflections of things (devoid of essence and lacking truth), the critics of Kanywood scold Hausa videos precisely because they do not reflect the right "things." What Hausa videos are lacking in the eyes of their critics is the representation of an imagined ideal of a genuine Hausa Muslim self whose religious and cultural integrity is untainted by immoral influences from the outside.

In Tanzania, the elitist critique of Bongo movies, though less vehement, is based on similar premises. Unlike Kano, however, religious overtones are absent in the critical debates of Dar es Salaam, where nationalist overtones run high. Bongo movies are criticized for misrepresenting Tanzanian ways of doing things and for lacking anything distinctively Tanzanian beyond the fact that they are produced in the national language Swahili. Copying from Nigerian Nollywood films is almost equated with a lack of national commitment on the part of the filmmakers. In Kano and Dar es Salaam, fears of the dangerous effects of imitation mix with anxieties about the loss of cultural integrity. In the eyes of their critics, Hausa videos and Bongo movies are capable of producing cultural mimics. However, unlike the "mimic men" often quoted in postcolonial theory, who are thought to imitate the European colonizers,[2] those feared by local critics in Kano and Dar es Salaam rather borrow from Indian and Nigerian films, respectively—that is, from cultural products originating outside the realm of the former colonizers.

APPROPRIATION AS PARTICIPATION
IN GLOBAL MEDIA FLOWS

African cultural producers are first among equals of African audiences of global mass culture. Through their own cultural production based on appropriation and mimesis, they not only cast the inspiration they receive from foreign media into a certain form but also regain agency as consumers of cultural artifacts produced by others. Here I find a certain parallel in the cultural "prosumers" of Western "convergence culture" (Jenkins 2006), who no longer content themselves with the passive consumption of the latest blockbuster movie or best-selling novel. Instead, they produce their own adaptations, which they share through social media platforms. The African cultural producers whose work I discuss are prosumers in their own right. Their own "convergence culture," which until recently was based on analogue media, precedes that of their Western counterparts, developed along with digital media and the web 2.0. In terms of their attitudes toward the artifacts of the dominant cultural industries, however, which translate into their own products, both have much in common. Here and there, the responses of the prosumers range from subversive counter readings of the originals to affirmative emulations and reenactments.

Among the cultural artifacts I discuss in this book, subversive readings are perhaps illustrated best by recalling some of the northern Nigerian interpretations of the "global war on terror" as expressed in video films such as *Ibro Saddam*, which ran counter to the dominant interpretations perpetuated by CNN and other hegemonic Western newscasters. Equally subversive, but in a somewhat paradoxical and more complex way, are the readings of Western representations of Africa by Nigerian cyber scammers. The paradox lies in the fact that it is precisely the perfect emulation of Western representations of Africa that helps them achieve their ultimate goal, cheating individuals from the Global North for personal gain, which constitutes a subversion of the international order of things that privileges the West. The majority of examples I discuss in this book, however, do not necessarily subvert the foreign cultural artifacts they relate to in any significant way. They rather emulate them. African appropriators have thus established themselves as brokers of global mass culture by providing local audiences with "copies with a difference," which are invested with both local meaning and the aura of globality. This is both a marketing strategy and a claim to participate in global media flows.

However, participation in global media flows must not stop at purely symbolic means. During the past ten years or so, some of the local culture industries I have taken my examples from, such as Kanywood in northern Nigeria and the Bongo movie industry of Tanzania, have been able to enter into transnational circulation and to thus open up to new audiences beyond their immediate constituencies. While Hausa videos travel along the Savannah belt of West Africa to the centers of the Hausa diaspora and all the way to Saudi Arabia, Bongo movies are watched throughout Swahili-speaking East Africa. Subtitled versions of films from both industries are also broadcast continent-wide, via Africa Magic Plus, a channel dedicated to film productions in African languages operated by the South African satellite pay-television network DSTV. The success of these industries is still surpassed by that of Nollywood, the video film industry of southern Nigeria whose English language films are watched across Africa and the African diaspora worldwide (cf. Krings and Okome 2013a). In terms of output, Nollywood has already been baptized the third largest film industry in the world (after Bollywood and Hollywood) by a UNESCO report in 2009. Even though it is still unclear whether it will be able to leave the continental and diasporic niche, Nollywood has most certainly become a player to reckon with in global media-scapes. Perhaps we will soon witness the appropriation of its aesthetics and the mimetical interpretation of its stories by cultural producers from elsewhere. I am already wondering what a Hollywood remake of a Nollywood classic such as *Karishika* would look like.

NOTES

INTRODUCTION

1. Plato's own use of *mimesis* has to be understood in a similar vein: throughout the text, he speaks via the figure of Socrates, his deceased teacher, rather than speaking himself.

2. Many authors, though, do not distinguish between *mimesis* and *mimicry* and tend to use both concepts interchangeably. However, as both differ in terms of the cultural functions they perform, it makes sense to differentiate them. "In mimicry, the dominant function is that of mischievous *imitation*—the kind of imitation that pays ironic homage to its object. Mimesis (although its function has always been disputed) usually refers to a wider process of *representation* that involves the mediation between different worlds and people—in essence between different symbolic systems" (Huggan 1997/1998: 94).

3. Earlier anthropological writing about "primitive" thought, such as James Frazer's (1978 [1890]) theory of "sympathetic magic" and Lucien Lévy-Bruhl's (1922) concept of "mystic participation," sought to come to terms with forms of thought and symbolic action in which similarity and mimetic behavior feature prominently. Tilman Lang (1998), who wrote a dissertation on Walter Benjamin's concept of mimesis, says that Benjamin was familiar with Lévy-Bruhl's work. However, it is not known whether he read Frazer's work as well.

4. Interestingly, Markus Verne (2007) has launched a critique on the concept of appropriation (*Aneignung* in German) on a similar account.

5. However, Jonathan Friedman (1990b: 161), who equates appropriation with consumption, points out that Congolese and Westerners, due to different "superordinate strategies of identification of self and world," appropriate for different ends: "Congolese internalize what is outside of themselves in order to become more than what they are. . . . Modern westerners appropriate what is outside of themselves in order to become what they are not" (161). I am not convinced of this binarism and would criticize it.

6. It is important to keep in mind, though, that the selling and buying of cultural property also occurs in African societies (Röschenthaler 2011).

7. For research that is rather concerned with the appropriation of more mundane consumer goods and technology in African societies, see Beck (2001), Hahn (2004), and Spittler (2002). See also Kohl (2001) for a summary of earlier studies of appropriation processes in anthropology.

NOTES TO PAGES 35-78

1. THE WICKED MAJOR

1. Of course, they spread much farther to the east and southeast than just to Maradi (Masquelier 2001). In 1993, a bori adept living in Zinder gave me a detailed list of more than forty Babule spirits' names. Throughout the 1990s, I met the Wicked Major and Caporal Salma (whose name goes back to the French officer Victor Salaman, Niamey's first commandant de cercle; he served from 1901 to 1905). I came across many other Babule spirits during bori dances in all parts of Hausaphone Nigeria and as far as Maiduguri in the northeastern part of the country (Krings 1997; see also Besmer 1983).

2. The Tuka movement in Fiji described by Peter Worsley (1957) is a particularly striking example of this.

3. The following account is based on the 1954 film and on a transcript of the film's audio track published in German (Rouch 1983). The quotes refer to this transcript that I have translated. I use Rouch's film as an ethnographic document, rather than discussing it as a film. For a summary of the critical debate about this highly controversial film, see Lim (2002).

4. The lyrics in the original Hausa look like this: "Babba'ku iyalan gwamna / Na gwamna ga rawa ga ya'ki / Soja birgimar hankaka / kowa ya ga ba'kinku / zai ga farinku."

2. LANCE SPEARMAN

1. For a contemporary account of Drum Publications' look-reads, I rely heavily on a short but very informative article by Stanley Meisler (1969), who was then based in Nairobi as a foreign correspondent of the *Los Angeles Times*. For the history of South African look-reads with white casts, see Saint (2010) and the steadily growing archives of the *South African Comic Books* blog (http://southafricancomicbooks.blogspot.co.uk).

2. The same seems to hold true for a number of other black characters, such as Supermask (another superhero); Chunky (also called Chunky Charlie, a corpulent black detective); Big Ben, whose "of London" epithet has a cosmopolitan sound to it; and the heroine, She, each of whom featured in his or her respective magazine in the southern African photo-novel landscape in the second half of the 1960s. I gathered this information on the *South African Comic Books* blog.

3. Later on, the East African and West African editions were printed in Tanzania (later Kenya) and Nigeria, respectively.

4. *African Film* was used as the title of the look-read in East Africa and West Africa, while the same content was published as *Spear* magazine in South Africa; similarly, *Boom* magazine, which contained the stories of Fearless Fang and The Stranger, was published in Nigeria and Kenya, while *The Stranger* served as the magazine title in South Africa. The South African photo-novel *True Love* appeared in East Africa and West Africa as *Sadness and Joy*.

5. All interviews are confidential, with the names of the interviewees withheld by mutual agreement.

6. I got a similar explanation for Spear's popularity from Richard Ndunguru, lecturer at University of Dar es Salaam, who avidly followed *African Film* as a child.

7. Interview with Faraji H. H. Katambula by Claudia Böhme, Dar es Salaam, October 20, 2009, translation of transcript by Uta Reuster-Jahn.

8. In the 1990s, this magazine, with a circulation of 10,000, was published every two weeks (Sturmer 1998).

9. According to Segun Sofowote, who was the first editor of West African Book Publishers' photo-play magazines *Atoka* and *Magnet*, the format was inspired by the look-reads of

Drum Publications, "which were the first to popularize the photoplay as a regular publishing format for Nigerian popular readership. Therefore in that sense, even though both magazines were imported from South Africa, they did demonstrate the feasibility of the format in Nigeria" (email, March 15, 2010).

10. The Tanzanian magazine *Femina* that is sponsored by the Swedish Development agency SIDA, for example, included a full-color three-page photo novel encouraging female empowerment in its 2006 issues. Another example is a set of photo novels "that addresses social issues such as alcoholism, HIV, and abuse in a compelling, fun and easy-to-understand format," produced by South African Strika Communications and the Goedgedacht Trust in 2006.

11. The blog *Kabozi: Notes from a Ugandan Abroad* may serve as an example: http://kabozi .wordpress.com/2012/03/19/looking-back-lance-spearman-and-the-african-photo-comic -magazines. The commentary by former readers, which can be found at the bottom of the essay, is particularly interesting, as it reveals a lot about past reading experiences.

12. See https://www.facebook.com/AfricanFilmComicMagazineLanceSpearmanMagazine.

3. BLACK *TITANIC*

1. The video can be viewed at http://www.youtube.com/watch?v=xaLcEKPeBhI.

2. Some sequences from *Masoyiyata/Titanic* can be viewed at http://www.youtube.com /watch?v=xaLcEKPeBhI.

3. One man of African descent was later identified on the passenger list: Joseph Philippe Lemercier Laroche, a Haitian gentleman traveling with his French wife and their two children (see http://www.encyclopedia-titanica.org/biography/486).

4. Since Mtani was kind enough to give me a full copy of his work—composed of all sixteen volumes he had initially planned to publish—as well as five colored paintings used as covers, I will base the following discussion on the work as it was meant to be published and consider the current cut-up continuation as only secondary.

5. For such information, I rely on Jigal Beez, who interviewed Mtani in June 2006 and subsequently published an article about his findings (2007), as well as on an interview Claudia Böhme conducted with the artist on my behalf in September 2006.

6. Original quote in Swahili and translation by Claudia Böhme, as is the case with all other quotes in this passage.

7. Church members remembered a preacher from Jamaica who visited their congregation in 2005 and indeed used the *Titanic* tragedy as a simile in his sermon.

8. The choir's share in each cassette sold by GMC was supposed to be one hundred Tanzania shillings (seven U.S. cents). In 2009, the parish council knew of only 332 copies sold, for which they had received their share in 2004. However, given the fact that the cassette was still available in Dar es Salaam in 2009, and in view of local piracy, the total circulation must have been considerably higher.

9. The song can be heard at http://www.youtube.com/watch?v=ga3Et4lLKZA&feature= related. Transcription and translation are by Claudia Böhme and Solomon Waliaula.

10. VCD stands for video compact disc. It is basically a CD that contains moving pictures and sound. The image quality is similar to VHS tape but not as sharp. The disc can be played on a computer or via DVD or VCD player, which is common in Africa.

11. The music video can be viewed at http://www.youtube.com/watch?v=iOW8zAIZ4iU.

12. The language of the song is Lingala, interspersed with Kikongo. As I am primarily interested in the song's message, I have omitted the "shouts" of the *atalaku*, and also I do not

indicate repetitions of lines and any other structural elements. Transcription and translation are by Jean-Baptiste Ndeke. Gracieux Mbuzukongira introduced me to the story behind the song, and Anna-Maria Brandstetter discussed Congolese cosmologies and the video clip with me.

13. The image of the three columns rising from the sea is probably inspired by TLC's video clip *Waterfalls* (1995), which contains a very similar image (http://www.mtv.de/musikvideos _artist/425-tlc?video=12024-waterfalls). Axel Brandstetter drew my attention to this video.

14. Jennifer Shamalla, of Nairobi, who was an eyewitness to the band's return home, provided this information. This event is also notorious for the violent clashes between rival groups that ensued when fans of Wenge Musica Maison Mère attacked Wenge BCBG's entourage along Kinshasa's Boulevard Lumumba (Tsambu Bulu 2004).

4. VICE AND VIDEOS

1. Several death sentences handed down to women found guilty of adultery by courts marks an extreme of these processes. The death sentences, however, were never executed, and the defendants in the two most prominent cases—Amina Lawal and Safiya Hussein—were discharged and acquitted by sharia courts of appeal.

2. As announced on the cover of the February 2003 issue of *Fim* magazine: "Ali Nuhu: Ba zan daina kwaikwayon Indiya ba."

3. See, for example, the transcript of his speech, which he gave at the launch of the first video film produced by members of the Muslim Brothers, published by the Hausa film magazine *Fim* (Zakzaky 2001).

4. Spelling as in English original; quote taken from a press briefing held by Director General Abubakar Rabo on February 11, 2008; an earlier version of the guidelines was announced by Rabo on September 21, 2007 (Sheme 2007c).

5. He was released in March 2009 after having served almost three months in prison; his case was ordered for retrial (Sheme 2009b) and finally waived in October 2010 as part of a reconciliation agreement between Iyan-Tama and Abubakar Rabo. The former had lodged a complaint of defamation against the latter at a court in Kaduna (McCain 2010b).

5. DAR 2 LAGOS

1. For an account of the history and problems of celluloid filmmaking in Tanzania, see Bryce (2010).

2. For more details on video narration in Tanzania, see Krings (2009), Englert and Moreto (2010), and Groß (2010).

3. His articles were published in the weekly tabloid *Ambha*, nos. 39, 43, and 45, July/ August 2007. These stirred controversy surrounding Bongo movies' production values and a reply written by Sultan Tamba, who discovered that the writer had plagiarized three British press articles about Nollywood for huge parts of his article series.

4. *Nsyuka* is based on a story Mussa Banzi once heard from a friend with a Nyakyusa ethnic background (Böhme 2013). Likewise, his other films—*Shumileta* (2005), *Chite Ukae* (2006), and *Kinyamkela* (2007)—are based on Tanzanian folk beliefs.

5. For example, *Sikitiko Langu* (2006), *Johari* (2006), and *Dangerous Desire* (2006), by director Vincent Kigosi, as well as *Penina—Jezebel's Daughter* (2007), by director Femi Ogedegbe.

6. Nollywood films surely have their share of these stereotypes and left an imprint on the public imagination, but jokes about Nigerians, their behavior, and their language seem to

be much older in Tanzania than the recent advent of Nigerian videos (Rose Nyerere, pers. comm., August 30, 2007).

6. BRANDING BIN LADEN

1. For a detailed history of Boko Haram, the ultraradical movement that developed out of the growing dissatisfaction with "political sharia"—as the half-hearted implementation of sharia laws was eventually called, see Loimeier (2012).

2. These terms refer to a functional element either no longer found in the posters or only present in miniature form—an annual calendar.

3. Eguzo Charley Izy, poster publisher, personal interview, September 6, 2003. All other interviews with poster publishers referred to in this and the following section were conducted in Mushin, Lagos, on September 6, 2003.

4. This information comes from a statement made by the publisher Onwane Emeka Frank (pers. comm., September 6, 2003). He was one of those who had been arrested.

5. One scene in the movie explicitly alludes to this correspondence of names. In the case of Clifford Orji and his treatment in Nigerian popular culture, compare Krings (2004a).

6. The movie is in the tradition of a whole series of comedies in which Danlasan impersonates famous characters that are part of local and international pop culture. The titles of these movies always combine his stage name with the figure satirized in the film, hence the film title *Ibro Usama*.

7. In the movie, the United Nations Organization is personified as a mere "henchwoman" of the American administration; a globe painted on her forehead, she is wearing a headscarf in the colors of the American flag. The female personification derives from the Hausa term for the United Nations General Assembly, the feminine noun *majalisar 'dinkin duniya* (as can be seen in figure 6.6).

8. In this context, refer to the work *Bearded Orientals: Making the Empire Cross,* by Australian artist Priscilla Joyce Brack. In this piece of art, Jesus Christ blends into bin Laden by means of a hologram (http://making-the-empire-cross.com/unleashed/bearded_orientals .html).

7. MASTER AND *MUGU*

1. Meanwhile, Jenna Burrell (2012) has published a very detailed ethnography of Ghanaian internet scamming, which parallels the Nigerian phenomenon in many ways.

2. In this section, citations like these pertain to personal online interviews with 419 scammers.

3. It is interesting to note that this attempted authentication through physical reference to media texts was also used in early-twentieth-century scam schemes of the Spanish prisoner type, for which newspaper clippings served the same purpose (Seltzer n.d.).

4. This coinage is obviously inspired by a practice called "flashing," which is very common in mobile phone communication throughout Africa. If mobile phone users do not want to waste minutes, they phone the person they wish to speak to and hang up before the person can answer (phone companies in Africa do not charge for in-coming calls). This way the phone number will show on the other person's display, who is now aware that a caller wishes to make contact and expects a call back.

5. Even if this account is not true, it certainly reveals what a successful scam should look like in the eyes of a scammer.

6. Previous forms of this confidence trick can be traced back to the late Middle Ages in Europe. Desiderius Erasmus describes a variant involving the transformation of coal into gold in "The Beggar's Dialogue," which he wrote around 1500 (Erasmus 1878). I would like to thank Daniel Künzler for drawing my attention to this.

7. The trick of transforming white notes into money by allegedly using special technology was practiced in neighboring Cameroon in the late 1990s—in particular, in circles involving the internationally active fraudster Donatien Koagne (Malaquais 2001). I would assume that the fraudsters for whom Tahir built the money machine took their inspiration from this.

8. Indeed, some fraudsters avail themselves of the ritual protection provided by magicians. The scammers I interviewed stated that while they did not turn to the magicians for assistance, other scammers are reputed to do this. For example, Ghana has been kept in suspense since 2009 by *sakawa*, an ideational complex, in which the success of email-initiated, advance-fee fraud is linked with occult practices (cf. Witte 2009).

9. The music video can be seen at http://www.youtube.com/watch?v=oqRsSDvQ1EQ. Ironically, former secretary of state Colin Powell danced to this song on stage during a black music festival in London (*BBC News* 2008).

8. "CRAZY WHITE MEN"

1. This is a characterization made by Espen Sørensen (aka Mzungu Kichaa) on the now-defunct website of his former band, Effigong (http://www.effigong.com/effigong/bio.html [accessed June 1, 2013; URL no longer active]).

2. Except when indicated otherwise, this biographical sketch is based on an interview I conducted with Espen Sørensen on November 14, 2013, in Hamburg, as well as on his web (http://www.mzungukichaa.com), Facebook (http://www.facebook.com/mzungukichaa), and Myspace (https://myspace.com/mzungukichaa) pages.

3. The information presented is based on an interview I conducted with Eric Sell on September 20, 2013, in Cologne, and on information gathered from his pages at diverse web sites, such as http://www.eesy-ees.com, http://www.yes-ja.com, http://www.facebook.com /eesmusic, and http://www.youtube.com/eesyees.

4. See http://www.facebook.com/eesmusic/info.

5. This biographical sketch is based on information gathered at http://www.facebook.com /WhiteNigerian and http://youtube.com/user/mohammedjammal, as well as from an essay published by Mohammed Jammal at http://www.bellanaija.com (White Nigerian 2013).

6. In Tanzania for example, the producers at the biggest private television station, ITV, must have been fully aware of Mzungu Kichaa's exoticism when calling on him to join the team of judges on *Bongo Star Search*, the Tanzanian version of *The X Factor*. Presumably, his being white adds glamor to the show and gives it more global appeal.

7. It is important to note, though, that Johnny Clegg was often called the "White Zulu." However, he never used this moniker as an official stage name.

8. In our interview, Mzungu Kichaa referred to working for the Danish jewelry company, Pilgrim, whose development-oriented foundation he helped build from 2006 to 2008. At the time, he coordinated the foundation's programs in Tanzania and also helped establish the company's fair-trade jewelry line. Moreover, his parents had also been involved in development work.

9. According to EES, the deal was meant to work both ways, as Gazza hoped to gain access to white Namibian audiences, who constitute a profitable segment of the Namibian music market.

10. The video is titled *White Nigerian with Aki and Paw Paw* (https://www.youtube.com /watch?v=Bu15CrKg7M4&list=UUok89vVPS5Rvxr_w97p3qhQ).

11. The show can be viewed at http://www.youtube.com/watch?v=-yKjBD9wxXU.

12. When I asked him about the significance of this representation, Mzungu Kichaa seemed a bit embarrassed. He laughed and admitted that he had produced the video clip himself and almost forgot about it. He said he was inspired by a popular rumor that he is a person with albinism, which was circulated among the people of Mwanza. In fact, the commentary on his video clip, *Jitolee!* is marked by recurring questions about his skin color: "Is he albino?" asks one user trying to make sense of Mzungu Kichaa's impressive command of Kiswahili. "No, he is a mzungu," replies another.

13. This and all other comments on White Nigerian's clips can be traced at http://www .youtube.com/watch?v=ONS8yDx4C3I.

14. The video clip may be viewed at http://www.youtube.com/watch?v=8cgVBKtGb9M.

15. The comment can be traced at http://www.youtube.com/watch?v=NunaOVDlicc.

16. The comment can be traced at http://www.youtube.com/user/eesyees/discussion.

17. This and all other quotes in this passage can be traced at http://www.youtube.com /watch?v=Zjs3JgMMbAw.

18. *Lekgoa* is the Sotho term for "white person." As a stage name, Lekgoa was used by a certain Francois Henning, a Boer, who released two Kwaito CDs in 1999 and 2001, and returned in the latter half of the 2000s with the new stage name Snotkop, performing pop and rock with Afrikaans lyrics. His all-white music videos reveal the kind of audience he seeks to address. In an interview given in 2011, he is quoted as saying: "I am the voice of SA's Afrikaner-Youth" (Angula 2011).

19. In *Das perfekte Dinner* (The perfect dinner; VOX 2011), EES prepared an "African" dish for the other guests on the show. On *Mieten, kaufen, wohnen* (To rent, to buy, to live; VOX 2013), he inspected several apartments with a real estate agent, as he was supposedly looking for a new domicile. On the game show *Rette die Million!* (Save the million! ZDF 2012), in which he took part with a friend, he won 275,000 euro, and on the *Millionärswahl* (Millionaire's poll; SAT1 2014), a talent show that earned its winner one million euros, EES was among the finalists, coming in fifth. Each of these shows gave him the chance to promote himself through interviews and clips about his personal background and music. On *Millionärswahl*, he also performed live, together with his dancers, who were flown in from Namibia.

20. This clip can be viewed at http://www.youtube.com/watch?v=3aLL38nLxgI.

21. Facebook's "people talking about this" score indicates a page's interaction rate. The score is the total of all users who have been active during the prior seven days, whereby each user is counted only once, even if he or she has been active more than once. Also, the nomenclature is somehow misleading because all sorts of user activities make up the score—not only the posting of texts or images but also activities such as "likes" (of the whole page or of individual posts but not of individual commentaries).

22. The origins of Facebook "likes" can be checked at http://www.sterntv-experimente .de/FacebookLikeCheck.

23. EES has a considerable number of likes from India (22.9 percent) and Serbia (10.8 percent), which puzzles me, as only very few users from these countries ever took part in the activities on his page (and the few that I could find did so only through "likes" and never through commentaries). So far, the most active writers of commentaries on EES's page are from Namibia, followed by users from Germany. If we exclude India's and Serbia's "likes" from the total number, the distribution is more similar to those of the other two musicians.

The percentage of "likes" from Namibia would rise to 52.5 percent and the "likes" from other African countries to 18.8 percent (with more than half of the latter, or 6,620 "likes," coming from Egypt, which is also somewhat strange).

24. If we exclude India's and Serbia's "likes" from the total of EES's "likes," the percentage from continental Europe, excluding Germany, would fall to 5.4 percent; the "likes" from Germany would rise to 8.6 percent.

25. EES has also created a fan page (http://www.megaphone-ghazzies.com) whose tagline reads, "This is where EES fans & community meet to show their support," and which has been used to coordinate support from German fans, encouraging them to hand out leaflets and send requests to radio stations to get EES's songs on playlists.

CODA

1. In a similar vein, Cassis Kilian (2012: 330), in her analysis of two Nigerian remakes of Hollywood movies, speaks about the remake's "oscillating" between projection and transformation, reenactment and modification of the foreign film.

2. Interestingly, V. S. Naipaul (2012: preface), whose novel *The Mimic Men* is often quoted in postcolonial studies, suggests a frequent misreading of his book's title: "The title gave trouble when the book was published. I should have been more careful. People thought 'the mimic men' was a way of saying 'the mimics' and this gave rise to a certain way of writing about the novel, in which colonial people became mimics. In fact, the matter here is more serious: colonial people, with their disturbed inner life, are mimicking the condition of men."

REFERENCES

A Daidaita Sahu. 2007. "Bud'ad'd'iyar wasika zuwa ga Kungiyar Masu Shirya Finafinai ta Jihar Kano" [Open letter to the Kano State Filmmakers Association]. *Bahaushe Mai Ban Haushi* (blog), August 22. http://ibrahim-sheme.blogspot.com/2007/08/daidaita-sahu.html.

Abdulaziz, Abdulaziz. 2010. "Kano Chief Censor in Alleged Child Abuse Scandal." *Leadership* (Abuja), August 30, 2.

Abu-Lughod, Lila. 1991. "Writing against Culture." In *Recapturing Anthropology: Working in the Present,* edited by Richard G. Fox, 137–162. Santa Fe, N.M.: School of American Research Press.

Adamu, Abdalla Uba. 2004. "Enter the Dragon: Shari'a, Popular Culture, and Film Censorship in Northern Nigeria." Paper presented at the Institute for African Studies, University of Cologne, Cologne, November 15.

———. 2007. *Transglobal Media Flows and African Popular Culture: Revolution and Reaction in Hausa Popular Culture.* Kano, Nigeria: Visually Ethnographic Productions.

———. 2008. "North of Nollywood, South of the Sahara: Cultural Dynamics in the Marketing of Hausa Home Video Films." Paper presented at the conference on Nollywood: Challenges of Production, Entertainment Value, and International Marketing Strategies, Pan-African University, Lagos, July 18–19.

———. 2010. "Islam, Hausa Culture, and Censorship in Northern Nigerian Video Film." In *Viewing African Cinema in the Twenty-First Century: Art Films and the Nollywood Video Revolution,* edited by Mahir Şaul and Ralph A. Austen, 63–73. Athens: Ohio University Press.

———. 2012. "Transnational Media Flows and Contra-Flows: Shifting Paradigms in South–South Entertainment Flows." *Hemispheres* 27:5–32.

Adogame, Afo. 2009. "The 419 Code as Business Unusual: Youth and the Unfolding of the Advance Fee Fraud Online Discourse." *Asian Journal of Social Science* 37 (4): 551–573.

Alhassan, Amina. 2012. "White Nigerian Serves Fatherland." *Weekly Trust,* November 7. http://weeklytrust.com.ng/index.php/entertainment/4264-white-nigerian-serves -fatherland.

Aliyu, Abdullahi. 2002. "Ashe Usama dan 419 ne!" [Osama is a fraudster!]. *Duniyar Fim* 1 (2): 26.

Aliyu, Ruqayyah Yusuf. 2010. "Rabo Arrested for Alleged Sex-Related Offence." *Trust Magazine* (Kaduna), August 29, 31.

Ames, David W. 1973. "A Sociocultural View of the Hausa Musical Activity." In *The Traditional Artist in African Societies,* edited by Warren L. d'Azevedo, 128–161. Bloomington: Indiana University Press.

Aminu, Abubakar. 2002. "Wai me ke damun Ibro ne?" [What's going on with Ibro?]. *Fim* (August): 9.

Ang, Ien. 1996. *Living Room Wars: Rethinking Media Audiences for a Postmodern World.* London: Routledge.

Angula, Conrad. 2011. "I Am the Voice of SA's AfrikanerYouth—Snotkop." *The Namibian,* September 16, 1.

Appadurai, Arjun, ed. 1986. *The Social Life of Things: Commodities in Cultural Perspective.* Cambridge: Cambridge University Press.

———. 1996. *Modernity at Large: Cultural Dimensions of Globalization.* Minneapolis: University of Minnesota Press.

Appiah, Kwame Anthony. 2007. *Cosmopolitanism: Ethics in a World of Strangers.* New York: Norton.

Aristotle. 1987. *The Poetics of Aristotle,* translation and commentary by Stephen Halliwell. Chapel Hill: University of North Carolina Press.

Armbrust, Walter. 2007. "Bravely Stating the Obvious: Egyptian Humor and the Anti-American Consensus." *Arab Media and Society* 3 (Fall). http://www.arabmediasociety .com/?article=413.

Ashcroft, Bill, Gareth Griffiths, and Helen Tiffin. 1989. *The Empire Writes Back: Theory and Practice in Post-colonial Literatures.* London: Routledge.

Askew, Kelly, and Richard R. Wilk, eds. 2002. *The Anthropology of Media: A Reader.* Malden, Mass.: Blackwell.

Banda, Tim Kamuzu. 2010. "Bongo Star's Latest Single a Big Hit." *Daily Nation* (Nairobi), January 29. http://www.nation.co.ke/News/-/1056/852120/-/vpwl27/-/index.html.

Barber, Karin. 2000. *The Generation of Plays: Yoruba Popular Life in Theatre.* Bloomington: Indiana University Press.

Barkiya, Ashafa Murnai. 2002. "Tsinuwa kan Ibro Usama: 'Ba ta yi mana komai ba!'—Mato" [The cursing of the film Ibro Usama: "I don't care"—Mato]. *Fim* (August): 21–22.

Barrot, Pierre, ed. 2005. *Nollywood: Le phénomène vidéo au Nigeria.* Paris: Harmattan.

Barz, Gregory. 2003. *Performing Religion: Negotiating Past and Present in Kwaya Music of Tanzania.* Amsterdam: Rodopi.

Basel Institute on Governance. 2007. "Banco Noroeste SA (Nigerian Scam 419)." http:// www.assetrecovery.org/kc/node/b7b13256-28f7-11de-900c-81c63910293a.2.

Bayart, Jean-François. 1999. "Conclusion." In *The Criminalization of the State in Africa,* edited by Jean-François Bayart, Stephen Ellis, and Béatrice Hibou, 114–116. Oxford: International African Institute.

BBC News. 2002. "Osama Baby Craze Hits Nigeria." January 3. http://news.bbc.co.uk/1/hi /world/africa/1741171.stm.

———. 2008. "Colin Powell Digs African Hip-Hop." October 15. http://news.bbc.co.uk/2 /hi/7670788.stm.

Bebeji, Rabee'u. 2003. "Khusufi 1." *Fim* 6:41–43.

Beck, Kurt. 2001. "Die Aneignung der Maschine." In *New Heimat,* edited by Karl-Heinz Kohl and Nicholas Schaffhausen, 66–77. New York: Lukas & Sternberg.

Becker, Heike. 2013. "Nollywood in Urban Southern Africa: Nigerian Video Films and Their Audiences in Cape Town and Windhoek." In *Global Nollywood: The Transnational Dimensions of an African Video Film Industry*, edited by Matthias Krings and Onookome Okome, 179–198. Bloomington: Indiana University Press.

Beek, Jan. 2007. "Miss Assoh Kabila und Prof. R. J. Felcher III: Scams und Scambaits als Alltagserzählungen des Fremden." Unpublished manuscript, Department of Anthropology and African Studies, Johannes Gutenberg University Mainz, Mainz, Germany.

Beez, Jigal. 2007. "The Swahili Titanic: The Tanzanian Appropriation of a Global Tragedy." *International Journal of Comic Art* 9 (1): 542–553.

———. 2009. "Stupid Hares and Margarine: Early Swahili Comics." In *Cartooning in Africa*, edited by John A. Lent, 137–157. Cresskill, N.J.: Hampton Press.

Behrend, Heike. 2009. "The Titanic in Northern Nigeria: Transnational Image Flows and Local Interventions." In *Transmission Image: Visual Translation and Cultural Agency*, edited by Birgit Mersmann and Alexandra Schneider, 224–239. Newcastle, U.K.: Cambridge Scholars Publishing.

Benjamin, Walter. 2005. "On the Mimetic Faculty." In *Selected Writings*, vol. 2, pt. 2, 1931–1934, edited by Michael Jennings, Howard Eiland, and Gary Smith, 720–722. Cambridge, Mass.: Harvard University Press.

Bergfelder, Tim, and Sarah Street, eds. 2004. *The Titanic in Myth and Memory: Representations in Visual and Literary Culture*. London: Tauris.

Bernstein, Matthew. 1999. "'Floating Triumphantly': The American Critics on *Titanic*." In *Titanic: Anatomy of a Blockbuster*, edited by Kevin S. Sandler and Gaylyn Studlar, 14–28. New Brunswick, N.J.: Rutgers University Press.

Besmer, Fremont E. 1983. *Horses, Musicians, and Gods: The Hausa Cult of Possession-Trance*. South Hadley, Mass.: Bergin & Garvey.

Bhabha, Homi. 1984. "Of Mimicry and Man: The Ambivalence of Colonial Discourse." *October* 28:125–133.

Biel, Steven. 1997. *Down with the Old Canoe: A Cultural History of the Titanic Disaster*. New York: Norton.

Blommaert, Jan, and Tope Omoniyi. 2006. "Email Fraud: Language, Technology, and the Indexicals of Globalisation." *Social Semiotics* 16 (4): 573–605.

Böhme, Claudia. 2007. "Der swahilisprachige Videofilm Girlfriend: Eine Sprachanalyse." Master's thesis, University of Hamburg. http://www.ifeas.uni-mainz.de/workingpapers/Ap63.pdf.

———. 2011. "White Elephant: Die Aushandlung von Kultur in der tansanischen Videofilmindustrie." Ph.D. diss., Johannes Gutenberg University Mainz.

———. 2013. "Bloody Bricolages: Traces of Nollywood in Tanzanian Video Films." In *Global Nollywood: The Transnational Dimensions of an African Video Film Industry*, edited by Matthias Krings and Onookome Okome, 327–346. Bloomington: Indiana University Press.

———. 2015. "'Look with Your Own Eyes!': Visualization of Spirit Media and Their Viewing Techniques in Tanzanian Video Films." In *Trance Mediums and New Media: Spirit Possession in the Age of Technical Reproduction*, edited by Heike Behrend, Anja Dreschke, and Martin Zillinger, 221–240. New York: Fordham University Press.

Bolter, Jay D., and Richard Grusin. 2000. *Remediation: Understanding New Media*. Cambridge, Mass.: MIT Press.

Boon, Marcus. 2010. *In Praise of Copying*. Cambridge, Mass.: Harvard University Press.

Britain-Tanzania Society. 1996. "Tanzania's 'Titanic' Disaster: MV Bukoba." *Tanzanian Affairs* 55:13.

———. 1997. "M.V. Bukoba: The Sequel." *Tanzanian Affairs* 56:7.

Brubaker, Rogers, and Frederick Cooper. 2000. "Beyond 'Identity.'" *Theory and Society* 29:1–47.

Bryce, Jane. 2010. "Outside the Machine? Donor Values and the Case of Film in Tanzania." In *Viewing African Cinema in the Twenty-First Century: Art Films and the Nollywood Video Revolution,* edited by Mahir Şaul and Ralph A. Austen, 160–177. Athens: Ohio University Press.

———. 2013. "'African Movies' in Barbados: Proximate Experiences of Fear and Desire." In *Global Nollywood: The Transnational Dimensions of an African Video Film Industry,* edited by Matthias Krings and Onookome Okome, 223–244. Bloomington: Indiana University Press.

Burrell, Jenna. 2012. *Invisible Users: Youth in the Internet Cafés of Urban Ghana.* Cambridge, Mass.: MIT Press.

Buse, Uwe. 2005. "Die Stadt der Cyber-Gangster." *Der Spiegel* 45:158–164.

Çaglar, Ayşe. 1990. "The Prison House of Culture in the Study of Turks in Germany." *Sozial-anthropologische Arbeitspapiere* 31. Berlin: Das Arabische Buch.

Carpenter, Edward Snow. 1972. *Oh, What a Blow That Phantom Gave Me!* New York: Holt, Rinehart & Winston.

Cartelli, Philip. 2007. "Nollywood Comes to the Caribbean." *Film International* 5 (4): 112–115.

Casey, Conerly C. 1997. "Medicines for Madness: Suffering, Disability, and the Identification of Enemies in Northern Nigeria." Ph.D. diss., University of California, Los Angeles.

Channel O. 2013. "Music Monday Interview: EES." *Channel O News* (website). http://channelo.dstv.com/2013/07/music-monday-interview-ees.

Comaroff, John L., and Jean Comaroff. 2004. "Criminal Justice, Cultural Justice: The Limits of Liberalism and the Pragmatics of Difference in the New South Africa." *American Ethnologist* 31 (2): 188–204.

———. 2009. *Ethnicity, Inc.* Chicago: University of Chicago Press.

Coombe, Rosemary. 1998. *The Cultural Life of Intellectual Properties: Authorship, Appropriation, and the Law.* Durham, N.C.: Duke University Press.

———. 2009. "The Expanding Purview of Cultural Properties and Their Politics." *Annual Review of Law and Social Science* 5:393–412.

Dan Fulani, Umar H. Dadem, and Sati U. Fwatshak. 2002. "Briefing: The September 2001 Events in Jos, Nigeria." *African Affairs* 101:243–255.

Debray, Régis. 2000. *Transmitting Culture.* New York: Columbia University Press.

Diawara, Mamadou. 2011. "Die Jagd nach den Piraten: Zur Herausbildung von Urheberrechten im Kontext der Oralität im subsaharischen Afrika." *Sociologus* 61 (1): 69–89.

Diers, Michael. 1997. *Schlagbilder: Zur politischen Ikonographie der Gegenwart.* Frankfurt: Fischer.

Dixon, Robyn. 2005. "Nigerian Cyber Scammers." *Los Angeles Times,* October 20. http://www.latimes.com/news/printedition/la-fg-scammers20oct20,1,1799691.story.

Doyle, Mark. 2001. "Nigeria Road Trip: Kano." *BBC News,* December 21. http://news.bbc.co.uk/1/hi/world/africa/1722164.stm.

Dyer, Richard. 2007. *Pastiche.* Milton Park, U.K.: Routledge.

Echard, Nicole. 1992. "Cultes et possession et changement social: L'exemple du bori Hausa de l'Ader et du Kurfey (Niger)." *Archives de Sciences Sociales des Religions* 79 (3): 87–100.

Edelson, Eve. 2006. *Scamorama: Turning the Tables on Email Scammers.* New York: Disinformation Company.

Eisner, Will. 1990. *Comics and Sequential Art.* Cincinnati, Ohio: North Light Books.

Englert, Birgit, with Nginjai Paul Moreto. 2010. "Inserting Voice: Foreign Language Film Translation into Kiswahili as a Local Phenomenon in Tanzania." *Journal of African Media Studies* 2 (2): 225–239.

Erasmus, Desiderius. 1878. *The Colloquies of Erasmus,* vol. 1, edited by Edwin Johnson. London: Reeves & Turner.

Evans-Pritchard, Edgar E. 1965. *Theories of Primitive Religion.* Oxford: Oxford University Press.

Fanon, Frantz. 1967. *Black Skin, White Masks.* New York: Grove Press.

Faulkingham, Ralph. 1975. *The Spirits and Their Cousins: Some Aspects of Belief, Ritual, and Social Organization in a Rural Hausa Village in Niger.* Research Report 15, Department of Anthropology, University of Massachusetts, Amherst.

Fehrmann, Gisela, Erika Linz, Eckhard Schumacher, and Brigitte Weingart. 2004. "Originalkopie: Praktiken des Sekundären—Eine Einleitung." In *Originalkopie: Praktiken des Sekundären,* edited by Gisela Fehrmann, Erika Linz, Eckhard Schumacher, and Brigitte Weingart, 7–17. Cologne: Dumont.

Ferguson, James G. 2002. "Of Mimicry and Membership: African and the 'New World Society.'" *Cultural Anthropology* 17 (4): 551–569.

Förster, Larissa. 2010. *Postkoloniale Erinnerungslandschaften: Wie Deutsche und Herero in Namibia des Krieges von 1904 gedenken.* Frankfurt: Campus.

Foucault, Michel. 1986. "Of Other Spaces." *Diacritics* 16 (1): 22–27.

Frazer, James George. 1978. *The Golden Bough: A Study in Magic and Religion.* London: Macmillan.

Friedman, Jonathan. 1990a. "The Political Economy of Elegance: An African Cult of Beauty." *Culture and History* 7:101–125.

———. 1990b. "Consuming Desires: Strategies of Selfhood and Appropriation." *Cultural Anthropology* 6 (2): 154–163.

Fugelsang, Minou. 1994. *Veils and Videos: Female Youth Culture on the Kenyan Coast.* Studies in Social Anthropology. Stockholm: Gotab.

Fuglestad, Finn. 1975. "Les Hauka: Une interprétation historique." *Cahiers d'Études Africaines* 58:203–216.

———. 1983. *A History of Niger, 1850–1960.* New York: Cambridge University Press.

Fuita, Franck Baku, and Godefroid Bwiti Lumisa. 2005. "Kinshasa: Quand les videos nigérianes chassaient les demons." In *Nollywood: Le phénomène vidéo au Nigeria,* edited by Pierre Barrot, 111–116. Paris: Harmattan.

Furnish, Timothy R. 2002. "Bin Ladin: The Man Who Would Be Mahdi." *Middle East Quarterly* (Spring): 53–59. http://www.meforum.org/article/159.

Furniss, Graham. 2003. "Hausa Popular Culture and Video Film: The Rapid Rise of Cultural Production in Times of Economic Decline." Working Paper 27, Department of Anthropology and African Studies, Johannes Gutenberg University Mainz, Mainz, Germany. http://www.ifeas.uni-mainz.de/Dateien/FurnissHausa.pdf.

Gebauer, Gunter, and Christoph Wulf. 1995. *Mimesis: Culture, Art, Society.* Berkeley: University of California Press.

———. 2003. *Mimetische Weltzugänge: Soziales Handeln, Rituale und Spiele, ästhetische Produktionen.* Stuttgart: Kohlhammer.

Geertz, Clifford. 1986. "Making Experiences, Authoring Selves." In *The Anthropology of Experience,* edited by Victor W. Turner and Edward M. Bruner, 373–380. Urbana: University of Illinois Press.

Gell, Alfred. 1998. *Art and Agency: An Anthropological Theory.* Oxford: Clarendon.

Getao, Kate. 2008. "How I Long for Those Comic Book Days." *The Nation* (Nairobi). http://
www. nation.co.ke/magazines/saturday/-/1216/490922/-/item/0/-/mgydua/-/index
.html (accessed February 12, 2009; URL no longer active).

Gilroy, Paul. 2004. *After Empire: Melancholia or Convivial Culture.* London: Routledge.

Ginsburg, Faye D., Lila Abu-Lughod, and Brian Larkin. 2002. *Media Worlds: Anthropology on
New Terrain.* Berkeley: University of California Press.

Giwa, Tunde. 2008. "Black Like Us." *Chimurenga Library* (website). http://chimurengalibrary
.co.za/black-like-us-an-essay-by-tunde-giwa.

Glickman, Harvey. 2005. "The Nigerian '419' Advance Fee Scams: Prank or Peril?" *Canadian
Journal of African Studies* 39 (3): 460–489.

Gondola, Didier. 2009. "Tropical Cowboys: Westerns, Violence, and Masculinity among the
Young *Bills* of Kinshasa." *Afrique et Histoire* 7:75–98.

Groß, Sandra-Katharina. 2010. "Die Kunst afrikanischer Kinoerzähler: Video Jockeys in Dar
es Salaam." Master's thesis, Johannes Gutenberg University Mainz.

Hacke, Gabriel. 2014. "Tanzanian Music Videos in the Black Atlantic: The Production,
Distribution, and Visual References of Bongo Flava Video Clips." In *Bongo Media Worlds:
Producing and Consuming Popular Culture in Dar es Salaam,* edited by Matthias Krings and
Uta Reuster-Jahn, 79–107. Cologne: Köppe.

Hahn, Hans Peter. 2004. "Global Goods and the Process of Appropriation." In *Between
Resistance and Expansion: Explorations of Local Vitality in Africa,* edited by Peter Probst and
Gerd Spittler, 211–230. Münster: Lit.

Hall, Stuart. 1992. "Encoding/Decoding." In *Culture, Media, Language: Working Papers in
Cultural Studies, 1972–79,* edited by Stuart Hall, Dorothy Hobson, Andrew Lowe, and Paul
Willis, 128–138. London: Routledge.

Halliwell, Stephen. 1987. "Commentary." In *The Poetics of Aristotle,* translation and commentary by Stephen Halliwell, 69–184. Chapel Hill: University of North Carolina Press.

Hannerz, Ulf. 1996. *Transnational Connections: Culture, People, Places.* London: Routledge.

Harnischfeger, Johannes. 2006. *Demokratisierung und Islamisches Recht: Der Scharia-Konflikt in
Nigeria.* Frankfurt: Campus.

Hayatu, Abubakar Baballe. 2002. "Saboda yawan kallon finafinan Indiya, ni da Ali Nuhu da
Rabi'u HRB muna jin yaren Indiya! Cewar Baballe Hayatu" [Because we are watching
Indian films so often, Ali Nuhu, Rabi'u HRB, and I understand the Indian language! Said
Baballe Hayatu]. *Fim* 11:46–47.

Haynes, Jonathan. 2000. *Nigerian Video Films.* Athens: Ohio University Press.

Hoesterey, Ingeborg. 2001. *Pastiche: Cultural Memory in Art, Film, Literature.* Bloomington:
Indiana University Press.

Höschele, Stefan. 2007. *Christian Remnant, African Folk Church: Seventh-Day Adventism in
Tanzania, 1903–1980.* Leiden, Netherlands: Brill.

Howells, Richard. 1999. *The Myth of the Titanic.* Houndmills, U.K.: Macmillan.

Huggan, Graham. 1997/1998. "(Post)Colonialism, Anthropology, and the Magic of Mimesis."
Cultural Critique 38:91–106.

Hunter, Rick. 2011. "Scammer Interview." *419 Eater* (website). http://www.419eater.com
/html/user_subs/interview/scammer_interview.htm.

Ibrahim, Yusha'u Adamu. 2007a. "Exodus of Artistes Hits Kannywood Despite Peace Parley
with KNSG." *Daily Trust* (Kaduna), November 3. http://allafrica.com/stories
/200711050273.html.

———. 2007b. "How Adam A. Zango Ended Up in Prison." *Weekly Trust* (Kaduna), October 1. http://allafrica.com/stories/200710011384.html.

———. 2008. "Resumption of Film Activities in Kano: Can Filmmakers Meet the New Conditions?" *Daily Trust* (Kaduna), February 17. http://allafrica.com/stories/200802181008.html.

Igwe, Chidi Nnamdi. 2007. *Taking Back Nigeria from 419*. New York: iUniverse.

Iyan-Tama, Hamisu Lamido. 2004. "Matsayin Fina-Finan Hausa a Musulunci" [The place of Hausa films in Islam]. In *Hausa Home Videos: Technology, Economy and Society*, edited by Abdalla Uba Adamu, Yusuf M. Adamu, and Umar Faruk Jibril, 421–429. Kano, Nigeria: Center for Hausa Cultural Studies and Adamu Joji Publishers.

Jameson, Fredric. 1993. "On 'Cultural Studies.'" *Social Text* 34:17–52.

Jenkins, Henry. 2006. *Convergence Culture: Where Old and New Media Collide*. New York: New York University Press.

Kane, Ousmane. 2003. *Muslim Modernity in Postcolonial Nigeria: A Study of the Society for the Removal of Innovation and Reinstatement of Tradition*. Leiden, Netherlands: Brill.

Kano's Censorship Laws. 2008. "Kano's Censorship Laws." *Bahaushe Mai Ban Haushi* (blog), February 14. http://ibrahim-sheme.blogspot.com/2008/02/kanos-censorship-laws.html.

Kazaure, Musa Umar. 2001. "Kano Ulama Declare Support for Bin Laden." *Daily Trust* (Kaduna), October 4. http://allafrica.com/stories/200110090433.html.

Keller, Alexandra. 1999. "'Size Does Matter': Notes on *Titanic* and James Cameron as Blockbuster Auteur." In *Titanic: Anatomy of a Blockbuster*, edited by Kevin S. Sandler and Gaylyn Studlar, 132–154. New Brunswick, N.J.: Rutgers University Press.

Kermani, Navid. 2001. "Sprich leise und mach die Poesie zu deiner Waffe." *Süddeutsche Zeitung* (Munich), October 12. http://www.sueddeutsche.de/politik/sz-artikel-sprich-leise-und-mach-die-poesie-zu-deiner-waffe-1.746922.

Kerr, David. 2011. "The Reception of Nigerian Video Drama in a Multicultural Female Community in Botswana." *Journal of African Cinemas* 3 (1): 65–79.

Kilian, Cassis. 2012. *Schwarz besetzt: Postkoloniale Planspiele im afrikanischen Film*. Bielefeld, Germany: transcript.

Kilpatrick, Kate. 2009. "Dancing around Possible Meanings of 'Yahoozee.'" *Online Nigeria* (website), July 25. http://newsnigeria.onlinenigeria.com/templates/?a=6337.

King, Alasdair. 2004. "Enzensberger's Titanic: 'The Sinking of the German Left and the Aesthetics of Survival.'" In *The Titanic in Myth and Memory: Representations in Visual and Literary Culture*, edited by Tim Bergfelder and Sarah Street, 73–83. London: Tauris.

Kohl, Karl-Heinz. 2001. "Aneignungen: Kulturelle Vielfalt im Kontext der Globalisierung." In *New Heimat*, edited by Karl-Heinz Kohl and Nicolaus Schaffhausen, 8–18. New York: Lukas & Sternberg.

Köster, Werner, and Thomas Lischeid, eds. 1999. *Titanic: Ein Medienmythos*. Leipzig, Germany: Reclam.

Koven, Mikel J. 2001. *Blaxploitation Films*. Harpenden, U.K.: Kamera Books.

Kramer, Fritz. 1993. *The Red Fez: Art and Spirit Possession in Africa*. London: Verso.

Krings, Matthias. 1997. *Geister des Feuers: Zur Imagination des Fremden im Bori-Kult der Hausa*. Hamburg: Lit.

———. 2004a. "Nigerianische Moritaten: Die Reproduktion des Bösen auf illustrierten Kalenderblättern." In *Africa Screams: Die Wiederkehr des Bösen in Kino, Kunst und Kult*, edited by Tobias Wendl, 174–187. Wuppertal, Germany: Peter Hammer.

——. 2004b. "Der Boom eines Mediums: Einblicke in die Werkstätten nigerianischer Plakat-verleger." In *Plakate in Afrika*, edited by Dieter Kramer and Wendelin Schmidt, 43–50. Frankfurt: Museum der Weltkulturen.

——. 2007. "Afrikanische Video-Vampire: Wiedergänger zwischen den Kulturen." In *All about Evil: Das Böse*, edited by Sike Seybold, 120–127. Mainz, Germany: Philipp von Zabern.

——. 2008. "Conversion on Screen: A Glimpse at Popular Islamic Imaginations in Northern Nigeria." *Africa Today* 54 (4): 44–68.

——. 2009. "Turning Rice into Pilau: The Art of Video Narration in Tanzania." *Intermédialités*. Electronic Supplement "Re-dire," edited by Vincent Bouchard, Ute Fendler, and Germain Lacasse. http://cri.histart.umontreal.ca/cri/fr/INTERMEDIALITES/interface/numeros.html.

Krings, Matthias, and Onookome Okome, eds. 2013a. *Global Nollywood: The Transnational Dimensions of an African Video Film Industry*. Bloomington: Indiana University Press.

——. 2013b. "Nollywood and Its Diaspora: An Introduction." In *Global Nollywood: The Transnational Dimensions of an African Video Film Industry*, edited by Matthias Krings and Onookome Okome, 1–22. Bloomington: Indiana University Press.

Kulick, Don, and Margaret Willson. 1994. "Rambo's Wife Saves the Day: Subjugating the Gaze and Subverting the Narrative in a Papua New Guinean Swamp." *Visual Anthropology Review* 10 (2): 1–13.

Kuper, Adam. 1999. *Culture: The Anthropologist's Account*. Cambridge, Mass.: Harvard University Press.

Lang, Tilman. 1998. *Mimetisches oder semiologisches Vermögen? Studien zu Walter Benjamins Begriff der Mimesis*. Göttingen, Germany: Vandenhoeck & Ruprecht.

Lange, Siri. 2002. "Managing Modernity: Gender, State, and Nation in the Popular Drama of Dar es Salaam." Ph.D. diss., University of Bergen.

Larkin, Brian. 1997. "Indian Films and Nigerian Lovers: Media and the Creation of Parallel Modernities." *Africa* 67:406–440.

——. 2002. "Bandiri Music, Globalization, and Urban Experience in Nigeria." *Cahiers d'Études Africaines* 42 (4): 739–762.

——. 2008. *Signal and Noise: Media, Infrastructure, and Urban Culture in Nigeria*. Durham, N.C.: Duke University Press.

Last, Murray. 2000. "La Charia dans le Nord-Nigeria." *Politique Africaine* 79:141–152.

——. 2008. "The Search for Security in Muslim Northern Nigeria." *Africa* 78 (1): 41–63.

Latour, Éliane de. 1992. *Le temps de pouvoir*. Paris: Éditions de l'École des Hautes Études en Sciences Sociales.

Lessig, Lawrence. 2008. *Remix: Making Art and Commerce Thrive in the Hybrid Economy*. New York: Penguin.

Lévy-Bruhl, Lucien. 1922. *La mentalité primitive*. Paris: Félix Alcan.

Lienhardt, Godfrey. 1961. *Divinity and Experience: The Religion of the Dinka*. Oxford: Oxford University Press.

Lim, Kien Ket. 2002. "Of Mimicry and White Man: A Psychoanalysis of Jean Rouch's *Les Maîtres Fous*." *Cultural Critique* 51 (Spring): 40–73.

Liman, Abubakar Aliyu. 2010. "Inversion of Hegemony in Contemporary Hausa Lyrical Expression." *Ker Review* 5 (1/2): 64–82.

Lips, Julius. 1937. *The Savage Hits Back or the White Man through Native Eyes*. New York: University Books.

Loimeier, Roman. 1997. *Islamic Reform and Political Change in Northern Nigeria*. Evanston, Ill.: Northwestern University Press.

———. 2012. "Boko Haram: The Development of a Militant Religious Movement in Nigeria." *Africa Spectrum* 47 (2/3): 137–155.

Luhmann, Niklas. 1996. *Die Realität der Massenmedien*. Opladen, Germany: Westdeutscher Verlag.

MacGaffey, Janet, and Remy Bazenguissa-Ganga. 2000. *Congo–Paris: Transnational Traders on the Margins of the Law*. Oxford: James Currey.

MacGaffey, Wyatt. 1968. "Kongo and the King of the Americans." *Journal of Modern African Studies* 6 (2): 171–181.

———. 1983. *Modern Kongo Prophets: Religion in a Plural Society*. Bloomington: Indiana University Press.

Macho, Thomas. 1996. "Gesichtsverluste: Faciale Bilderfluten und postindustrieller Animismus." *Ästhetik und Kommunikation* 25:25–28.

Malaquais, Dominique. 2001. "Arts de feyre au Cameroun." *Politique Africaine* 82:101–118.

Marks, Laura U. 2000. *The Skin of the Film: Intercultural Cinema, Embodiment, and the Senses*. Durham, N.C.: Duke University Press.

Masquelier, Adeline. 1993. "Narratives of Power, Images of Wealth: The Ritual Economy of Bori in the Market." In *Modernity and Its Malcontents: Ritual and Power in Postcolonial Africa*, edited by Jean Comaroff and John Comaroff, 3–33. Chicago: University of Chicago Press.

———. 2001. *Prayer Has Spoiled Everything: Possession, Power, and Identity in an Islamic Town of Niger*. Durham, N.C.: Duke University Press.

Mazarella, William. 2004. "Culture, Globalization, Mediation." *Annual Review of Anthropology* 33:345–367.

Mboti, Nyasha. 2011. "Wife and/or Whore: Depicting African Women in the Last King of Scotland and Blood Diamond." *drnayshamboti* (blog). http://drnyashamboti.wordpress .com/2011/07/14/wife-andor-whore-depicting-african-women-in-the-last-king-of-scotland -and-blood-diamond.

McCain, Carmen. 2009. "Award-Winning Film Lands Director in Jail." *Inter Press Service News Agency*, February 16. http://www.ipsnews.net/2009/02/culture-nigeria-award-winning -film-lands-director-in-jail.

———. 2010a. "Hausa Rapper Ziriums Releases Album 'This Is Me' and Music Single Online." *A Tunanina* (blog), September 7. http://carmenmccain.wordpress.com/2010/09/07 /hausa-rapper-ziriums-releases-album-this-is-me-and-music-video-single-online-lyrics -included-here.

———. 2010b. "Iyan Tama Reaches Settlement with Director General of the Kano State Censorship Board." *A Tunanina* (blog), October 17. http://carmenmccain.wordpress.com /2010/10/17/iyan-tama-reaches-settlement-with-director-general-of-the-kano-state -censorship-board.

———. 2013. "Nollywood, Kannywood, and a Decade of Hausa Film Censorship in Nigeria." In *Silencing Cinema: Film Censorship around the World,* edited by Daniel Biltereyst and Roel Vande Winkel, 223–240. London: Palgrave Macmillan.

McCain, Carmen, Nazir Ahmed Hausawa, and Ahmad Alkanawy. 2009. "Censorship Crisis in Kano: Arrests and Fines for Hausa-Language Film Industry Figures." *Pambazuka* 415. http://www.pambazuka.org/en/category/comment/53222.

McCloud, Scott. 1994. *Understanding Comics: The Invisible Art*. New York: Harper Collins.

Meisler, Stanley. 1969. "Look-Reads." *Africa Report* 14 (5/6): 80–83.

Meyer, Birgit. 2003. "Visions of Blood, Sex, and Money: Fantasy Spaces in Popular Ghanaian Cinema." *Visual Anthropology* 16:15–41.

———. 2005. "Religious Remediations: Pentecostal Views in Ghanaian Video Movies." *Postscripts* 1 (2/3): 155–181.

———. 2006. "Impossible Representations." In *Religion, Media, and the Public Sphere,* edited by Birgit Meyer and Annelies Moors, 290–311. Bloomington: Indiana University Press.

———. 2010. "Ghanaian Popular Video Movies between State Film Policies and Nollywood." In *Viewing African Cinema in the Twenty-First Century: Art Films and the Nollywood Video Revolution,* edited by Mahir Şaul and Ralph A. Austen, 42–62. Athens: Ohio University Press.

Miller, Daniel. 1992. "The Young and the Restless in Trinidad: A Case of the Local and the Global in Mass Consumption." In *Consuming Technologies: Media and Information in Domestic Spaces,* edited by Roger Silverstone and Eric Hirsch, 163–182. London: Routledge.

Mkamba, Ibrahim. 2008. "Kweli Bongo Dar es Salam Wasanii" [There are truly many artistes in Dar es Salaam]. *Raia Mwema* (Dar es Salaam), March 19. http://www.raiamwema.co.tz/kweli-bongo-dar-es-salaam-wasanii.

Mtani, Joshua Amandus. 2000. *Mkasa wa Mapenzi ndani ya Titanic* [A romantic tragedy on the Titanic]. Vol. 1. Dar es Salaam: Mtania Artwork Production.

Naipaul, V. S. 2012. *The Mimic Men* (Kindle edition). New York: Picador.

Nava, Mica. 2007. *Visceral Cosmopolitanism: Gender, Culture, and the Normalization of Difference.* Oxford: Berg.

Noor, Farish. 2004. "When Osama and Friends Came a-Calling: The Political Deployment of the Overdetermined Image of Osama ben Laden in the Contestation for Islamic Symbols in Malaysia." In *Media, War, and Terrorism: Responses from the Middle East and Asia,* edited by Peter van der Veer and Shona Munshi, 197–223. London: Routledge.

Noyes, Dorothy. 2010. "Traditional Culture: How Does It Work?" Concepts and Institutions of Cultural Property 1/2010, Interdisciplinary Research Group on Cultural Property, University of Göttingen, Göttingen, Germany. http://webdoc.sub.gwdg.de/ebook/serien/qu/cp101/01_2010.pdf.

Nye, Russel B. 1977. "Miroir de la vie: The French Photoroman and Its Audience." *Journal of Popular Culture* 10 (4): 744–751.

Obiechina, Emanuel N. 1973. *An African Popular Literature: A Study of Onitsha Market Literature.* Cambridge: Cambridge University Press.

Ojetade, Balogun. 2013. "African Pulp: The Spear in Racist Pulp Fiction's Heart!" http://chroniclesofharriet.com/2013/12/13/african-pulp-the-spear-in-racist-pulp-fictions-heart.

Olivier de Sardan, Jean-Pierre. 1982. *Concepts et conceptions songhay-zarma.* Paris: Nubia.

———. 1984. *Les societies songhay-zarma (Niger–Mali): Chefs, guerriers, esclaves, paysans. . . .* Paris: Karthala.

———. 1993. "La surinterprétation politique: Les cultes de possession Hawka du Niger." In *Religion et modernité politique en Afrique noire: Dieu pour tous et chacun pour soi,* edited by Jean-François Bayart, 163–213. Paris: Karthala.

Ondego, Ogova. 2005. "Le Kenya sous dependance." In *Nollywood: Le phénomène vidéo au Nigeria,* edited by Pierre Barrot, 117–122. Paris: Harmattan.

Ong, Walter J. 2010. *Orality and Literacy: The Technologizing of the Word.* London: Routledge.

Packalén, Leif. 2009. "Tanzanian Comic Art: Vibrant and Plentiful." In *Cartooning in Africa,* edited by John A. Lent, 307–322. Cresskill, N.J.: Hampton Press.

Parisi, Paula. 1998. *Titanic and the Making of James Cameron: The Inside Story of the Three-Year Adventure That Rewrote Motion Picture History.* New York: Newmarket Press.

Pasteur, Georges. 1982. "A Classificatory Review of Mimicry Systems." *Annual Review of Ecology and Systematics* 13:169–199.

Peel, Michael. 2006. *Nigeria-Related Financial Crime and Its Links with Britain.* London: Royal Institute of International Affairs.

Peterson, Mark Allen. 2005. *Anthropology and Mass Communication: Media and Myth in the New Millennium.* New York: Berghahn.

Plato. 2008. *The Republic,* translated by Benjamin Jowett. Project Gutenberg Ebook. http://www.gutenberg.org/files/1497/1497-h/1497-h.htm.

Potolsky, Matthew. 2006. *Mimesis.* New York: Routledge.

Powdermaker, Hortense. 1962. *Coppertown: Changing Africa.* New York: Harper & Row.

Pratt, Marie-Louise. 1991. "Arts of the Contact Zone." *Profession* 91:33–40.

Probst, Peter. 2008. "A Matter of Mimicry: Visual Publics." *Critical Interventions* 1 (2): 7–10.

Probst, Peter, Jan-Georg Deutsch, and Heike Schmidt. 2002. "Introduction: Cherished Visions and Entangled Meanings." In *African Modernities: Entangled Meanings in Current Debate,* edited by Jan-Georg Deutsch, Peter Probst, and Heike Schmidt, 1–17. Oxford: James Currey.

Pype, Katrien. 2012. *The Making of the Pentecostal Melodrama: Religion, Media, and Gender in Kinshasa.* New York: Berghahn.

Rabo, Abubakar. 2008. "On Kano Censors Board." *This Day* (Lagos), August 14. http://allafrica.com/stories/printable/200808140660.html.

Ratering, Jörn. 2014. "Don't Mess with an Angel: A Mexican Telenovela on Tanzanian Television." In *Bongo Media Worlds: Producing and Consuming Popular Culture in Dar es Salaam,* edited by Matthias Krings and Uta Reuster-Jahn, 148–166. Cologne: Köppe.

Reichelt, Leisa. 2007. "Ambient Intimacy." *disambiguity* (blog). http://www.disambiguity.com/ambient-intimacy.

Rejholec, Jutta. 1986. "Überraschung am Samstag: Liebe und Leid in westafrikanischen Photoromanen." In *Afrika, Literatur, Kultur, Politik, Alltag,* edited by Hans-Jürgen Heinrichs, 366–373. Frankfurt: Qumran.

Reuster-Jahn, Uta. Forthcoming. "Private Entertainment Magazines and Popular Literature Production in Socialist Tanzania." In *African Print Cultures,* edited by Stephanie Newell, Emma Hunter, and Derek R. Peterson. Ann Arbor: University of Michigan Press.

Reuster-Jahn, Uta, and Gabriel Hacke. 2014. "The Bongo Flava Industry in Tanzania and Artists' Strategies for Success." In *Bongo Media Worlds: Producing and Consuming Popular Culture in Dar es Salaam,* edited by Matthias Krings and Uta Reuster-Jahn, 24–42. Cologne: Köppe.

Ribeiro, Gustavo Lins. 2001. "Cosmopolitanism." *International Encyclopedia of Social and Behavioral Sciences,* 4:2842–2845. London: Elsevier.

Ricoeur, Paul. 1981. *Hermeneutics and the Human Sciences.* Cambridge: Cambridge University Press.

Röschenthaler, Ute. 2011. *Purchasing Culture: The Dissemination of Associations in the Cross River Region of Cameroon and Nigeria.* Trenton, N.J.: Africa World Press.

Rouch, Jean. 1956. *Migrations au Ghana (Gold Coast): Enquête 1953–1955.* Paris: Société des Africanistes, Musée de l'Homme.

———. 1960. *La religion et la magie Songhay.* Paris: Presses Universitaires de France.

———. 1978. "Jean Rouch Talks about His Films to John Marshall and John W. Adams." *American Anthropologist* 80:1005–1022.

———. 1983. "Les maîtres fous: Protokoll des Films über das Ritual der Hauka." In *Colon: Das schwarze Bild vom weissen Mann,* edited by Jens Jahn, 217–232. Munich: Rogner & Bernhard.

Rubin, Martin. 1993. *Showstoppers: Busby Berkeley and the Tradition of Spectacle.* New York: Columbia University Press.

Ryan, Pauline. 1976. "Color Symbolism in Hausa Literature." *Journal of Anthropological Research* 32 (4): 141–160.

Sacks, Harvey. 1984. "On Doing 'Being Ordinary.'" In *Structures of Social Action,* edited by John M. Atkinson and John Heritage, 413–429. Cambridge: Cambridge University Press.

Sagna, Najib. 2006a. "Emigration clandestine: Les clandestines de rufisque veulent rallier les USA." *Wal Fadjri* (Dakar), June 22. http://fr.allafrica.com/stories/printable /200606220585.html.

———. 2006b. "Le Titanic rendu à son propriétaire, le fabricant aurait déjà ecaissé 26 millions." *Wal Fadjri* (Dakar), November 24. http://fr.allafrica.com/stories/printable /200611270632.html.

Saint, Lily. 2010. "Not Western: Race, Reading, and the South African Photocomic." *Journal of Southern African Studies* 36 (4): 939–958.

———. 2013. "'You Kiss in Westerns': Cultural Appropriation in Moustapha Alassane's *Le retour d'un aventurier.*" *Journal of African Cinemas* 5 (2): 203–217.

Sampson, Anthony. 2005. *Drum: The Making of a Magazine.* Johannesburg: Jonathan Ball.

Sanders, Todd. 2001. "Save Our Skins: Structural Adjustment, Morality, and the Occult in Tanzania." In *Magical Interpretations, Material Realities: Modernity, Witchcraft, and the Occult in Postcolonial Africa,* edited by Henrietta L. Moore and Todd Sanders, 160–183. London: Routledge.

Sandler, Kevin S., and Gaylyn Studlar, eds. 1999. *Titanic: Anatomy of a Blockbuster.* New Brunswick, N.J.: Rutgers University Press.

Sanga, Imani. 2011. "Mzungu Kichaa and the Figuring of Identity in Bongo Flava Music in Tanzania." *International Review of the Aesthetics and Sociology of Music* 42 (1): 189–208.

Sanusi, Sa'idu Mohammed. 2008. "Making a Scapegoat of . . . ." *Leadership* (Abuja), October 13, 1.

Schimming, Ulrike. 2002. *Fotoromane: Analyse eines Massenmediums.* Frankfurt: Lang.

Schneider, Arnd. 2003. "On 'Appropriation': A Critical Reappraisal of the Concept and Its Application in Global Art Practices." *Social Anthropology* 11 (2): 215–229.

———. 2006. *Appropriation as Practice: Art and Identity in Argentina.* New York: Palgrave Macmillan.

Schwartz, Hillel. 2000. *The Culture of the Copy: Striking Likeness, Unreasonable Facsimiles.* New York: Zone Books.

Sell, Eric. n.d. *Esisallesoreidt: NAM-släng—Deutsch.* Windhoek: EES Records Namibia.

Sheme, Ibrahim. 2007a. "Nude Video Causes a Stir." *Bahaushe Mai Ban Haushi* (blog), August 13. http://ibrahim-sheme.blogspot.com/2007/08/nude-video-causes-stir.html.

———. 2007b. "Film Burning in Kano." *Bahaushe Mai Ban Haushi* (blog), September 26. http://ibrahim-sheme.blogspot.com/2007/09/film-burning-in-kano.html.

———. 2007c. "Censoring Movies and Books in Kano." *Bahaushe Mai Ban Haushi* (blog), September 25. http://ibrahim-sheme.blogspot.com/2007/09/censoring-movies-and -books-in-kano.html.

———. 2009a. "Iyan-Tama: Another Case of Injustice." *Bahaushe Mai Ban Haushi* (blog), January 2. http://ibrahim-sheme.blogspot.com/2009/01/another-case-of-injustice.html.

———. 2009b. "Iyan-Tama: Matters Arising." *Bahaushe Mai Ban Haushi* (blog), March 20. http://ibrahim-sheme.blogspot.com/2009/03/iyan-tama-matters-arising.html.

———. 2009c. "An Kulle Bashir Dandago a Jarun" [Bashir Dandago has been jailed]. *Bahaushe Mai Ban Haushi* (blog), August 6. http://ibrahim-sheme.blogspot.com/2009 /08/kulle-bashir-dandago-jarun.html.

———. 2009d. "Kano Censorship: Aminu Ala Arrested, Jailed." *Bahaushe Mai Ban Haushi* (blog), July 8. http://ibrahim-sheme.blogspot.com/2009/07/kano-censorship-aminu-ala -arrested.html.

———. 2010. "Shekarau's Hausa Movie Script." *Bahaushe Mai Ban Haushi* (blog), July 9. http:// ibrahim-sheme.blogspot.de/2010/07/shekaraus-hausa-movie-script.html.

Simon, Okolo Ben. 2009. "Demystifying the Advance-Fee Fraud Criminal Network." *African Security Review* 18 (4): 6–18.

Smith, Andrew. 2009. "Nigerian Scam E-mails and the Charms of Capital." *Public Culture* 23 (1): 27–47.

Smith, Daniel Jordan. 2007. *A Culture of Corruption: Everyday Deception and Popular Discontent in Nigeria.* Princeton, N.J.: Princeton University Press.

Spittler, Gerd. 2002. "Globale Waren—Lokale Aneignungen." In *Ethnologie der Globalisierung: Perspektiven kultureller Verflechtungen,* edited by Brigitta Hauser-Schäublin and Ulrich Braukämper, 15–30. Berlin: Reimer.

Sreberny-Mohammadi, Annabelle, and Mohammadi, Ali. 1994. *Small Media, Big Revolution: Communication, Culture, and the Iranian Revolution.* Minneapolis: University of Minnesota Press.

Stiebel, Lindy. 2002. "Black 'Tecks: Popular Thrillers by South African Black Writers in the Nineties." In *Readings in African Popular Fiction,* edited by Stephanie Newell, 187–192. Oxford: James Currey.

Stoller, Paul. 1984. "Horrific Comedy: Cultural Resistance and the Hauka Movement in Niger." *Ethos* 12 (2): 165–188.

———. 1994. "Embodying Colonial Memories." *American Anthropologist* 69 (2): 634–648.

———. 1995. *Embodying Colonial Memories: Spirit Possession, Power, and the Hauka in West Africa.* New York: Routledge.

Strang, Veronica, and Mark Busse, eds. 2011. *Ownership and Appropriation.* Oxford: Berg.

Studlar, Gaylyn, and Sandler, Kevin S. 1999. "Introduction: The Seductive Waters of James Cameron's Film Phenomenon." In *Titanic: Anatomy of a Blockbuster,* edited by Kevin S. Sandler and Gaylyn Studlar, 1–13. New Brunswick, N.J.: Rutgers University Press.

Sturmer, Martin. 1998. *The Media History of Tanzania.* Salzburg: Afro-Asiatisches Institut.

Sutton, Tony. 2006. "Drum 1976–1980." In *Drum 1976–1980: An Exhibition from the Pages of Drum Magazine,* 6–12. http://www.coldtype.net/Assets.06/Essays.06/0606.DrumBook .pdf.

Taussig, Michael. 1993. *Mimesis and Alterity: A Particular History of the Senses.* New York: Routledge.

———. 2003. "Viscerality, Faith, and Skepticism: Another Theory of Magic." In *Magic and Modernity: Interfaces of Revelation and Concealment,* edited by Birgit Meyer and Peter Pels, 272–306, 338–341. Stanford, Calif.: Stanford University Press.

Thompson, John B. 1995. *The Media and Modernity: A Social Theory of the Media.* Cambridge: Polity.

Tive, Charles. 2006. *419 Scam: Exploits of the Nigerian Con Man*. New York: iUniverse.

Todorov, Tzvetan. 1977. *The Poetics of Prose*. Oxford: Blackwell.

Trouillot, Michel-Rolph. 2003. *Global Transformations: Anthropology and the Modern World*. New York: Palgrave Macmillan.

Tsambu Bulu, Léon. 2004. "Musique et violonce à Kinshasa." In *Ordre et désordre à Kinshasa: Réponses populaires à la faillite de l'état*, edited by Theodore Trefon, 193–212. Paris: Harmattan.

Tyoden, Sonni. 1989. "The Importance of the Military." In *Nigeria since Independence: The First Twenty-Five Years*, edited by Yusufu Bala Usman, 1:89–110. Ibadan, Nigeria: Heinemann.

Ukah, Asonzeh F.-K. 2004. "Religiöse Propaganda in Afrika." In *Plakate in Afrika*, edited by Dieter Kramer and Wendelin Schmidt, 83–88. Frankfurt: Museum der Weltkulturen.

———. 2008. "Roadside Pentecostalism: Religious Advertising in Nigeria and the Marketing of Charisma." *Critical Interventions* 1 (2): 125–141.

Ukpabi, Sam C. 1976. "The Changing Role of the Military in Nigeria, 1900–1970." *Africa Spectrum* 11 (1): 61–77.

Ultrascan. 2010. "419 Advance Fee Fraud Statistics 2009." *Ultrascan* (website). http://www.ultrascan-agi.com/public_html/html/public_research_reports.html.

Van der Veer, Peter. 2002. "Colonial Cosmopolitanism." In *Conceiving Cosmopolitanism: Theory, Context, and Practice*, edited by Steven Vertovec and Robin Cohen, 165–179. Oxford: Oxford University Press.

Veal, Michael E. 2000. *Fela: The Life and Times of an African Musical Icon*. Philadelphia: Temple University Press.

Verne, Markus. 2007. "Die Rückkehr kultureller Stimmigkeit: Eine Kritik des Aneignungskonzepts—Nicht nur in Hinblick auf den Verlauf von Mikrokreditprojekten." *Sociologus* 57 (2): 227–265.

Vertovec, Steven, and Robin Cohen. 2002. "Introduction: Conceiving Cosmopolitanism." In *Conceiving Cosmopolitanism: Theory, Context, and Practice*, edited by Steven Vertovec and Robin Cohen, 1–24. Oxford: Oxford University Press.

Wallace, Anthony. 1956. "Revitalization Movements." *American Anthropologist* 58:264–281.

Weiss, Brad. 2009. *Street Dreams and Hip Hop Barbershops: Global Fantasy in Urban Tanzania*. Bloomington: Indiana University Press.

Wendl, Tobias. 2002. "Try me! Reklame und visuelle Kultur in Afrika." In *Afrikanische Reklamekunst*, edited by Tobias Wendl, 12–30. Wuppertal, Germany: Hammer.

———. 2004a. "Medien und ihre kulturelle Konkretion: Eine ethnologische Perspektive." In *Die Kommunikation der Medien*, edited by Jürgen Fohrmann and Erhard Schüttpelz, 37–67. Tübingen, Germany: Niemeyer.

———. 2004b. "Wicked Villagers and the Mysteries of Reproduction: An Exploration of Horror Movies from Ghana and Nigeria." In *African Media Cultures: Transdisciplinary Perspectives*, edited by Rose-Marie Beck and Frank Wittmann, 263–285. Cologne: Köppe.

Werner, Jean-François. 2006. "How Women Are Using Television to Domesticate Globalization: A Case Study on the Reception and Consumption of Telenovelas in Senegal." *Visual Anthropology* 19 (5): 443–472.

White, Bob W. 2008. *Rumba Rules: The Politics of Dance Music in Mobutu's Zaire*. Durham, N.C.: Duke University Press.

White Nigerian. 2013. "'White Nigerian' Mohammed Jammal Shares His NYSC Experience with BN." *Bella Naija* (website). http://www.bellanaija.com/2013/01/28/white-nigerian-mohammed-jammal-shares-his-nysc-experience-with-bn.

Wiedemann, Charlotte. 2006. "Zum Frieden verdammt." *Die Zeit* (Hamburg), March 23. http://www.zeit.de/2006/13/Nigeria.

Witte, Marleen de. 2009. "Financial Crisis Worldwide, 5: Sakawa Money in Ghana." *Standplaats Wereld* (website), November 26. http://standplaatswereld.nl/2009/11/26/financial-crisis-worldwide-5-sakawa-money-in-ghana.

Wizard, Brian. 2000. *Nigerian 419 Scam: "Game Over!"* Wallowa, Ore.: Starquill International.

Wolf, Mark J. P. 2004. "The Technical Challenge of Emotional Realism and James Cameron's *Titanic.*" In *The Titanic in Myth and Memory: Representations in Visual and Literary Culture,* edited by Tim Bergfelder and Sarah Street, 215–224. London: Tauris.

Woodward, Ian, and Zlatko Skrbis. 2012. "Performing Cosmopolitanism." In *Routledge Handbook of Cosmopolitanism Studies,* edited by Gerard Delanty, 127–137. Milton Park, U.K.: Routledge.

Worsley, Peter. 1957. *The Trumpet Shall Sound: A Study of "Cargo" Cults in Melanesia.* London: MacGibbon & Kee.

Yanoshak, Nancy. 2008. "Mr. West Mimicking 'Mr. West': America in the Mirror of the Other." *Journal of Popular Culture* 41 (6): 1051–1068.

'Yarshila. 2007. "Hausa Porn Video—The Naked Truth." *Daily Trust* (Kaduna), September 6. http://allafrica.com/stories/200709060383.html.

Yusha'u, Muhammad Jameel. 2004. "Hausa Home Videos: The Moral Question and Political Economy of the Media." In *Hausa Home Videos: Technology, Economy and Society,* edited by Abdalla Uba Adamu, Yusuf M. Adamu, and Umar Faruk Jibril, 129–136. Kano, Nigeria: Center for Hausa Cultural Studies and Adamu Joji Publishers.

Zakzaky, Ibrahim Yakub. 2001. "Matsayin shirya fim a Musulunci" [The place of filmmaking in Islam], pts. 1 and 2. *Fim* 20:48–49; 21:52–53.

Ziff, Bruce, and Pratima V. Rao. 1997. "Introduction to Cultural Appropriation: A Framework for Analysis." In *Borrowed Power: Essays on Cultural Appropriation,* edited by Bruce Ziff and Pratima V. Rao, 1–30. New Brunswick, N.J.: Rutgers University Press.

FILMS

Billionaires Club, dir. Afam Okereke, Nigeria, 2003
Blood Diamond, dir. Edward Zwick, United States, Germany, 2006
Chite Ukae, dir. Mussa Banzi, Tanzania, 2006
Christ in Me, dir. Sunday Nnajiude, Nigeria, 2003
Dangerous Desire, dir. Mtitu Game, Tanzania, 2006
Dar 2 Lagos, dir. Femi Ogedegbe, Tanzania, 2006
Friday the 13th, dir. Sean S. Cunningham, United States, 1980
Gidauniya, dir. Sani Danja, Nigeria, 2004
Girlfriend, dir. George Tyson, Tanzania, 2003
Hiyana, dir. Ali Nuhu, Nigeria, 2006
Hotel Rwanda, dir. Terry George, United Kingdom, United States, Italy, South Africa, 2004
Ibro Aloko, dir. Lawan Kaura, Nigeria, 2006
Ibro Kauran Mata, dir. Rabilu Musa Danlasan, Nigeria, 1998
Ibro Saddam, dir. Kabeer Umar, Nigeria, 2003
Ibro Usama, dir. Malam Auwalu Dare, Nigeria, 2002
Johari, dir. Vincent Kigosi, Tanzania, 2006
Judah! dir. Saifullahi Tukr Yola, Nigeria, 2003 (Parts 1 and 2)
Karishika, dir. Christian Onu, Nigeria, 1998
Khusufi, dir. Ali Nuhu, Nigeria, 2003
King Solomon's Mines, dir. J. Lee Thompson, United States, 1985
Kinyamkela, dir. Mussa Banzi, Tanzania, 2007
Maîtres fous, les, dir. Jean Rouch, France, 1953/1954
Majonzi, dir. Kulwa Abdallah, Tanzania, 2007
Masoyiyata/Titanic, dir. Farouk Ashu-Brown, Nigeria, 2003
Master, The, dir. Andi Amenechi, Nigeria, 2005
Nsyuka, dir. Mussa Banzi, Tanzania, 2003
Omereme, dir. Sunday Nnajiude Nigeria, 2002
Osama Bin La, dir. Mac-Collins Chidebe, Nigeria, 2002
Out of Africa, dir. Sydney Pollack, United States, 1985

Pains of Love, dir. Chidi Chikere, Nigeria, 2003
Penina—Jezebel's Daughter, dir. Femi Ogedegbe, Tanzania, 2007
Private Affair, dir. Chinedu Nwoko, Nigeria, 2003
Sauran kiris, dir. Muhammad Bashir Abdulgani, Nigeria, 2000
Shaheed, dir. Zikiflu Mohammed, Nigeria, 2002 (Part 1), 2003 (Part 2)
Shumileta, dir. Mussa Banzi, Tanzania, 2005
Sikitiko Langu, dir. Vincent Kigosi, Tanzania, 2006
Suicide Mission, dir. Fred Amata, Nigeria, 1998
Super Love, dir. Andi Amenechi, Nigeria, 2003
Taal, dir. Subhash Ghai, India, 1999
Titanic, dir. James Cameron, United States, 1997
True Love, dir. Kabat Ebosa Egbon, Nigeria, 2003
Tsintsiya, dir. Hamisu Lamido Iyan-Tama, Nigeria, 2008

INDEX

Italic page numbers indicate material in the figures.

MATTHIAS KRINGS

———— ✍ ————

is Professor of Anthropology and African Popular Culture at
Johannes Gutenberg University Mainz. He is editor with Onookome Okome of *Global Nollywood: The Transnational Dimensions
of an African Video Film Industry* (Indiana University Press, 2013)
and with Uta Reuster-Jahn of *Bongo Media Worlds: Producing and
Consuming Popular Culture in Dar es Salaam* (Köppe, 2014).